Colloquial

Tamil

THE COLLOQUIAL SERIES
Series Adviser: Gary King

The following languages are available in the Colloquial series:

Afrikaans
Albanian
Amharic
Arabic (Levantine)
Arabic of Egypt
Arabic of the Gulf
Basque
Bengali
Breton
Bulgarian
Burmese
Cambodian
Cantonese
Catalan
Chinese (Mandarin)
Croatian
Czech
Danish
Dutch
English
Estonian
Finnish
French
German
Greek
Gujarati
Hebrew
Hindi
Hungarian
Icelandic
Indonesian
Irish
Italian
Japanese
Kazakh
Korean
Latvian
Lithuanian
Malay
Mongolian
Norwegian
Panjabi
Persian
Polish
Portuguese
Portuguese of Brazil
Romanian
Russian
Scottish Gaelic
Serbian
Slovak
Slovene
Somali
Spanish
Spanish of Latin America
Swahili
Swedish
Tamil
Thai
Tibetan
Turkish
Ukrainian
Urdu
Vietnamese
Welsh
Yiddish
Yoruba
Zulu (forthcoming)

COLLOQUIAL 2s series: *The Next Step in Language Learning*

Chinese
Dutch
French
German
Italian
Portuguese of Brazil
Russian
Spanish
Spanish of Latin America

Colloquials are now supported by FREE AUDIO available online. All audio tracks referenced within the text are free to stream or download from www.routledge.com/cw/colloquials. If you experience any difficulties accessing the audio on the companion website, or still wish to purchase a CD, please contact our customer services team through www.routledge.com/info/contact.

Colloquial
Tamil

The Complete Course for Beginners

R. E. Asher and E. Annamalai

Routledge
Taylor & Francis Group
LONDON AND NEW YORK

First published 2002
by Routledge
2 Park Square, Milton Park, Abingdon, Oxon, OX14 4RN

and by Routledge
711 Third Avenue, New York, NY 10017

Routledge is an imprint of the Taylor & Francis Group, an informa business

Reprinted with corrections in 2004

British Library Cataloguing in Publication Data
A catalogue record for this book is available from the British Library

Library of Congress Cataloging in Publication Data
A catalog record for this book has been requested

ISBN: 978-1-138-96034-3 (pbk)

Typeset in Times by
Florence Production Ltd, Stoodleigh, Devon

Printed and bound in the United States of America
by Edwards Brothers Malloy on sustainably sourced paper.

Contents

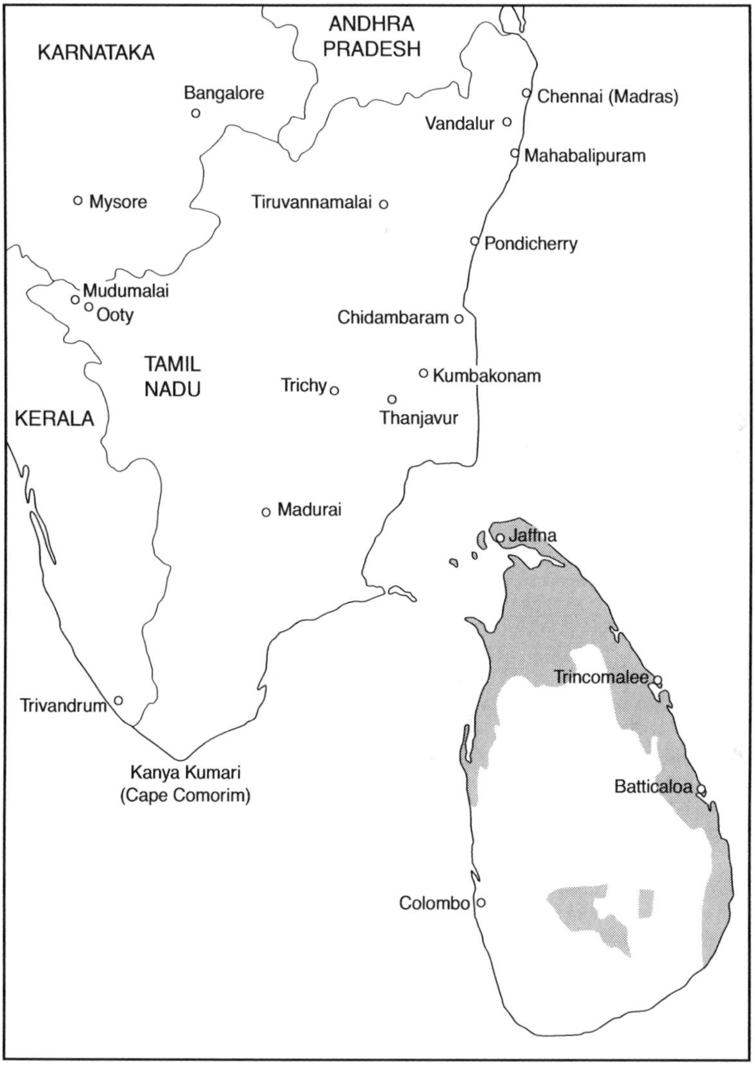

SOUTH INDIA AND SRI LANKA. In India, Tamil Nadu is the main Tamil area. The parts of Sri Lanka where more than half of the population are Tamil-speaking are shaded.

Dedicated to the memory of our teachers
T.P. Meenakshisundaran and
M. Varadarajan

– R.E.A.
E.A.

Introduction

Where Tamil is spoken

The number of speakers of Tamil worldwide is in excess of 65 million. The two principal homelands of the language are India, where it is the mother tongue of 87 per cent of the population of the state of Tamil Nadu in the south-east of the country, and Sri Lanka, where a quarter of the inhabitants are Tamil speakers. In the northern and eastern provinces of Sri Lanka, Tamil speakers are in the majority. During the nineteenth and twentieth centuries, considerable numbers of Tamilians migrated from both India and Sri Lanka to other countries. These countries include Malaysia, Singapore, Mauritius, Fiji, South Africa, the United Kingdom, Germany, the United States, and Canada.

The history of the language

Tamil has a very long recorded history. Inscriptions in the language date back to the middle of the third century BC, and the earliest Tamil poetry – some of the finest poetry ever written – is thought to have been produced not less than two millennia ago. Good modern translations of the lyrical and bardic poetry of this so-called Sangam age are available in English.

The hundreds of languages spoken in India belong to four distinct language families, of which the two with the largest numbers of speakers are Indo-Aryan and Dravidian. The former are related to the languages of western Europe as members of the larger Indo-European family. The thirty or more Dravidian languages of which Tamil is one are not so related. There has, however, been mutual influence, particularly through the borrowing of words. Modern Tamil, especially the spoken variety, also makes use of a number of English words, as you will see as you progress through this book.

Enjoying Tamil culture

Tamil has a very rich culture, and a visit to Tamil Nadu is particularly rewarding from this point of view alone. One of the dialogues in this volume relates to the renowned rock sculptures and monolithic temples near the shore of the Bay of Bengal at Mahabalipuram – carved in the seventh century. Somewhat later comes the magnificent Dravidian style architecture of the great temples, with their towering gopurams, that are to be found in ancient cities throughout the state. The history of Tamil sculpture is a study in itself. Stone is the more commonly used medium, but bronze too has been used over a long period, notably for sculptures of Siva as Nataraja, Lord of the Dance. One famous temple, at Chidambaram, has carvings of poses in the unique Tamil classical dance form – *bharatha natyam*. Dance recitals in this style are given throughout the year, but the most opportune time to see them is in December in Chennai (Madras), where each year there is a great festival of dance and of classical music, both vocal and instrumental. There is a thriving film industry too, and the production of films in Tamil is second in India only to that of Hindi films.

Quite a different aspect of life in Tamil Nadu relates to the fact the state is in the forefront of information technology. Coinciding with the dawn of a new millennium is the creation of a new science city at Taramani in Chennai.

Colloquial and written Tamil

The language of writing differs considerably from the language of everyday conversation – so much so that there is no universally accepted way of writing the colloquial variety in Tamil script. This book concentrates on the colloquial language, but devotes a modest amount of space to introducing the written language, on the assumption that learners will want at the very least to decipher signs they might see in travelling in Tamil-speaking parts of the world. What we are calling written language is also the language of formal speech – as in platform speaking, lecturing, reading news bulletins on the radio or television, and so on. A knowledge of this formal style is inadequate for anyone who wishes to converse, whether it is to ask the way or to buy a train ticket, a meal, or a postage stamp. Formal speech and writing on the one hand and colloquial speech on the other differ from each other in a number of ways, for instance, in the important grammatical endings that are added to nouns and verbs and also in the choice of words. You will see something of the nature of these differences in Unit 16.

Varieties of colloquial Tamil

No language is without its dialects, and colloquial Tamil varies from region to region and from social group to social group. However, partly through the influence of films and popular radio and television programmes, something approaching a standard variety has evolved in South India. This, being the one most widely used and understood, is the variety introduced in this book.

Language and society

Cultural differences often show up in the impossibility of transferring conventional items of conversation from one language community to another. In the dialogues presented in this book, therefore, you should not expect to find in all situations exact translation equivalents of common English social interchange. English often expresses politeness by such words as ‘please’ or ‘thank you’. In Tamil, such lubrication of vocal interaction is done by tone of voice, facial expression, and sometimes by grammatical features. One effect of this sort of thing is that a Tamil dialogue that is totally natural and authentic may have features that seem slightly strange in an English translation the aim of which is to assist in the understanding of what is there in Tamil. You should try to get the feel of this aspect of the language just as much as the basic grammatical structures.

Pronunciation (Audio 1: 2–8)

To understand spoken Tamil and to speak it intelligibly, it is necessary to become familiar with a number of sounds that are not found in English. Points of pronunciation that a learner needs to be aware of are explained in this section in terms of the Roman transcription used in the sixteen units of this book. The letters used, including some that are not part of the Roman alphabet as used for English, are: a, aa, i, ii, u, uu, e, ee, o, oo; k, g, c, j, ʈ, ɖ, t, d, p, b, ɳ, n, m, y, v, r, l, ɭ ʐ, j, s, ʂ, h.

You will notice that the vowels listed come in pairs of one long (these are indicated by double letters) and one short. This distinction is very important, as it is the only difference in quite a large number of pairs of words. Just as it is necessary to distinguish in English between such words as 'beat' and 'bit', so such words as **paattu** 'having seen' and **pattu** 'ten' must be kept apart in Tamil. We give below examples of the ten vowels, providing hints as to the pronunciation with English words. It is important to remember, however, that these are only approximations, above all because long vowels in English are in many cases phonetically diphthongs – that is to say that the nature of the sound is not constant throughout – as contrasted with pure vowels. In this sense, the vowels of Tamil are more akin to, say, the vowels of French or Italian, or to the vowels of northern (British) English or Scots. It is important, therefore, that you listen to how native speakers pronounce words, either in person or by using the recordings that accompany this book. Examples:

a	**pattu**	ten	as in *cat* (northern English)
aa	**paaru**	see!	as in *part* (southern English)
i	**sinna**	small	as in *pin*
ii	**miin**	fish	as in *keen*
u	**uppu**	salt	as in *put*
uu	**uuru**	town	as in *cool*
e	**vele**	price	as in *bell*
ee	**veele**	work	as in *vain*
o	**oru**	one	as in *olive*
oo	**ooḍu**	run	as in *own*

One set of vowels used in colloquial Tamil (though not in formal Tamil) that is not found in English is nasal vowels. These occur only in the final syllable of words and are indicated in the transcription by a vowel followed by **m** or **n**. Similar vowels are found in French. You will be readily understood if you pronounce the consonant, but you should try to copy the nasal vowels. The two sequences **-am** and **-oom** are very similar, being distinguished, if at all, only by the slightly greater length of the second. The same is true of the pair **-an** and **-een**. For the benefit of those who are familiar with them, standard phonetic symbols are given in square brackets. Examples:

-aam	**varalaam**	may come	as in French *avant*	[ɑ̃]
-aan	**vandaan**	he came	as in French *avant*	[ɑ̃]
-am	**maram**	tree	as in French *bon*	[ɔ̃]
-oom	**vandoom**	we came	as in French *bon*	[ɔ̃]
-an	**avan**	he	as in French *vin*	[ẽ]
-een	**vandeen**	I came	as in French *vin*	[ẽ]
-um	**varum**	it will come		[ũ]

For some speakers, the last sound, [ũ], has merged with [ɔ̃] in some words, so that a variant of **innum** [ũ] 'still, yet' is **innom** [ɔ̃]. If, because something is added to the word, the **m** or **n** in these words no longer comes at the end, you should pronounce it as a consonant. For example, **-aa** can be added to the last word of a sentence to turn a statement into a question. So, while **vandaan** means 'he came', **vandaanaa** means 'did he come?'

Careful listeners will notice subtle differences between the consonants of Tamil and those of English that are written with the Roman symbols we are using for Tamil. We concentrate here on features of pronunciation that are vital for clear understanding.

In accordance with conventions for transcribing words from Indian languages into Roman, **c** is used for a sound similar to that represented by 'ch' in English 'church'. This sound often alternates with **s** at the beginning of a word.

It is important not to pronounce the letters **t** and **d** as in English. Used for Tamil, these letters represent dental sounds (as in French). When you articulate them, make sure that the tip of your tongue touches the upper front teeth. This is important in order that these shall be clearly distinct from the sounds **ʈ** and **ɖ** which are discussed in the next paragraph but one.

Careful listening will show that **d** has a different pronunciation depending on what other sounds come next to it. At the beginning of a word, and after **n** in the middle of a word, it has the sound of a French *d*, as just mentioned. When it occurs between vowels in the middle of a word, however, it sounds more like the 'th' in English 'other'. The case of **g** is somewhat similar to this. At the beginning of a word (where it occurs only rarely), and after **n** in the middle of a word, it has the sound of English 'g'. When it occurs between vowels in the middle of a word, however, it may have the sound of English 'h' or the sound of 'ch' in the Scottish pronunciation of 'loch'. Examples of these are:

teru	street
ettane	how many
denam	daily
anda	that
adu	it
gaandi	Gandhi
ange	there
magan	son

One set of sounds needs special mention. These sounds are often labelled 'retroflex', because the tip of the tongue is turned backwards when they are pronounced. It is thus the underside of the tongue that approaches or touches the roof of the mouth. All these sounds are represented here by special Roman letters which share the feature of ending in a tail that turns upwards. This should remind you of what to do with your tongue! Listen very carefully to words on the tape containing these sounds. Except in some words borrowed from another language (as shown in the first word listed), these sounds do not occur at the beginning of a word. You may well notice that the preceding vowel has a special quality too. This will help you to distinguish the consonants. Here are a few examples:

ʈii	tea
paaʈʈu	song
paaɖu	sing
paɳam	money
paʐam	fruit, banana
puɭi	tamarind
kaʂʈam	trouble, difficulty

You will observe frequent occurrences of a sequence of two identical consonant letters. It is important to remember that this indicates that the consonant sound in question is noticeably longer than for a single letter. If you think about how the spelling system works, you will realise that this is quite unlike what happens in English: the 'm' sound of 'hammer' is no longer than that of 'farmer'. With this, compare the pairs of Tamil words in the list below (where the consonants illustrated are those where the distinction between long and short is most important). To get a similar 'long' consonant in English, one has to think of instances where, for example, an 'm' at the end of one word is followed by an 'm' at the beginning of another. Try saying these two sentences, and see if you can feel and hear a difference: 'Tom makes all sorts of things; Tom aches all over'.

paɳam	money	**paɳɳu**	make
manam	mind	**kannam**	cheek
aamaa	yes	**ammaa**	mother
kale	art	**kallu**	stone
puɭi	tamarind	**puɭɭi**	dot
vara	to come	**varraa**	she is coming
payan	usefulness	**payyan**	boy

This difference between single and double consonants is particularly important for those in the above table (**ɳ/ɳɳ**, **n/nn**, **m/mm**, **l/ll**, **ɭ/ɭɭ**, **r/rr** and **y/yy**). It is less significant for such pairs as **k/kk**, **t/tt**, and **p/pp**.

Finally, you should take some care with what are called intonation and stress patterns. Intonation has to do with the way the pitch of the voice goes up and down in speech. You will observe that the pattern of this rise and fall is not the same for Tamil and English. As far as stress is concerned, the contrast between weakly and strongly stressed syllables is much greater in English than in Tamil. You will find it helpful in listening to the tapes to observe all such points and then try to imitate as closely as possible what you hear.

Writing system

The Tamil writing system is introduced in stages through a short section on the script at the end of each of the first eleven units. The principal purpose of this is to put the reader in the position of being able to read the various signs to be seen in a Tamil-speaking town. The presentation of the writing system is done in such a way as to allow those who wish to do so to concentrate solely on the spoken language in the early stages of their study of Tamil.

The script is unique to Tamil. It is sometimes described as syllabic. The reason for this will soon become apparent: a sequence (in sound) of consonant + vowel has to be read as a single unit, since the sign indicating the vowel may come before the consonant letter (as well as after, above, underneath, and part before and part after). The system shares something with an alphabet, however, in that in a given complex symbol it is usually possible to see which parts represent the consonant and which the vowel. In this respect it is not a 'true' syllabary (as compared, for instance, with the *hiragana* and *katakana* syllabaries of Japanese). It has therefore been classified, along with most of the writing systems used for the languages of South Asia and many of Southeast Asia, as an 'alphasyllabary'. An appendix at the end provides a chart of the simple and combined symbols.

Tamil grammar

To any one with a knowledge of only western European grammar, the grammar of Tamil provides a number of surprises. We look at just two of these here. First, the basic order of words in a sentence is different, in that most usually the last word in a Tamil sentence is a verb; corresponding to English 'Tom saw her', Tamil, one might say, has 'Tom her saw'. After a little exposure to the language you will soon get used to this. The second major characteristic is that a Tamil word can seem very complex, in that information carried in English by a number of separate words may be carried in Tamil by something (or a sequence of somethings) added to the end of a word. Thus, the Tamil equivalent of the sequence 'may have been working' would be in the form of one word made of the parts 'work-be-have-may'. To talk about such sequences of parts and to explain how they work it is unavoidable that a certain number of grammatical terms are used. So the equivalent of 'work' will sometimes be spoken of as a 'stem' and each of the additional items as a 'suffix'. Labels will also be attached to regularly recurring endings or suffixes. The aim will be that the meaning of such labels is as transparent as possible. Thus, when something is added to a verb to indicate that the action of the verb is completed, the label 'completive' will be used. It is clearly not important to be able to reproduce such slightly technical terms; what matters is to remember, by practice, what an item added to a basic word means.

1 en peeru Murugan

My name is Murugan

In this unit you will learn to:

- use simple greetings
- introduce yourself
- use personal pronouns
- use verb forms that are appropriate to the different pronouns
- ask questions
- make requests
- express politeness

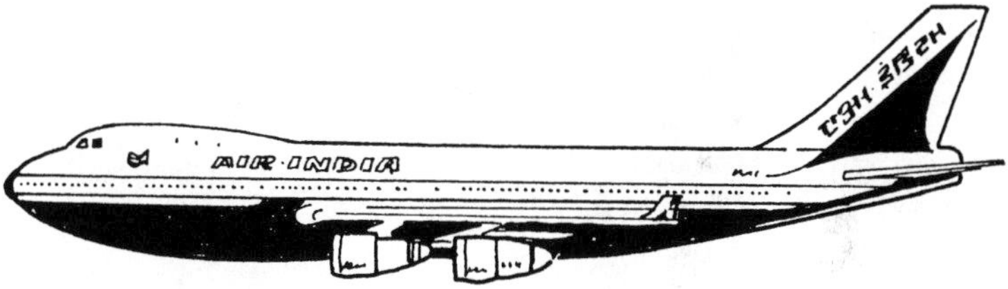

Dialogue 1 (Audio 1: 9)

Arriving in Chennai

Robert Smith, on his first visit to India, is met at Chennai (Madras) airport by a student of a friend of his.

MURUGAN: vaṉakkam. niinga Robert Smith-aa?
SMITH: aamaa. naandaan Robert Smith. vaṉakkam.
MURUGAN: en peeru Murugan. peeraasiriyar Madivaaṉanooḍa maaṉavan.

SMITH: romba magiẓcci.
MURUGAN: vaanga, ooṭṭalukku poovoom. ange konjam ooyvu eḍunga.
SMITH: sari. vaanga, poovoom.

MURUGAN: *Greetings. Are you Robert Smith?*
SMITH: *Yes. I* am *Robert Smith. Greetings.*
MURUGAN: *My name is Murugan. Professor Madhivanan's student.*
SMITH: *Pleased to meet you.* (lit. *Much pleasure*)
MURUGAN: *Come. Let's go to the hotel. You can rest up a bit.* (lit. *Take some rest there*)
SMITH: *Fine. Come, let's go.*

Vocabulary

vaṇakkam	greetings
niinga(ḷ)	you (plural and polite)
peeru	name
aamaa	yes
naan	I
taan (-daan, -ttaan)	(emphatic word)
en	my
peeraasiriyar	professor
maaṇavan	student (masc)
romba	very; very much
magiẓcci	happiness, pleasure
vaa (var-, varu-, va-)	come
ooṭṭal	hotel
ange	there
poo (poog-)	go
konjam	a little
ooyvu	rest
eḍu	take

Pronunciation tips

1 The intonation rises slightly at the end of the sentence when it is a question.
2 **g** between vowels is commonly pronounced **h**.
3 Vowels **i** and **e** in the beginning of a word are pronounced with a preceding **y** tinge (e.g. ^{y}**eḍu**). Vowels **u** and **o** in the beginning of a word have a **w** tinge (e.g. ^{w}**onga**).
4 In a few phrases, **n** at the end of a word, when followed by a word beginning with **p**, is pronounced as **m**; e.g. **en peeru** is normally pronounced as **em peeru** (or even **embeeru**).
5 The word final **u** is not pronounced when followed by a vowel.

Language points

Greeting

vaṉakkam is an expression of greeting generally used in formal encounters with elders and equals. It signifies bowing, but the physical gesture which accompanies the expression is the placing of the palms of one's hands together near the chest.

Case endings

English often relates nouns to verbs by the use of prepositions such as 'to', 'in', 'by', 'of', 'from'. Very often, the equivalent of these in Tamil will be a 'case' ending or suffix added to a noun. Two such endings are introduced in this unit (see the sections on 'Genitive' and 'Dative').

Genitive (possessive)

Pronouns of first and second person ('I', 'we', 'you') have two forms. One is when they occur without any case suffix, i.e. when they occur as the subject of a sentence. The other is when they occur with a case suffix. We shall call this the 'non-subject' form. The genitive (or possessive) case suffix is **-ooḍa**. This is optional for both nouns and pronouns, but you should learn to recognise it. It is more commonly omitted with pronouns. The pronouns mentioned have the second form ('non-subject') in the genitive even when the case suffix is omitted.

niinga you; **onga** your (full form **ongaḷooḍa**)
peeraasiriyar professor; **peeraasiriyarooḍa** professor's

In phrases indicating possession, the possessor precedes the thing possessed (as in English):

onga viiḍu your house
peeraasiriyarooḍa pustagam the professor's book

Questions

The question suffix is **-aa** for questions which are answered by 'yes' or 'no'. It may be added (1) at the end of the sentence; or (2) to any word (other than the modifier of a noun) which is questioned in a sentence. Notice that in these examples, there is nothing corresponding to the English verb 'be'. Verbless sentences of this sort are discussed in the next paragraph. Examples occur in Exercises 1–3.

1 **niinga Murugan-aa?** Are you Murugan?
2 **niingaḷaa Murugan?** Are *you* Murugan?

Verbless sentences

It is not necessary for all sentences to have a verb. Some sentences have as their predicate (1) nouns or pronouns, or (2) other parts of speech without a verb. You will notice that in many such instances an English sentence will have the verb 'be'.

1 **en peeru Murugan.**	My name (is) Murugan.
idu enakku.	This (is) for me.
2 **ooṭṭal enge?**	Where (is) the hotel?

Exercise 1 (Audio 1: 9)

Let us indicate what a person's name is. Suggested subjects are provided in English. Use a different name (Tamil or English) for each. Masculine names include **Raaman**, **Goovindan**, **Arasu** and feminine names: **Lakşmi**, **Kalyaaṉi**, **Nittilaa**. A correct answer does not, of course, necessarily mean that you chose the name found in the key. The Tamil writing system does not distinguish capital letters and small letters. However, in the Roman transcription used in this book, to help you distinguish proper nouns (e.g. names of persons) from common nouns, the former are spelt with a capital letter.

Example: **naan Murugan.** I am Murugan.

1 you
2 he
3 you (polite)
4 professor
5 professor's student

Exercise 2

Now provide information on these lines by using the word **peeru** 'name' preceded by a possessive form.

Example: **naan Murugan. en peeru Murugan.**

1 niinga
2 en maaṉavan
3 onga maaṉavan

Exercise 3

You are not sure that you have got someone's name right. Find out by asking. Remember to use masculine or feminine names in appropriate places!

Example: **niinga Muruganaa?**

1 avan (he)
2 avaru (he (polite))
3 ava (she)
4 onga peeru
5 onga maaṉavan peeru

Linking sounds

Final **l** and **ḷ** disappear in certain words when these words occur alone, that is to say when they are not followed by a suffix; **l** and **ḷ** reappear when there is a following suffix and this suffix begins with a vowel. For this reason, these consonant letters occur in parentheses in vocabulary lists:

niinga you

but

niingaḷaa you?

Emphasis

Emphasis is of different kinds. One kind is expressed by **-taan** (which has variant forms **-daan** and **-ttaan**). It roughly means 'not other than'; contrastive stress is sometimes used in English to convey this meaning.

naandaan Murugan.	*I* am Murugan.
en peerudaan Murugan.	*My* name is Murugan.

Commands and requests

The simple form of the verb without any suffix is used for making a request and giving an order. When a request is made to an elder or a superior, it should be polite, and for this the plural suffix **-nga** is added to the verb. If in doubt, use the **-nga** form.

vaa	come	**vaanga**	please come
poo	go	**poonga**	please go

Exercise 4

Show that you know how to be polite by modifying the verb forms and pronouns in the examples below. You will realise that in the two examples given in the model, it is the second which is the polite form. The pronouns **nii** and **niinga** are optional in these 'imperative' forms.

Example: **nii vaa** **niinga vaanga**

1 nii poo
2 nii iru
3 nii kuḍu (give)

Future tense

The future tense suffix is **-v-** or **-pp-** added to two different sets of verbs to be explained later.

poovoom. We shall go.
eḍuppoom. We shall take.

The future tense has more than one sense or function. One of the senses is that the action of the verb takes place at a time in the future, i.e. after the time when the sentence is uttered:

1 **naan naaḷekki pooveen.** I shall go tomorrow.

Another very frequent use is with first person subject which includes the hearer. As you will see from the section below headed 'Pronouns', where English has 'we', Tamil makes a distinction, depending on whether 'we' includes or does not include the person spoken to. When the person spoken to is included, the future tense suffix commonly has the sense of a suggestion to do the action of the verb; it translates in English as 'let us'.

2 **(naama) naaḷekki poovoom.** Let's go tomorrow.

Notice that in (1), the pronoun **naan** and the ending **-een** convey the same information, namely 'I'. The same is true of the meaning 'we' **naama** and **-oom** in (2). The result is that the meaning of a sentence is clear, even if a subject pronoun is dropped – and this often happens.

Dative case: 'to'

Noun forms, with the exception of the subject of a sentence, generally take a case suffix, which relates the noun to the verb. The dative case suffix, often to be translated in English by the preposition 'to', is **-(u)kku** or **-kki** depending on the final vowel of the noun. If the noun ends in **i** or **e**, the suffix is **-kki**. As you can see from the list below, with some pronouns it is **-akku**.

ooṭṭalukku to the hotel
tambikki to the younger brother
enakku to me
onakku to you
namakku to us

The dative case is used in a variety of meanings, of which recipient and destination are the most common. A noun with this case is the recipient of the action of verbs like **kuḍu** 'give' (1) and the destination of verbs like **poo** 'go' (2).

1 **enakku kuḍu.** Give (it) to me.
2 **ooṭṭalukku poo.** Go to the hotel.

Dialogue 2 (Audio 1: 10)

Going out

Smith and Murugan arrange to meet later at a favourite spot for a walk in the relative cool of the evening.

SMITH: saayangaalam enge poovoom?
MURUGAN: biiccukku poovamaa?
SMITH: poovoom. biic peeru Meriinaavaa?
MURUGAN: aamaa. inda biic Cennekki perume.
SMITH: Cenneyooḍa ingliṣ peeru Meḍraasaa?
MURUGAN: adu paẓeya peeru.

SMITH: *Where shall we go in the evening?*
MURUGAN: *Shall we go to the beach?*
SMITH: *Yes. Is the name of the beach Marina?*
MURUGAN: *Yes. This beach is the pride of Chennai.*
SMITH: *Is the English name of Chennai, Madras?*
MURUGAN: *That's the old name.*

Vocabulary

saayangaalam	evening	**biiccu**	beach (also **biic**)
Meriinaa	Marina	**inda**	this
Cenne	Chennai	**perume**	pride, renown
ingliṣ	English	**Meḍraas**	Madras
adu	that, it	**paẓeya**	old

Language points

Dative case

The dative case (**-kku** or **-kki**) may also give the meaning of 'possessing a property or quality':

Cennekki perume pride of Chennai

Adjectives

Specific adjectives are few in Tamil. Among them is **paẓeya** in Dialogue 2. But nouns too can be placed before a noun to modify it, as in **konja neeram** 'some time'. The final sounds of a noun functioning as an adjective may undergo some change. One change is the nouns that end in **-am** drop **-m** – a point illustrated by **konja**, the related noun being **konjam**.

Variations in vowel sounds

Vowels of first and second person suffixes may be changed before the interrogative suffix **-aa**. Remember that **-oom** in **poovoom** is pronounced as a nasalised vowel, while **-m-** in **poovamaa** is pronounced as a consonant. Notice also the linking sound **y** in **pooviyaa**.

poovoom + **aa** → **poovamaa**
poove + **aa** → **pooviyaa**

Distance from the speaker

Third person pronouns and related adjectives and adverbs indicate relative distance from the speaker. The distance indicated is either near the speaker (called 'proximate') or away from the speaker (called 'remote'). The part that indicates proximity is **i-** and the part indicating remoteness is **a-**. By a happy coincidence, these can be remembered from the vowels in English 'this' and 'that'. A fairly full set of such words is given below. At this stage you may care simply to note the pattern, learning the words when they appear in context in dialogues.

idu	this	**adu**	that
inda	this (adj)	**anda**	that (adj)
inge	here	**ange**	there
ippa	now	**appa**	then
iɳɳekki	today	**aɳɳekki**	on that day
ittane	this many	**attane**	that many
ivʅavu	this much	**avʅavu**	that much
ipḍi	in this way, thus	**apḍi**	in that way, so

Exercise 5

Distinguish between 'this' one and 'that' one.

Example: **inda ʈæksi** **anda ʈæksi**

1 ooʈʈalu
2 viiḍu
3 ruum
4 maaɳavan
5 peeraasiriyar

Pronouns

So far you have met five pronoun forms: **naan** 'I', **naama** 'we', **nii** 'you (singular)', **niinga** 'you (plural)', and **adu** 'it'. For future reference, we list all pronouns here, but you may wish to learn them only as they occur. Pronouns are divided into three persons – first person (the speaker), second person (the person spoken to), and third person (the person spoken about). They also vary for number, that is to say singular and plural.

As already mentioned, there are two different pronouns corresponding to 'we'; one of these (**naama**(**ʅ**)) includes the person spoken to, and the other (**naanga**(**ʅ**)) excludes the person spoken to.

You will also notice that Tamil, like many European languages but unlike most dialects of English, has two words for 'you'. The plural form **niinga** is also used as a polite form when speaking to just one person. If in doubt, use **niinga** in preference to **nii**.

The third person pronoun is further divided into three genders – human masculine ('he'), human feminine ('she'), and other ('it') – and two distances (see previous section 'Distance from the speaker'). When the speaker wishes to be polite about a person being referred to, a different form from the 'singular' pronoun is used. Talking about a man, one says **avaru**; and talking about a woman **avanga** – which you will see is the same as the plural form. Politeness is expressed for elders and superiors. In the list of pronouns that follows, the 'non-subject' stems (mentioned above as the form on to which case endings are added) are given for first and second persons.

List of pronouns

	Singular		*Plural*	
	Nominative	*Non-subject*	*Nominative*	*Non-subject*
First person	**naan** I	**en-**	**naama(ɭ)** we (inclusive)	**nam/namma(ɭ)**
			naanga(ɭ) we (exclusive)	**enga(ɭ)**
Second person	**nii** you	**on-**	**niinga** you (plural and polite)	**onga(ɭ)**
Third person				
proximate	**ivan** he		**ivanga(ɭ)** they	
	ivaru he (polite)			
	iva(ɭ) she		**ivanga(ɭ)** they	
	ivanga(ɭ) she (polite)		**ivanga(ɭ)** they	
	idu this, it		**iduga(ɭ)** these	
remote	**avan** he		**avanga(ɭ)** they	
	avaru he (polite)			
	ava(ɭ) she		**avanga(ɭ)** they	
	avanga(ɭ) she (polite)			
	adu that, it		**aduga(ɭ)** those	

Verb endings

The verb in the main sentence agrees with the subject in person and number. With third person pronouns (and nouns) it also agrees in gender. This is to say that, as a general rule, each pronoun will have a particular verb ending associated with it. Exceptions are pointed out below. Since it is a frequently used verb, the endings are illustrated here as they occur in the verb **iru** 'be'. The forms are illustrated here as they occur in the verb **iru** 'be'. The forms given are future tense, this being the only tense mentioned so far. Present and past tense forms will be introduced later. Notice the third person neuter form, where **-kk-** is found rather than **-pp-**. As will become apparent later, the ending **-um** is not used in past and present tense forms.

Verb forms: iru *'be'*

naan irupp*een* I shall be	**naama irupp*oom*** We shall be
	naanga irupp*oom* We shall be
nii irupp*e* You will be	**niinga irupp*iinga*(ḷ)** You (pl) will be
avan irupp*aan* He will be	**avanga irupp*aanga*(ḷ)** They (masc. and fem.) will be
avaru irupp*aaru* He (pol.) will be	
ava irupp*aa*(ḷ) She will be	
avanga irupp*aanga*(ḷ) She (pol.) will be	
adu irukkum It will be	**aduga irukkum** They (neut.) will be

You will see from this that the first person plural ending (**-oom**) is the same for each of the two pronouns **naama** and **naanga**. Note also that for third person neuter (**adu** and **aduga**), singular and plural – 'it' and 'they' – have the same ending.

Exercise 6 (Audio 1: 10)

Ask if various people will be going to the beach.

Example: **niinga biiccukku pooviingaḷaa?**

1 nii
2 ava
3 avanga
4 Murugan
5 Kalyaaṇi
6 peeraasiriyar
7 onga maaṇavan

Exercise 7

Make similar enquiries about whether people are going (a) to the hotel, and (b) to Chennai.

Word order

The common word order in a sentence is subject, object, verb. However, these elements can be moved around with greater freedom than is possible, for example, in English. Reordering does not alter the essential meaning of the sentence, but it does have such effects as bringing into greater prominence a word moved from its 'basic' position. Modifying words like adjective and adverb precede the word they modify, but an adverb that is not a modifier of an adjective or adverb can be reordered.

naama ooṭṭalukku poovoom.	We will go to the hotel.
ooṭṭalukku naama poovoom.	To the hotel we will go.
saayangaalam enge poovoom?	Where shall we go in the evening?
enge poovoom saayangaalam?	In the evening where shall we go?

Subjectless sentences

The subject may be absent in any sentence, and this is frequently so in imperative sentences (i.e. sentences giving an order or making a request). The identity of the subject is understood from the ending of the verb (1) or from the context (2).

1	**ooṭṭalukku poovoom.** (***naama*** **ooṭṭalukku poovoom.)**	Let (us) go the hotel.
	ooyvu eḍunga. (***niinga*** **ooyvu eḍunga.)**	(You) take a rest.
2	**peeraasiriyarooḍa maaṇavan.** (***naan*** **peeraasiriyarooḍa maaṇavan.)**	(I am) the professor's student.

Dialogue 3 (Audio 1: 11)

On the beach

Smith has gone with Murugan to Madras beach, where he learns from him about the vendors of items to eat and drink there.

MURUGAN:	niinga murukku saapḍuviingaḷaa?
SMITH:	adu inikkumaa?
MURUGAN:	ille. karumbu caaru inikkum. adu kuḍinga.
SMITH:	karumbu caaru kuḍippaangaḷaa?
MURUGAN:	aamaa. kuḍippaanga.
SMITH:	inge keḍekkumaa?
MURUGAN:	keḍekkum. vaanga, ange naḍappoom.

MURUGAN:	*Will you eat some murukku?*
SMITH:	*Is it sweet?*
MURUGAN:	*No. Sugar cane juice is sweet. Try that.*
SMITH:	*Do people drink sugar cane juice?*
MURUGAN:	*Yes, they do.*
SMITH:	*Is it available here?*
MURUGAN:	*It is. Come. Let's walk over there.*

Vocabulary

murukku	a snack (shaped like pretzel)	**saapḍu**	eat
		ini	be sweet
karumbu	sugar cane	**caaru**	juice
kuḍi	drink	**keḍe**	be available, get
naḍa	walk		

Language points

Future tense

This dialogue illustrates another use of the future tense, namely to describe habitual or customary action (where English uses the present tense): **karumbu caaru kuḍippaangaḷaa?** 'Do they drink sugar cane juice?'

Exercise 8 (Audio 1: 12)

Ask what different people habitually drink. Suggested subjects: **Goovindan**, **Lakṣmi**, **niinga**, **avanga**. Suggested drinks: **karumbu caaru**, **ṭii** 'tea', **paalu** 'milk', **mooru** 'buttermilk', **kaapi** 'coffee'.

Tamil script

As you already know, written and colloquial Tamil differ considerably. Colloquial forms are not often written in the Tamil script. However, moving around in Tamil-speaking parts of the world is much easier if one can read signs written in the Tamil script. Accordingly, each of the first eleven units will contain some words, and later sentences, in the script for you to practise. We start with just one word, **ooṭṭalu** 'hotel'. This word is borrowed from English and is found in two forms, one without and one with 'h'. First without: ஓட்டல், which is made up of ஓ = **oo**, + ட் = **ṭ**, + ட = **ṭa**, + ல் = **l**. The alternative is ஹோட்டல், which differs from the first in beginning with ஹோ (= **hoo**) rather than ஓ. These two variant spellings of one word illustrate all the main features of the Tamil writing system:

- A vowel at the beginning of a word is represented by an independent letter, here ஓ.
- A vowel preceded by a consonant is represented by a sign attached to the consonant; this sign may be located to the right of, to the left of, on both sides of, or under the consonant symbol; in the case of ஹோ, **oo** is made up of the two elements ே and ா.
- A consonant followed by the vowel **a** is represented by the consonant letter on its own, with no attachment. For this reason, the vowel **a** is said to be 'inherent' in the consonant letter. We have an example of this in ட.
- A consonant not followed by a vowel (i.e. occurring at the end of a word or followed by another consonant) has a dot, called **puḷḷi** in Tamil, above it; examples are ட் and ல்.

Note that the final **u** of the colloquial form of **ooṭṭalu** is not present in the written form. Remember also that there are no capital letters in the Tamil writing system.

Exercise 9

Match the Tamil syllables in the second column with the appropriate transcribed form in the first:

1 la	a டோ
2 ha	b ல
3 ṭoo	c லோ
4 loo	d ஹ

2 naan viiṭṭukku pooreen

I'm going home

In this unit you will learn to:

- get a taxi
- hire an autorickshaw
- check into a hotel
- ask how many
- use present tense forms
- use adjectives
- read some words in Tamil script

Dialogue 1 (Audio 1: 13)

Getting a taxi

Murugan is taking Smith to see a friend who lives in the Nungambakkam area of Chennai. They go there by taxi.

MURUGAN:	Nungambaakkam varriyaa?
TAXI DRIVER:	ille, naan viiṭṭukku pooreen.
MURUGAN:	inda ṭaaksikkaarangaḷee ipḍittaan.
SMITH:	paravaayille. konja neeram kaattiruppoom.
MURUGAN:	idoo, innoru ṭaaksi varudu . . . ṭaaksi, Nungambaakkam varriyaa?
TAXI DRIVER:	eerunga.
MURUGAN:	Mr Smith, niinga pinnaale ukkaarunga. naan munnaale ukkaarreen.
SMITH:	ille, ille. niingaḷum pinnaale ukkaarunga.
MURUGAN:	sari.

MURUGAN:	*Will you take us to Nungambakkam?* (lit. *Are you coming to . . . ?*)
TAXI DRIVER:	*No, I'm going home.*
MURUGAN:	*These taxi drivers are like this.*
SMITH:	*Never mind. Let's wait a little while.*
MURUGAN:	*Look, another taxi's coming . . . Taxi, will you take us to Nungambakkam?*
TAXI DRIVER:	*Get in.*
MURUGAN:	*Mr Smith, You sit in the back. I'll sit in front.*
SMITH:	*No, no. You too sit in the back.*
MURUGAN:	*Fine.*

Vocabulary

Nungambaakkam	Nungambakkam, an area in Madras (now officially referred to in English as Chennai (from Tamil **Cen̲n̲ai** – colloquial form **Cenne**))
ille	no
viiḍu	house
ṭaaksikkaaranga(ḷ)	taxi people, taxi drivers
ipḍi	like this, in this manner
paravaayille	does not matter, all right

neeram	time
kaattiru	wait
idoo	look here, here it is
innoru	another
ṭaaksi/ṭæksi	taxi
pinnaale	behind, in the back
munnaale	before, in the front
ukkaaru	sit down

Pronunciation tips

1 Words borrowed into Tamil from English are normally pronounced according to the Tamil sound system. Thus English 't' becomes Tamil **ṭ**. Nevertheless, for some speakers some new sounds have been introduced into Tamil from English; e.g. where we have **ṭaaksi** in the dialogue, some speakers use the English vowel sound: **ṭæksi** (the letter **æ** is used to represent the sound of 'a' in (southern) English 'taxi' or 'man').

2 As pointed out in Unit 1, the vowel **e** in the second person singular ending is more like **i** before a suffix beginning with a vowel. For this reason, **varre** + **-aa** in Dialogue 1 is written **varriyaa**.

Language points

Present tense

The present tense suffix is **-r-** or **-kkir-** added to two different sets of verbs to be explained later. The verbs which take **-pp-** for future tense take **-kkir-** for present. The tense suffix is omitted in third person neuter forms. With the verb **iru** 'be', the suffix is **-kk-**.

ukkaar*r*aan	He is sitting down
eḍu*kkir*aan	He is taking
ukkaa*r*udu	It is sitting down
iru*kk*u	It is

Note the third person neuter singular ending **-udu** in **ukkaarudu**. The verb 'be' (**irukku**) is exceptional in having only **-u**. The present tense has a number of different senses. These include (1) that the action of the verb takes place in the present time, i.e. at the same time as the utterance; (2) that the action takes place in future time but the speaker indicates that it will definitely take place:

1	**ṭæksi varudu.**	A taxi is coming.
2	**Nungambaakkam varriyaa?**	Will you come to Nungambakkam?

The present tense in first person singular also indicates a suggested action (see explanation for future tense with first person (inclusive) plural after the first dialogue in Unit 1):

paakkireen. Let me see. I'll see.

If you listen to the tapes accompanying this book carefully, you will observe that the **i** of **-kkir-** is commonly dropped, so that you hear something more like **paakreen**.

Linking sounds

As already indicated, when a suffix beginning with a vowel sound follows, some change may take place at the end of the word to which the suffix is added: (1) if the word ends in **i**, **ii**, **e** or **ee**, a **y** is inserted between this final vowel and the vowel suffix; (2) if the word ends in **uu**, **oo**, **a** or **aa**, a **v** is inserted; (3) final **u** disappears; (4) in a number of words, the consonants **l** and **ḷ** have been given in parentheses, as they are not pronounced when the words occur alone. These consonants are, however, pronounced when followed by a suffix beginning with a vowel:

1	**ṭæksi** + **aa** → **ṭæksiyaa**	taxi?
2	**Amerikkaa** + **aa** → **Amerikkaavaa**	America?
3	**ooṭṭalu** + **aa** → **ooṭṭalaa**	hotel?
4	**niinga** + **aa** → **niingaḷaa**	you?

Non-subject form of nouns

In Unit 1, 'non-subject' forms of pronouns were given (i.e. the forms used when the pronoun is not the subject of the sentence). Certain nouns also have a 'non-subject' form, i.e. a special form to which a case suffix is added. A noun that ends in **-ḍu** preceded by a long vowel or more than one syllable changes the ending to

-ṭṭu in the 'non-subject' form. In the examples below, the simple 'non-subject' form is followed by the dative case of the same noun.

viiḍu house → **viiṭṭu** **viiṭṭukku** to the house
odaḍu lip → **odaṭṭu** **odaṭṭukku** to the lip(s)

Members of one large set of nouns referring to non-human beings or things end in **-am**. This changes to **-att**(**u**) before any suffix is added:

maram tree → **marattu** **marattukku** to the tree

Exercise 1 (Audio 1: 14)

Indicate that different people are going somewhere. Use a variety of destinations (e.g. home, hotel, beach, Chennai (**Cenne**), London (**Laṇḍan**)).

Example: **naan**: **naan sinimaavukku pooreen.**

1 naama
2 naanga
3 nii
4 niinga
5 avan
6 ava
7 avaru
8 avanga
9 Murugan
10 Mr Smith
11 peeraasiriyar
12 adu
13 ṭæksi

Exercise 2

Let the action be in the future. Change all the sentences you have made for Exercise 1 into the future tense.

Example: **naan sinimaavukku pooveen.**

Derived nouns

It is very common to derive one noun from another by adding **-kaaran** (masculine), **-kaari** (feminine), **-kaararu** (polite masculine), or **-kaaranga(ḷ)** (plural), according to the gender indicated:

ṭæksikkaaranga(ḷ)	taxi people, taxi drivers
ooṭṭalkaaran	hotel man (hotel clerk, hotel owner, etc.)
viiṭṭukkaararu	man of the house (husband, owner of the house)
viiṭṭukkaari	wife (informal)

Emphasis

In Dialogue 1 of Unit 1, **taan** was given as an emphatic form. Another form used for emphasis is **-ee**, among the meanings of which are 'contrary to the expected', 'exclusively':

naanee pooreen.	I am myself (which is not usual) going.
naanee eḍukkireen.	I myself (without others) will take (it).

Demonstrative and interrogative pronouns

'Proximate' and 'remote' pronouns (beginning with the vowels **i-** and **a-** respectively) were introduced after Dialogue 2 of Unit 1. Corresponding to these is a set of interrogative pronouns beginning with the vowel **e-**. These are used to ask the question 'which' in relation to a set of persons already mentioned. To ask 'who' in a more general sense, **yaaru** is used:

	Demonstrative		*Interrogative*
	Proximate	*Remote*	
Masculine	**ivan**	**avan**	**evan, yaaru**
Feminine	**iva(ḷ)**	**ava(ḷ)**	**eva(ḷ), yaaru**
Polite masculine	**ivaru**	**avaru**	**evaru, yaaru**
Plural	**ivanga(ḷ)**	**avanga(ḷ)**	**evanga(ḷ), yaaru**

Some manner adverbs

In the dialogue, **ipḍi** 'like this' occurred. In connection with what is said in the preceding paragraph, note also **apḍi** 'like that', and **epḍi** 'like what?', 'how?'.

Exercise 3

Match each word in the first column with the appropriate one in the second:

1	peeraasiriyar	a	varriyaa
2	Kalyaaṇi	b	poovoom
3	naanga	c	iruppaan
4	nii	d	irukkum
5	Murugan	e	varraa
6	adu	f	poovaaru

 Dialogue 2 (Audio 1: 15)

Hailing an autorickshaw

A cheap and convenient way to get around most Indian cities is by autorickshaw. Murugan hails an autorickshaw by raising and waving his right hand and shouting 'aaṭṭoo!'

AUTO DRIVER:	enge pooriinga?
MURUGAN:	rayilvee sṭeeṣanukku.
AUTO DRIVER:	ukkaarunga. nuuru ruubaa kuḍunga.
MURUGAN:	enna? nuuru ruubaayaa? pattu kiloomiiṭṭardaan irukkum. miiṭṭar pooḍu.
AUTO DRIVER:	miiṭṭar rippeer, saar.
MURUGAN:	aaṭṭookkaaranga ellaarum ipḍidaan solriinga. janangaḷe eemaatturiinga.
AUTO DRIVER:	peṭrool liṭṭar muppadu ruubaaykki vikkidu. pooliskaarangaḷukku maamuul kuḍukkaṉum.
MURUGAN:	sari, sari. embadu ruuba kuḍukkireen. poo.

AUTO DRIVER:	*Where are you going?*
MURUGAN:	*To the railway station.*
AUTO DRIVER:	*Sit down. Give me a hundred rupees.*
MURUGAN:	*What? A hundred rupees? It's only ten kilometres. Set the meter.*
AUTO DRIVER:	*The meter's under repair, sir.*
MURUGAN:	*All you auto drivers say this. You cheat people.*
AUTO DRIVER:	*Petrol costs thirty rupees a litre. We have to give bribes to the police.*
MURUGAN:	*OK, OK. I'll give eighty rupees. Go.*

Vocabulary

rayilvee sṭeeṣan	railway station	**nuuru**	hundred
ruubaa(y)	rupee (basic unit of Indian currency)	**kuḍu**	give
		enna	what
		kiloomiiṭṭar	kilometre
miiṭṭar	meter	**rippeer**	repair
saar	sir, a term of address	**aaṭṭookkaaranga(ḷ)**	autorickshaw drivers
ellaarum	all	**sollu**	say
jananga(ḷ)	people	**eemaattu**	cheat
peṭrool	petrol, gas	**liṭṭar**	litre
muppadu	thirty	**villu**	sell
pooliskaaranga(ḷ)	policemen	**maamuul**	bribe (*lit.* customary thing)
embadu	eighty		
sari	OK		

Language points

Accusative case

This case marks the object of the sentence and its suffix is **-e**. An object noun that does not refer to a human being may not have this case suffix if it is not particularised.

paalu kuḍi.	Drink milk.
inda paale kuḍi.	Drink this milk.

'All'

As mentioned in the previous unit, most words that modify a noun (including adjectives and numerals) come before the noun, as in English. One important exception to this is **ellaarum** 'all', which occurs after the noun, as in **aaṭṭookkaaranga ellaarum** 'all auto-drivers'. An alternative is to put **ellaa** before the noun and **-um** after it: **ellaa aaṭṭookkaarangaḷum**.

Note the use of **rippeer** (borrowed from English) in the dialogue to mean 'under repair'.

Exercise 4

Where is Gopalan going? Give him a variety of destinations.

Example: to the hotel **avan ooṭṭalukku pooraan**

1 home
2 to the room
3 to Madras
4 to London
5 to America

Exercise 5

Locate things at the back and then at the front.

Example: **ṭæksi pinnaale irukku** **ṭæksi munnaale irukku**

1 ooṭṭalu
2 viiḍu
3 ruum

4 maaṉavan
5 peeraasiriyar
6 Murugan
7 Mr Smith

Dialogue 3 (Audio 1: 16)

Checking into a hotel

With Murugan's help, Smith checks into a hotel.

MURUGAN:	ruum irukkaa?
CLERK:	risarveeṣan irukkaa?
SMITH:	ille.
CLERK:	irunga, paakkireen . . . irukku. ettane naaḷekki?
SMITH:	oru vaarattukku.
CLERK:	ee si ruumaa? saadaaraṇa ruumaa?
SMITH:	saadaaraṇa ruumee poodum.
MURUGAN:	ille. veyil romba aḍikkidu. ee si ruumee nalladu.
SMITH:	sari. adeyee kuḍunga.

MURUGAN:	*Do you have a room?* (lit. *Is there a room?*)
CLERK:	*Do you have a reservation?* (lit. *Is there a reservation?*)
SMITH:	*No.*
CLERK:	*Wait. I'll see . . . I have one.* (lit. *There is*) *For how many days?*
SMITH:	*For a week.*
CLERK:	(*Do you want*) *an AC (air-conditioned) room or an ordinary room?*
SMITH:	*An ordinary room will do.*
MURUGAN:	*No. It's very hot. An AC (air-conditioned) room* (*will be*) *better.*
SMITH:	*Fine. Give* (*me*) *an AC room.*

Vocabulary

ruum	room	**iru**	be, have, wait
risarveeṣan	reservation	**paaru**	see, check, try
ettane	how many	**naaḷu**	day
oru	one (adj)	**vaaram**	week

ee si	AC (air conditioned)	**aḍi**	hit, beat
saadaaraṇam	ordinary, common	**veyil**	sunshine
poodum	enough, sufficient	**veyil aḍi**	be hot
nalladu	good, good thing	**kuḍu**	give

Language points

Note on iru *'be'*

When the verb **iru** 'be' occurs with the dative case with human nouns, it translates as 'have'. The dative/locative noun may be understood (i.e. not expressed) in a dialogue:

ruum irukkaa? Do you have a room? (*lit.* Is there a room?)

If, on making an enquiry at a hotel reception, one wished to be more specific, one could choose either of the following: **ooṭṭalle ruum irukkaa** or **ongagiṭṭe ruum irukkaa**.

If you were asking another (prospective) guest if he has a room, you would ask **ongaḷukku ruum irukkaa?** From these examples you will see that to indicate possession, or the person who has something, there is a choice between **-kku** (dative case) and **-giṭṭe** or **-ṭṭe** (locative case). The second of these is used if a thing possessed is in principle available for giving away. Thus one might say:

ongagiṭṭe kaaru irukkaa? Do you have a car?

With this compare:

ongaḷukku piḷḷe irukkaa? Do you have (any) children?

In many cases the use of **-giṭṭe** resembles the use of 'on' in English; e.g. 'Do you have money on you?' (**ongagiṭṭe paṇam irukkaa?**).

Exercise 6

Ask Raman if he has:

1 a younger brother (tambi)
2 an elder brother (aṇṇan)
3 a younger sister (tangacci)
4 an elder sister (akkaa)
5 a pen (peenaa)

Noun as 'adjective' in predicate

Words having the form of an adjective do not occur as predicates, but only before a noun as a modifier. A noun of quality occurring as a predicate translates as an adjective. There is usually no verb 'be' in such sentences: **inda ruum nalladu** 'This room (is) a good one'. With this can be compared the adjective **nalla** 'good' occurring before a noun, as in **nalla ruum** 'a good room'. An alternative structure to the one given (and with a somewhat different meaning) is: **inda ruum nallaa irukku** 'This room is good'. Note the adverbial ending **-aa** when the verb **iru** ('be') is used; see the paragraph on adverbs on page 70.

Numerals (Audio 1: 17)

A few numerals have been introduced in dialogues. A few more follow. With one exception, the same form is used both in counting and before a noun. The exception is 'one': **oru viiḍu** 'one house' (also 'a house'), but **oṇṇu** in the sequence '1, 2, 3, . . .'. Similarly when a larger numeral ends in 'one': **padinoṇṇu** 'eleven', but **padinoru viiḍu** 'eleven houses'.

oṇṇu	1	**padinoṇṇu**	11
reṇḍu	2	**panireṇḍu**	12
muuṇu	3	**padimuuṇu**	13
naalu	4	**padinaalu**	14
anju	5	**padinanju**	15
aaru	6	**padinaaru**	16
eeẓu	7	**padineeẓu**	17
eṭṭu	8	**padineṭṭu**	18
ombadu	9	**pattombadu**	19
pattu	10		
iruvadu	20	**aruvadu**	60
muppadu	30	**eẓuvadu**	70
naappadu	40	**embadu**	80
ambadu	50	**toṇṇuuru**	90
nuuru	100	**aayiram**	1000

Exercise 7

Read aloud the numbers 1–20 in ascending order.

Exercise 8

Find out how many. Notice that neuter nouns, even when referring to more than one thing, do not usually take the plural suffix **-ga(ḷ)**. Plural nouns referring to humans, on the other hand, always take this suffix. Provide answers to your questions.

Example: **ettane ruum irukku? muppadu ruum irukku.**

1 ooṭṭalu
2 viiḍu
3 ṭæksi
4 naaḷu
5 maaṇavanga

Tamil script

We look here at some of the signs you will see as you go around Chennai and other cities. Since you have learnt a little about travelling by bus, note that in buses some seats are often reserved for female passengers. This is indicated by மகளிர் மட்டும் **magaḷir maṭṭum** 'women only'. In this phrase you see

- two examples of consonant letters with the 'inherent' vowel **a**: ம and க (**ma** and **ka**)
- three examples of consonant letters with **puḷḷi**: ர் (**r**), ட் (**ṭ**) and ம் (**m**)
- a letter made up of consonant + the vowel **i**: ளி (**ḷi**), showing that a vowel **i** coming immediately after a consonant is represented by ി
- a letter made up of consonant + the vowel **u**: டு. If you compare this with ட, you will see that, in the case of some consonant + vowel symbols, the vowel is not simply the addition of vowel symbol to the basic consonant shape; there are other modifications. This applies to short **u** and long **uu**. For each, there are several different possibilities, depending on the consonant. It is therefore probably easier to learn each of these separately, though in doing so you will begin to see certain patterns.

You may be puzzled by the fact that க is transcribed above by both **ka** and **ga**. This is because the Tamil writing system does not distinguish between the two members of such pairs of consonants as **k/g**, **ṭ/ḍ**, **t/d** and **p/b**. With native Tamil words, this causes no problem; the position in the word determines which sound is used. For words borrowed from other languages, the pronunciation of each has to be learnt separately. The fact that many of these borrowings are from English will reduce the difficulty; e.g. பஸ், written 'pas' but pronounced **bas**. In Tamil words, only the first member of each pair of sounds – i.e. **k**, **ṭ**, **t** and **p** – occurs at the beginning of a word.

Here are a few more words: கட்டணக் கழிப்பறை **kaṭṭaṇak kaẓippaṟai** 'public (paying) toilet'; ஆண் **aaṇ** 'men'; பெண் **peṇ** 'women'. Can you work out which Tamil letters correspond to which Roman letters? In றை, the vowel (or, more exactly, the diphthong) **ai** is represented by ை. What other vowel symbol here comes before the consonant in writing what is a consonant-vowel sequence? You will have observed that, in such signs as those given here, ஆண் and பெண் are singular in form. With regard to 'r' sounds, the script differentiates between ர் (**r**) and ற் (**ṟ**). For the standard colloquial dialect, however, **r** alone is required.

Exercise 9

Match the Tamil letters or syllables in the first set with the appropriate transcribed form in the second:

1 ஆ	2 ம்	3 பெ	4 ஓ	5 ண்	6 ட	7 க
a **ṇ**	b **ka**	c **m**	d **oo**	e **ṭa**	f **aa**	g **pe**

3 enna veeɳum?

What would you like?

In this unit you will learn to:

- order food in a restaurant
- buy things in a shop
- buy stamps in a post office
- express desire and need
- state alternatives
- use question words
- express obligation
- use verbs borrowed from English

Dialogue 1 (Audio 1: 18)

Eating in a restaurant

Smith orders breakfast for himself in a restaurant.

Waiter: enna veeɳum?
Smith: doose irukkaa?
Waiter: irukku. saadaa dooseyaa? masaalaa dooseyaa?
Smith: masaalaa doose. saambaarum kuɖunga. iɳɳekki enna saambaar?
Waiter: kattarikkaa saambaar. kaapi veeɳumaa? ʈiiyaa?
Smith: kaapi. cakkare veeɳɖaam.
(*After eating*)
Smith: billu kuɖunga.
Waiter: indaanga billu. pattu ruubaa.

WAITER: *What would you like?*
SMITH: *Do you have dosa?*
WAITER: *Do you want plain dosa or masala dosa?*
SMITH: *Masala dosa. Let me have* (lit. *give*) *sambar also. What sambar* (*is it*) *today?*
WAITER: *Brinjal sambar. Would you like coffee or tea?*
SMITH: *Coffee. Without sugar, please.* (lit. *I don't want sugar*)
(After eating)
SMITH: *Give me the bill please.*
WAITER: *Here's your bill, sir. Ten rupees.*

Vocabulary

veeṇum	want
saadaa	ordinary, not special (short for **saadaaraṇa(m)**)
doose	pancake made of fermented rice and black gram flour
masaalaa	curry made of potatoes and ground spices
saambaar	sauce made of yellow split peas and spices
kattarikkaa(y)	brinjal, aubergine, egg-plant
kaapi	coffee
ṭii	tea
cakkare	sugar
billu	bill

Language and cultural points

Starting the day

Tamil breakfast in middle-class families generally consists of some fried or steamed snack made of rice or wheat flour that is eaten with some spicy side dish. Two possibilities – **doose** and **iḍli** – are mentioned in the dialogue. Others are **puuri** (flat wheat cake, fried), **vaḍe** (small savoury cake made of black gram or split peas, fried) and **uppumaa** (cooked cream of wheat). The savoury snack is followed by coffee or tea, which is generally taken with milk and sugar.

Question words

From examples already given (see p. 30), you will have noticed that most question words begin with **e-** : **enna** 'what', **enge** 'where', **enda** 'which (adjective)', **edu** 'which (pronoun)', **epḍi** 'how', **ettane** 'how many', **evḷavu** 'how much', **eppa** 'when'. An exception to this generalisation is **yaaru** 'who'.

Expression of desire and need

veeṇum expresses want or need when it occurs alone with a noun. The equivalent of its subject in English is in the dative case in Tamil, as in:

enakku kaapi veeṇum.	I want coffee.
avanukku ṭii veeṇum.	He wants tea.

When **veeṇum** occurs with the infinitive of a verb, it abbreviates to **-ṇum** and the 'want' or 'need' has to do with the meaning of the verb. It translates into English as 'want to (do)' or 'must (do)'. Examples of this construction will be given later. The negative of **veeṇum** is **veeṇḍaam**, which is not abbreviated.

Exercise 1 (Audio 1: 18)

People want different things and often they do not know what they want. Provide questions and then answers based on the hints given below.

Example: **avangaɭukku enna veeɳum?** What do they want?
avangaɭukku doose veeɳum. They want dosa.

1 avanukku	iɖli
2 avaɭukku	puuri
3 Muruganukku	uppumaa
4 Robert-ukku	vaɖe

Exercise 2 (Audio 1: 18)

They do not want what you guessed. Tell the waiter that they do not want the thing you said.

Example: **avangaɭukku doose veeɳɖaam.**

-um *'also', 'and'*

When **-um** is added to a noun or an adverb, it has the meaning 'also': **saambaarum** 'sambar also'. If it is added to each of a succession of two or more words, it acts as a co-ordinator, that is to say it is the equivalent of English 'and': **dooseyum saambaarum kaapiyum** 'dosa, sambar and coffee'. Note that while in such a list in English 'and' occurs only once, **-um** is added to each item listed.

Alternative questions

When more than one interrogative form with **-aa** occurs in a row, this (as the translations in Dialogue 1 show) implies these are alternatives and gives the meaning of 'or'. The word **alladu** 'or' may be used additionally: **kaapiyaa alladu ʈiiyaa?** 'Tea or coffee?'

Linking sounds

The linking sound **y** has been shown in Unit 1 to appear after certain words when they are followed by a vowel. This rule was shown to apply when the word in question ended in **i**, **ii**, **e** or **ee**. In some words, **y** also occurs after other vowels. These words are indicated by (**y**) at the end in vocabularies.

Exercise 3 (Audio 1: 18)

Give each of the same people in Exercise 2 a choice and ask them which one they want. They all want the first thing you mention.

Example:
ongaḷukku kaapi veeṇumaa? ṭii veeṇumaa?
Do you want coffee or tea?

enakku kaapi veeṇum. I want coffee.

1 paalu (milk)	kaapi
2 juus (juice)	paalu
3 caṭni (chutney)	saambaar
4 vengaaya (onion) saambaar	kattarikkaa saambaar

Exercise 4

Tell us what each one does not want (which in each case will be the second of the options you offered).

Example: **enakku ṭii veeṇḍaam.** I don't want tea.

Dialogue 2 (Audio 1: 19)

Buying groceries

SHOPKEEPER:	vaanga. niinga uurukku pudusaa?
SMITH:	aamaa. viiṭṭukku konjam saamaan vaanganum.
SHOPKEEPER:	nalla arisi irukku. evḷavu veeṇum?
SMITH:	anju kiloo kuḍunga. koodume maavu irukkaa?
SHOPKEEPER:	irukku. adu anju kiloo kuḍukkireen. veere enna veeṇum?
SMITH:	samayalukku veere enna veeṇum?

SHOPKEEPER:	tovaram paruppu, eṇṇe, puḷi, masaalaa saamaan. idu poodumaa?
SMITH:	poodum, poodum . . . oo, uppu veeṇum.
SHOPKEEPER:	aamaa, aamaa. indaanga.
SMITH:	evḷavu aagudu?
SHOPKEEPER:	irunga, kaṇakku pooḍreen. munnuuru ruuba aagudu.

SHOPKEEPER:	*Good morning.* (lit. *Come*) *Are you new to the town?*
SMITH:	*Yes, I want to buy a few things for the house.*
SHOPKEEPER:	*There's some good rice. How much do you want?*
SMITH:	*Give me five kilos. Do you have wheat flour?*
SHOPKEEPER:	*We do. I'll give you five kilos. What else do you want?*
SMITH:	*What else do I need for cooking?*
SHOPKEEPER:	*Split lentils, oil, tamarind, spices. Will this be enough?*
SMITH:	*That's enough . . . Oh, I need some salt.*
SHOPKEEPER:	*Yes. Here you are.*
SMITH:	*How much is it?*
SHOPKEEPER:	*Wait, I'll work it out. It's three hundred rupees.*

Vocabulary

uuru	town, place where people live	**pudusu**	new
		vaangu	buy
saamaan	thing, provision	**nalla**	good
arisi	rice (uncooked)	**evḷavu**	how much
kiloo	kilogram	**anju**	five
koodume	wheat	**maavu**	flour
samayal	cooking	**veere**	else, other
eṇṇe	oil	**tovaram paruppu**	split lentil
puḷi	tamarind	**masaalaa**	spice
poodum	enough	**uppu**	salt
aagu	become, be	**kaṇakku**	calculation
pooḍu	put, make	**munnuuru**	300

Language points

Rice

As noted in the vocabulary, **arisi** is rice in its uncooked state. Rice when boiled for eating is **sooru**, while a rice crop growing in a field is **nellu**.

Dative case

Notice the use of the dative case (**-ukku**) in instances where English has ‘for’: **viiʈʈukku saamaan** ‘things for the house’, and **samay-alukku** ‘for cooking’.

Enough

To express the idea that one has enough of something, **poodum** ‘(it) is enough/sufficient’ is used. The corresponding negative form is **poodaadu** ‘(it) is insufficient/not enough’.

Hundreds

Here are a few numerals, in steps of 100 (**nuuru**), to add to those in Unit 2:

eranuuru	200	**aranuuru**	600
munnuuru	300	**eẓanuuru**	700
naanuuru	400	**eɳɳuuru**	800
aynuuru	500	**toɭaayiram**	900

Exercise 5

Imagine that you are at the vegetable market. Play the part of the shopkeeper and answer the questions put by the customer. Imagine the vegetable in the picture for your answer.

Example:	**idu enna?**	What is this?
	idu kattarikkaa.	This is brinjal.

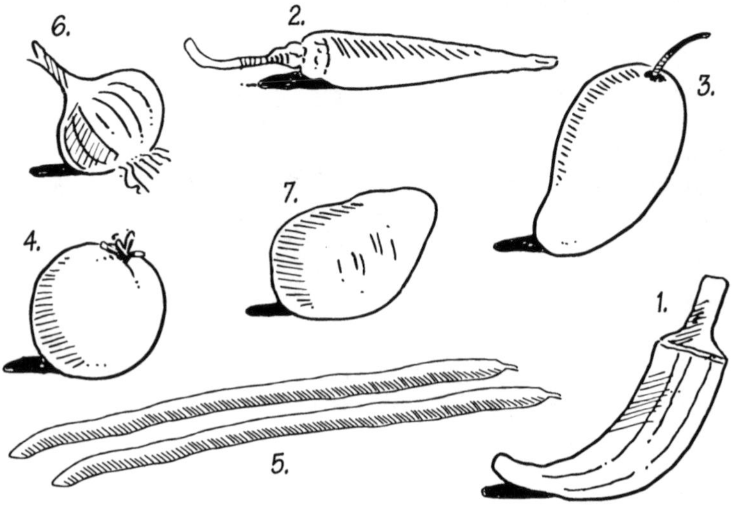

1	veṇḍekkaa(y)	okra, lady's finger
2	meḷagaa(y)	chilli
3	maangaa(y)	unripe mango
4	takkaaḷi	tomato
5	biins	beans
6	vengaayam	onion
7	uruḷekkeẓangu	potato

Exercise 6

Now play the part of the customer and ask for the names of the vegetables in the picture above in their given order. Give the shopkeeper's answer.

Example: **idu kattarikkaayaa?** Is this aubergine?
aamaa, idu kattarikkaa. Yes, it is aubergine.

Dialogue 3 (Audio 1: 20)

Post office

SMITH: inda kavarukku evḷavu sṭaampu oṭṭaṇum?
CLERK: idu enge poogudu? Laṇḍanukkaa?

SMITH: aamaa.
CLERK: rijisṭar-paṉriingaḷaa?
SMITH: ille. saadaaraṉa tabaaldaan.
CLERK: nuuru graam irukku. padinanju ruubaaykki sṭaampu oṭṭaṉum.
SMITH: pattu padinanju ruubaa sṭaampu kuḍunga. Madurekki oru kavarukku evḷavu aagum?
CLERK: muuṉu ruubaa aagum.
SMITH: muuṉu ruubaa sṭaampu pattu kuḍunga.

SMITH: *How much will it cost to send this letter?* (lit. *How much worth of stamps should I stick on this envelope?*)
CLERK: *Where is it going? To London?*
SMITH: *Yes.*
CLERK: *Are you registering it?*
SMITH: *No. Just ordinary post.*
CLERK: *It's a hundred grams. You need to put stamps to fifteen rupees.*
SMITH: *Give me ten fifteen-rupee stamps. How much is it for a letter to Madurai?*
CLERK: *It'll be three rupees.*
SMITH: *Give me ten three-rupee stamps.*

Vocabulary

kavaru	envelope, cover
Laṇḍan	London
tabaal	mail
Madure	Madurai, a major city in Tamil Nadu
sṭaampu	stamp
oṭṭu	stick, paste
graam	gram

Language points

The use of -ṇum *to express need or obligation*

When **-ṇum** (which, as mentioned earlier in this unit, is the short form of **veeṇum**) is added to the infinitive of a verb, it can have the sense of need or obligation. Thus, in the dialogue, **oṭṭaṇum** means 'should/must stick'. In the sentences in which it occurs here, no subject is expressed. If it were, the noun or pronoun would be in the nominative (i.e. subject) case. Compare this (in the notes following Dialogue 2) with the use of the dative case when **veeṇum** is used to express the sense of 'wanting' something, and the something is represented by a noun. Examples of infinitive + **-ṇum**:

naan evḷavu sṭaampu oṭṭaṇum?	How much (worth of) stamps should I stick?
niinga kuḍukkaṇum.	You should give (it).
Murugan varaṇum.	Murugan should come.

Using English verbs in Tamil

Quite often English words are used in Tamil conversation, even by speakers whose knowledge of English is small. In the case of verbs, however, Tamil grammatical endings are not added directly to the borrowed word. Instead, the verb **paṇṇu** 'do' is first added to the English word to make it a verb. This will come in handy when you cannot recall a particular Tamil verb. More on this mixing of English words in Tamil is to be found in the dialogues in Unit 11. So, in Dialogue 3, we see **rijisṭar-paṇṇu** for English 'register'.

Order of words in number phrases

As is clear from Dialogue 2, there are two possible positions for a numeral when used along with a noun. One might say that the basic position, as with all adjectives, is before the noun. However, a numeral can follow a noun, particularly if there is another modifier of the noun incorporating a numeral, as in 'five-rupee stamp' (**anju-ruubaa sʈaampu**). If one wants six of such an item, for example, one can say **aaru anju-ruubaa sʈaampu** or **anju-ruubaa sʈaampu aaru**. If the number is 'one', the form of the numeral varies with its position: **oru anju-ruubaa sʈaampu** or **anju-ruubaa sʈaampu oɳɳu**.

Exercise 7 (Audio 1: 21)

Buy the following items at the post office:

Example: **irubadu ruubaa sʈaampu reɳɖu kuɖunga.**
Please let me have two twenty-rupee stamps.

1 Five ten-rupee stamps
2 Ten five-rupee stamps
3 Three fifteen-rupee stamps
4 Fifteen three-rupee stamps
5 Four air letters (eer meyil)
6 Five inland letter forms (inlaanɖ)

Exercise 8 (Audio 1: 21)

Tell the clerk that your letter is going to one of the following places, and ask how much it will cost. Practise with each of the place names.

Example: **idu Fransukku poogudu; evɭavu aagum?**

1 London (Laɳɖan)
2 Chennai (Cenne)
3 Paris (Paaris)
4 The USA (Amerikkaa)

Exercise 9

Sort the following items into two separate categories:

doose **uppu** **maavu** **arisi**
puḷi **iḍli** **cakkare** **sooru** **vaḍe**

Tamil script

Let's look at some of the names of towns and cities you may see on the front of buses or at railway stations. These will be in the form in which you would see them, that is to say in the standard written style, and will in most cases be rather different from the form you would use in conversation. This list of place names serves as a reminder that the Tamil writing system does not distinguish between capitals and lower case letters.

சென்னை	**cen̲n̲ai**	Chennai/Madras
எழும்பூர்	**ez̤umbuur**	Egmore (an area of Chennai and the name of a railway station)
பாரிமுனை	**paari mun̲ai**	Parry's Corner (a part of Chennai)
மதுரை	**madurai**	Madurai
சிதம்பரம்	**cidambaram**	Chidambaram
புதுச்சேரி	**puducceeri**	Pondichery
கன்னியாகுமரி	**kan̲n̲iyaakumari**	Cape Comorin
யாழ்ப்பாணம்	**yaaz̤ppaaṇam**	Jaffna (Sri Lanka)
மட்டக்களப்பு	**maṭṭakkaḷappu**	Batticaloa (Sri Lanka)

The syllable னை (**n̲ai**) is in the modern reformed script and has now widely replaced the earlier form னை. Three other consonants used to combine with **ai** in this way: ணை, லை and ளை (**ṇai**, **lai**, and **ḷai**), but these have largely given way to ணை, லை and ளை. In the remainder of this book, only these modern forms will be used. Note that ர் (**r**) is also printed as ா்.

Exercise 10

From the examples in the above list match the Tamil script items below with the appropriate items in transcription:

1	ண	2	னை	3	கு	4	ழு	5	னி
6	பூ	7	சே	8	மு	9	சி	10	து
a	**ṉai**	b	**ʐu**	c	**cee**	d	**ɳa**	e	**puu**
f	**ci**	g	**ku**	h	**tu**	i	**ṉi**	j	**mu**

4 haloo, naan Smith peesureen

Hello, this is Smith

In this unit you will learn to:

- make a telephone call
- travel by bus
- buy a train ticket
- tell the time
- order things numerically
- use the verb **poo** 'go' to express future action
- use postpositions
- indicate the location of something

Dialogue 1 (Audio 1: 22)

Making a telephone call

Smith phones Professor Madhivanan to make an appointment to see him.

SMITH: haloo, naan Smith peesureen. peeraasiriyar irukkaaraa?

MADHIVANAN: naandaan Madivaaṇan peesureen. epḍi irukkiinga?

SMITH: nallaa irukkeen. iṇṇekki ongaḷe paakka muḍiyumaa?

MADHIVANAN: naalu maṇikki viiṭṭukku vaanga. epḍi vara pooriinga?

SMITH: basle.

MADHIVANAN: onga ooṭṭal munnaale eṭṭaam nambar bas nikkum. adule vaanga.

SMITH: adu neere onga viiṭṭupakkam varudaa?

MADHIVANAN: aamaa. niinga Layoolaa kaaleej sṭaaple erangunga. pattu miiṭṭarle eḍadu pakkam oru teru poogum. adule modal viiḍu enga viiḍu. viiṭṭu nambar oṇṇu.
SMITH: nalladu. apḍiyee seyreen.
MADHIVANAN: sari. naalu maṇikki paappoom.

SMITH: *Hello. This is Smith. Is the professor in?*
MADHIVANAN: *This is Madhivanan speaking. How are you?*
SMITH: *I'm fine. Is it possible to see you today?*
MADHIVANAN: *Come to the house at four o'clock. How will you get here?* (lit. *How will you come?*)
SMITH: *By bus.*
MADHIVANAN: *The number 8 bus stops in front of your hotel. Take that one.* (lit. *Come in that*)
SMITH: *Does it stop near your house?* (lit. *Does it come direct to the vicinity of your house?*)
MADHIVANAN: *Yes. Get off* (lit. *down*) *at the Loyola College stop. After ten metres there is a street on the left.* (lit. *Ten metres on left side a street goes*) *Our house is the first one.* (lit: *The first house in it is our house*) *House number one.*
SMITH: *Fine. I'll do that.*
MADHIVANAN: *Right. We'll meet at four o'clock.*

Vocabulary

nallaa	well, good	**iṇṇekki**	today
paaru	see, meet	**muḍiyum**	can, be able, be possible
naalu	four	**maṇi**	hour, time
bas	bus	**eṭṭu**	eight
nambar	number	**nillu**	stop, stand
neere	straight, directly	**pakkam**	side, towards, in the direction of, nearby
kaaleej	college		

sṭaap	stop	**pattu**	ten
miiṭṭar	metre	**eḍadu**	left (side)
teru	street	**modal**	first
nalladu	good, fine	**apḍi**	like that, so

Language points

Speaking on the telephone

Note the convention for identifying yourself at the beginning of a telephone call: use the first person singular pronoun **naan** 'I', followed by your name, followed by the first person singular present tense of the verb **peesu** 'speak'. The name may be used on its own, without the pronoun, but the verbal ending will still be first person. Thus Kalyani may say either **naan Kalyaaṇi peesureen** or **Kalyaaṇi peesureen** for 'This is Kalyani speaking.'

Asking if someone is in

Look again at Smith's first question. If you telephone somewhere or call at a place and wish to ask if X is there, you ask simply 'Is X?', that is to say that no adverb is necessary. The appropriate personal ending on the verb, of course, must be used: **ammaa irukkaangaḷaa?** 'Is mother (there)?'; **Murugan irukkaanaa?** 'Is Murugan (in)?'

Exercise 1 (Audio 1: 23)

Telephone your office and ask if each of the following is there (Lakshmi and Murugesan are senior female and male colleagues respectively, Raman is the office boy and Mullai is a junior typist):

Example: **haloo, naan Raajaa peesureen. Smith irukkaaraa?**

1 Lakṣmi 2 Murugeesan 3 Raaman 4 Mulle

Telling the time

Stating the time on the hour is done by giving a number preceded by **maṇi** 'hour': **maṇi pattu** 'The time is ten', 'It's ten o'clock.' To indicate 'at' a certain time, **maṇi** in the dative case is preceded by the appropriate number: **pattu maṇikki** 'at ten o'clock'. For times on the quarter hour, the following three items are used: **kaal** 'quarter', **are** 'half', and **mukkaa(l)** 'three quarters'. You will need to keep in mind two other points: (a) **-ee** is added to the numeral when **kaal** or **mukkaa** follows; (b) the final **-u** of a numeral is dropped when **are** follows:

maṇi enna?	What's the time?
maṇi anjee kaal.	It's a quarter past five.
maṇi anjare.	It's half past five.
maṇi anjee mukkaa.	It's a quarter to six.

'At' these various times is: **anjee kaal maṇikki**, **anjare maṇikki**, **anjee mukkaa maṇikki**.

Time can also be told in minutes. There are two ways of saying it: (a) by juxtaposing a numeral for the hour and a numeral for the number of minutes – exactly as in English; (b) by adding **-aagi** after the numeral for the hour and following this with the second numeral + the word **nimiṣam** 'minute':

a	**anju pattu**	five ten
b	**anjaagi pattu nimiṣam**	ten minutes past five

Exercise 2 (Audio 1: 24)

Tell the time. Imagine that someone asks you the time every hour from 5 o'clock until 10.

Example: **maṇi enna?** What's the time?
maṇi anju. It's 5 o'clock.

Exercise 3

Time can be a fraction of the hour. Imagine that someone asks you the time every quarter of an hour from 5 o'clock until 7 and you tell the time.

Exercise 4

Tell the time ten minutes after the hour from 5.10 to 10.10.

Expression of possibility and ability

muḍiyum preceded by the infinitive of a verb means that the subject of the sentence is able to do the action of the verb or that it is possible for the subject to do the action. This subject can take one of two different forms. The first is the one that occurs most frequently as subject (referred to by some as the nominative case). The second is with the ending **-aale** (which, because it may be used to refer to the person by whom an action was done, or the instrument with which an action was performed, you may see referred to as the agentive case or instrumental case). The following sentences show the two alternatives:

naan vara muḍiyum.	I can come.
ennaale vara muḍiyum.	

The equivalent negative form is **muḍiyaadu** 'cannot': **naan/ennaale solla muḍiyaadu** 'I can't say.'

Future action: poo

The infinitive of a verb + **poo** 'go' in the present tense expresses a future action that is going to take place: **naan vara pooreen** 'I shall come.' Compare the use of 'be going to' in English.

Postpositions

Where English uses prepositions, Tamil often uses postpositions. As the name implies, these follow the noun. Many postpositions are spatial terms and indicate location. An example in Dialogue 1 is **pakkam** 'near', in the phrase **onga viiṭṭupakkam** 'near your house'. Notice that **pakkam** here follows the 'non-subject' form of the noun **viiḍu**.

Location

Location in a fairly general sense is expressed by the 'locative' case suffix **-le**, which translates into English as 'in, 'on', 'at', etc. In **basle** in the dialogue it translates as 'by'.

Ordinal numbers

Ordinal forms of numerals (equivalent to English '-th' forms, as in 'fourth') are formed by adding **-aavadu** to the numeral; an alternative form is **-aam**, and this is preferred before some nouns like **nambar** 'number'. For 'first' there is an additional form **modal**, as well as **oṉṉaavadu**.

Verb forms

When the present tense suffix of a verb is **-kkir-** and the future tense suffix is **-pp-** or **-kk-**, the final consonant **r** or **l** of the simple form of the verb disappears; e.g.

nillu	stop	**nikkum.**	It will stop.
paaru	see	**paappoom.**	We shall see.

Remember that the suffix **-kk-** as an indicator of future occurs only with third person neuter forms.

Exercise 5

A few numerals were introduced in Unit 2. Remind yourself of those for one to ten, and say them aloud.

Exercise 6

Order the classes from one to ten, using the suffix **-aam**:

Example:
oṉṉu one + **vaguppu** class → **oṉṉaam vaguppu** first class

Exercise 7

Change 'class' into 'house'. Use **-aavadu** instead of **-aam**.

Example:
oṉṉu one + **viiḍu** house → **oṉṉaavadu viiḍu** first house

Exercise 8

Somebody gives you the number of the streets up to ten and you count them and give their order.

Example: **oru teru** one street **oɳɳaavadu teru** first street

Dialogue 2 (Audio 1: 25)

Travelling by bus

Smith travels by bus from the centre of Chennai to Loyola College.

Bus conductor:	enge poogaɳum?
Smith:	Layoolaa kaaleejukku.
Bus conductor:	oɳɳare ruubaa kuɖunga.
Smith:	oɳɳare ruubaa ille; pattu ruubaaykki sillare irukkumaa?
Bus conductor:	kuɖunga. munnaale eɖam irukku. ange ukkaarunga; vaẓile nikkaadinga.
Smith:	munnaaledaan erangaɳumaa?
Bus conductor:	aamaa.

Bus conductor:	*Where do you want to go?*
Smith:	*To Loyola College.*
Bus conductor:	*That'll be* (lit. *Give me*) *one and a half rupees.*
Smith:	*I don't have one and a half rupees; would you have change for ten rupees?*
Bus conductor:	*I do.* (lit. *Give*) *There's space in front. Sit down there; don't stand in the gangway.*
Smith:	*Should I get off at the front?*
Bus conductor:	*Yes.*

Pronunciation tips

1 **oɳɳare** 'one and a half' is also pronounced as **oɳɖre**. Before **ruubaa** 'rupee' it may be abbreviated to **oɳɳaa**: **oɳɳaa ruubaa** 'one and a half rupees'.
2 In rapid speech, short vowels before **r** or **l** may be dropped, in which case the double consonant before the dropped vowel

becomes a single one; e.g. **sillare** – **silre**; **kattarikkaa** – **katrikkaa**; **viiṭṭule** – **viiṭle**.

Vocabulary

oṇṇare	one and a half
sillare	small change
vaẓi	pathway, path, way

Language points

Negative imperative

To make a request or to give an instruction not to do something, **-aade** is added to the verb stem. For plural (or polite singular), **-aadinga** is added. In the case of verbs where the indicator of present tense is **-kkir-** (and future **-pp-** or **-kk-**), **-kk-** is first added before **-aade** or **-aadinga**:

varaade/varaadinga.	Don't come.
kuḍukkaade/kuḍukkaadinga.	Don't give.
nikkaade/nikkaadinga.	Don't stand.

Future tense and politeness

Note the use of the future tense form **irukkumaa** in Dialogue 2 instead of the present form **irukkaa**, even though the reference is to present time. This has the effect of making the utterance more polite – rather like English 'would you have' in contrast to 'do you have'.

Exercise 9 (Audio 1: 26)

Tell someone not to perform the following actions. Alternate singular and plural (polite) forms.

1 look 2 speak 3 stand 4 sit down
5 eat 6 drink

Exercise 10 (Audio 1: 26)

Ask Murugan if he can do certain things. Alternate positive and negative answers.

Example: **Murugan, niinga viiṭṭukku vara muḍiyumaa?**
Murugan, can you come to (my) house?

muḍiyum. Yes, I can.
muḍiyaadu. No, I can't.

1	kaaleejule peesa	to speak in the college
2	kaḍekki pooga	to go to the shop
3	peeraasiriyare paakka	to see the professor
4	enakku odavi seyya	to help me

Exercise 11

Now list the things Murugan can do and cannot do from the answers. Use the **-aale** form (instrumental case) instead of the nominative.

Example: **Muruganaale viiṭṭukku vara muḍiyum.**
Murugan can come home.

Exercise 12

Different things are in different places. Put the given things in the given places. (Note the difference in the meaning of the locative ending **-le** with different nouns and verbs.)

Example: **Kumaar kaaleej*le* irukkaan.**
Kumar is in the college.

1	Raajaa	viiḍu	irukkaan
2	peenaa	payyi (bag)	irukku
3	pustagam	meese (table)	irukku
4	payyi	sovaru (wall)	tongudu (hangs)
5	nii	bas	vaa
6	peenaave	kayyi (hand)	piḍi (hold)
7	kayye	taṇṇi (water)	kaẓuvu (wash)

Exercise 13

Make the above sentences negative.

Example: **Kumaar kaaleejle ille.**
Kumar is not in the college.

Exercise 14

Poor Raja got instructions to do several different things at 9 o'clock. Write down the things he must do.

Example: **Raajaa ombadu maɳikki kaaleejukku poogaɳ*um*.**
Raja must go to college at 9 o'clock.

1 kaaleejle (peesu)
2 peeraasiriyare (paaru)
3 viiʈʈule (iru)
4 tambikki pustagam (kuɖu)

Exercise 15

Tell those asking the questions that follow that they have no choice and they should do what they were asked to do.

Example: **naan kaaleejukku varaɳumaa?**
Should I come to college?

aamaa, varaɳum.
Yes, you should come.

1 Kumaar kaɖekki poogaɳumaa?
2 Raajaa kaaleejle peesaɳumaa?
3 Maalaa peeraasiriyare paakkaɳumaa?
4 Murugan viiʈʈule irukkaɳumaa?

Dialogue 3 (Audio 1: 27)

Buying a train ticket

Smith goes to Chennai Egmore station to book a seat from there to Madurai.

SMITH: (*to the clerk at the information counter*) Madurekki oru tikkaṭ risarv-paṇṇanum.
CLERK: eṇṇekki pooganum?
SMITH: pattaam teedi.
CLERK: enda ṭreynle pooriinga?
SMITH: Paaṇḍiyanle.
CLERK: eḍam irukku . . . inimee boorḍule niingaḷee paakkaṇum . . . inda faaratte nerappunga. peragu anda varisele nillunga.

SMITH: (to the clerk at the information counter) *I want to book a ticket to Madurai.*
CLERK: *When do you want to go?*
SMITH: *The tenth.*
CLERK: *What train are you going on?*
SMITH: *The Pandian.*
CLERK: *There are seats . . . In future you should check on the board . . . Please fill in this form. Then stand in that queue.*

Vocabulary

eṇṇekki	what day, when	**teedi**	day, date
ṭreyn	train	**eḍam**	seat, place

Paaṉḍiyan	Pandian, name of a train	**boorḍu**	board (now computerised)
paaru	look up, see	**faaram**	form
peragu	then, afterwards	**varise**	line, queue
nillu	stand		

Language points

Emphasis

The emphatic suffix **-ee** at the end of words translates into English as 'oneself', 'right', 'even', etc. depending on the context.

niiyee vaa.	You yourself come.
pinnaaleyee vaa.	Come right behind.
naanee varreen.	I myself will come/Even I am coming.

An English word becomes a Tamil word

Notice that the English word 'form' has become Tamil **faaram** (and, for some speakers, **paaram**). It takes on the same sort of 'non-subject' form as Tamil words ending in **-am**, i.e. **faarattu**, so that 'to the form' is **faarattukku**, and 'on the form' is **faarat(tu)le**.

Exercise 16

You ask the booking clerk at what time the train leaves: **ṭreyn ettane maṉikki porappaḍum?** Give her answers for a few different times of day: 2.00, 3.15, 4.30, 10.45.

Exercise 17

Ask questions about what he – or she, as appropriate – is doing, using the question word given in each instance.

Example:

avan pustagam paḍikkiraan.	He is reading a book.
avan enna paḍikkiraan?	What is he reading?

1	avan kaḍekki pooraan.	enge?
2	avan basle varraan.	edule? epḍi?

3 avan aaru maṉikki peesapooraan. ettane? eppa?
4 ava pattu pustagam vaangapooraa. ettane?
5 ava pattu ruubaa kuḍuppaa. evḷavu?
6 ava Raajaave paappaa. yaare?

Tamil script

The earlier sections on the script have aimed to give a general idea of how it works, with a somewhat miscellaneous set of examples. We turn now to a more structured presentation and begin by focusing on the vowels. We have already seen that vowels at the beginning of a word appear as separate letters, but a vowel occurring in the middle of the word is not represented by one of these but by a different, dependent sign. This sign, depending on the vowel, may occur above, below, after, before, or on both sides of the consonant that occurs before the vowel in speech. Remember that the vowel **a** is 'inherent' in the consonant letter, that is to say that it is represented by the absence of any other sign. To the ten vowels used by all speakers in colloquial forms (**a**, **aa**, **i, ii**, **u**, **uu**, **e**, **ee**, **o**, **oo**) it is necessary to add the diphthongs **ai** and **au** for the written language. As the following table shows, the sign **aa** follows the consonant letter; **i** and **ii** are attached to the top right of the consonant; **u** and **uu** are attached to the bottom of the consonant; **e**, **ee**, and **ai** precede the consonant, and **o**, **oo**, and **au** have two components, one before and one after the consonant. Two vowels, namely **u** and **uu**, need special attention, in that the signs for them have three (**u**) or four (**uu**) distinct forms. In the table, only one out of two slightly differing signs each is given for **i** and **ii**, and only one of the various possibilities is represented for **u** and **uu**. For the sake of simplicity, only one consonant is used in the third column namely '**p** (ப்) + vowel'. The examples in the next column, however, present the vowels in company with a variety of different consonants, with a view to providing examples of more commonly occurring words.

Vowel letter	*Vowel sign*	***p** + vowel*	*Examples*		
அ		ப	அவன்	**avan**	he
ஆ	ா	பா	ஆமா	**aamaa**	yes
இ	ி	பி	இப்படி	**ippaḍi**	like this

Vowel letter	*Vowel sign*	***p*** *+ vowel*	*Examples*		
ஈ	ீ	பீ	ஈ	**ii**	fly
			நீ	**nii**	you
உ	ு	பு	உப்பு	**uppu**	salt
ஊ	ூ	பூ	ஊர்	**uur**	town, village
			பூ	**puu**	flower
எ	ெ	பெ	என்	**en**	my
			பெண்	**peṇ**	girl, woman
ஏ	ே	பே	ஏன்	**een**	why
			பேர்	**peer**	name
ஐ	ை	பை	ஐயோ	**aiyoo**	oh dear! alas!
			பையன்	**paiyan**	boy
ஒ	ெ ா	பொ	ஒலி	**oli**	sound, noise
			பொடி	**poḍi**	powder
ஓ	ே ா	போ	ஓட்டல்	**ooṭṭal**	hotel, restaurant
			போ	**poo**	go
ஔ	ெ ள	பௌ	ஔஷதம்	**auṣadam**	medicine
			வௌவால்	**vauvaal**	bat (mammal)

Before the script was reformed, three consonants had irregular forms for the addition of **aa**. These were ணா (**ṇaa**, modern ணா), றா (**r̲aa**, modern றா) and னா (**n̲aa**, modern னா). These forms were also used with the vowels **o** and **oo**: e.g. ணொ (**ṇo**, modern ணொ) and ணோ (**ṇoo**, modern ணோ). In this book the modern, regular forms are used for these symbols.

In dictionaries, words beginning with vowels precede words beginning with consonants. Vowels follow the order in which they are listed above. The last vowel (ஔ) occurs in only a very small number of words. The 'alphabetical order' for consonants will be presented in the next unit.

Exercise 18

Put the following twelve words in dictionary order:

இந்த; ஓட்டல்; ஈ; அது; உப்பு; ஒரு; ஏன்;

ஆம்; ஊசி; ஐந்து; ஔஷதம்; என்

5 mannikkaɳum, taamadamaa varradukku

I'm sorry I'm late

In this unit you will learn to:

- report an activity
- offer congratulations
- rent a house
- express politeness and gratitude
- make negative statements
- ask different kinds of questions
- form verbal nouns
- use adjectives and adverbs

Dialogue 1 (Audio 1: 28)

Expressing sentiments

Smith apologises for arriving late for his appointment with Professor Madhivanan.

Smith:	mannikkaɳum, taamadamaa varradukku.
Madhivanan:	paravaayille. enna aaccu?
Smith:	basle oree kuuʈʈam. Layoolaa kaaleej sʈaappe paakka muɖiyale. kaɳɖakʈarum sollale.
Madhivanan:	kaɳɖakʈar sollamaaʈʈaan. peragu enna aaccu?
Smith:	Layoolaa kaaleej sʈaaplerundu reɳɖaavadu sʈaap peeru enna? angerundu varreen.
Madhivanan:	aɖa paavamee! ukkaarunga. kaɭeppaa irukkum. kaapi saapɖriingaɭaa?

Smith: saapɖreen. konjam taɳɳiyum kuɖunga.

(*After some time*)

Madhivanan: naan aaru maɳikki oru kuuʈʈattukku poogaɳum. neeram aaccu. naama romba neeram peesa muɖiyale. mannikkaɳum.

Smith: ille, ille. en tappudaan. innoru naaɭekki varreen. nidaanamaa peesalaam.

Madhivanan: sari.

Smith: *I'm sorry I'm late.* (lit. *Please excuse me for coming late*)

Madhivanan: *That's all right. What happened?*

Smith: *The bus was very crowded. I couldn't see the Loyola College stop. And the conductor didn't say.*

Madhivanan: *The conductor never says. Then what happened?*

Smith: *What's the name of the second stop from the Loyola College stop? I've come from there* (lit. *I'm coming from there*)

Madhivanan: *What a pity! Sit down. You'll be tired. Will you have a coffee?*

Smith: *Yes. Please give me a little water also.*

(After some time)

Madhivanan: *I have to go to a meeting at six o'clock. It's time. We couldn't talk for a long time. I'm sorry.* (lit. *Please excuse me*)

Smith: *No, no. It's my fault. I'll come on another day. We can talk at leisure.*

Madhivanan: *Fine.*

Vocabulary

manni	excuse, pardon	**taamadamaa**	late
aaccu	happened	**oree**	too much, excessive
kuuʈʈam	crowd, meeting	**kaɳɖakʈar**	bus conductor
aɖa paavamee	what a pity	**kaɭeppaa**	tired

saapɖu eat (also used, as here, for 'to drink', for which there is another word, **kuɖi**, used only for liquids)

konjam a little, some, somewhat (used to make requests, statements, etc. less assertive)

taṇṇi	water	**peesu**	talk, speak
tappu	mistake, fault	**innoru**	another
nidaanamaa	leisurely, unhurriedly		

Language points

Expressing politeness

In English conversation certain words and phrases such as 'please', 'thank you' and 'sorry' occur frequently in the explicit expression of politeness or regret. While what one might call verbal equivalents of these can be found, they are not part of informal Tamil, in which such notions are expressed by tone of voice, intonation, facial expression, and also grammatically. You have already seen different forms of pronouns used for this purpose, as well as the plural form of the imperative (e.g. **kuḍunga** as opposed to **kuḍu**) used in addressing a single person. In Dialogue 1, **-ṇum**, which, as explained in Unit 3, can express obligation or need ('must', 'should', 'want'), is used in this way in **mannikkaṇum** 'Please excuse me'. Bilingual Tamils may also use English 'sorry' in addition in such cases.

Exercise 1 (Audio 1: 28)

You are not talking to your equal or your junior. Change the following instructions to be:

(a) more polite; (b) suggestive and indirect:

Example: **naaḷekki vaa.** Come tomorrow!

a **naaḷekki vaanga.** Come tomorrow! (polite)
b **naaḷekki varaṇum.** Please come tomorrow!

1 meduvaa peesu (Speak slowly!)
2 avanukku sollu (Tell him!)
3 pinnaale ukkaaru (Sit at the back!)

Negation

To negate an action taking place in present or past time, **ille** 'not' (in its short form **-le**, except in cases of emphasis) is added to the infinitive of the verb. This is unchanged whatever the number, gender or person of the subject. The preceding dialogue provides the example **sollale** 'did not say'. Other examples are **varale** 'did not come', **kuḍukkale** 'did not give', **paakkale** 'did not see'. For actions in the future, the negative form, which also follows the infinitive of the verb, is **maaṭṭ-**, to which the appropriate personal ending is added. This generalisation applies only when the subject of the sentence refers to a human being:

naan vara maaṭṭeen.	I won't come.
peeraasiriyar vara maaṭṭaaru.	The professor won't come.

When the subject of the sentence is a neuter noun, **-aadu** is added to the stem of the verb:

bas varaadu.	The bus won't come.

Exercise 2

Raja is grouchy and answers 'no' to every question. He also makes his answers as short as possible. What answers does he give to the following questions? Note that with the verb **peesu**, the noun denoting the person one speaks to takes the ending **-ṭṭe**: **Maalaaṭṭe** 'to Mala', 'with Mala'.

Examples:

Q **on peeru raajaavaa?**	A **ille.**
Q **nii ange poo!**	A **maaṭṭeen.**
Q **onakku ṭii veeṇumaa?**	A **veeṇḍaam.**

1 nii Tamiẓ paḍikkiriyaa?
2 nii Maalaaṭṭe peesuviyaa?
3 nii konjam veḷiye pooriyaa?
4 nii paalu kuḍippiyaa?
5 onakku paalu veeṇumaa?
6 nii paalu kuḍikkiriyaa?
7 nii viiṭṭukku pooganumaa?
8 nii basle viiṭṭukku pooga muḍiyumaa?

Verbal nouns

Noun forms can be made from verbs by the addition of **-adu**. This can follow the present or past stem. An example in the dialogue is **varradukku**. This is made up of **varr-** (the present stem of **vaa** 'come') + **-adu** + the dative case. The dative here has the sense of 'for': 'Excuse (me) *for* coming late.' Such forms function as verbs, in that they can be modified by adverbs, and also as nouns, in that they can take case endings – as shown by **varrad*ukku*** here.

Adverbs

A common way of forming adverbs (as modifiers of verbs) is by the addition of **-aa** to a noun. Thus **taamadam** 'delay' + **-aa** gives **taamadamaa** 'late'; similarly, **nidaanamaa** 'in a leisurely fashion'. Such adverbs are generally adverbs of manner. **kaḷeppaa**, from **kaḷeppu** 'tiredness', is a rather different case, in that it modifies the verb **iru** 'be'. In such contexts, adverbs ending in **-aa** are often best translated by adjectives in English. The meaning of **-aa** is much broader than English '-ly' – a point illustrated by **kaḷeppaa** in this dialogue, **naaḷaa** 'for days' in Dialogue 2 and **munpaṇamaa** 'as an advance' in Dialogue 3. There are also adverbs without this adverbial suffix; e.g. **neere** 'straight', 'directly'.

'From'

To express the meaning 'from', **-lerundu** (sometimes called the ablative case) is added to a noun stem. As you can see from **sṭaaplerundu**, this ending is added to words borrowed from English as well as to native Tamil words: **viiṭṭulerundu** 'from (the) house'.

This ending can also be added to an adverb which itself expresses the idea of location in a place. In that event a shorter form is used, namely **-rundu**; this, added to **ange** ‘there’, gives us **angerundu** ‘from there’.

Possibility and permission

The verb ending **-laam**, which is added to the infinitive form of a verb (as in **peesalaam** in Dialogue 1) has two main senses: the possibility for an action to take place, as here; and the granting of permission: **niinga naaḷekki varalaam** ‘You may come tomorrow.’

Exercise 3

Select from among the list of words that follow, those which can fit in the slot in this sentence: **Murugan ——— kuḍippaan.**

paalu, iḍli, doose, ṭii, karumbu caaru, murukku, kaapi, sooru

Exercise 4

Answer, in Tamil, the following questions based on Dialogue 1, using full sentences.

1 Who came late?
2 How did he come?
3 What did Smith drink?
4 Why was Madhivanan short of time?

Dialogue 2 (Audio 1: 29)

Congratulations

Madhivanan and Kannappan exchange news and congratulate each other.

MADHIVANAN: vaanga, vaanga. romba naaḷaa ongaḷe paakka muḍiyale. neettu kuuṭṭattulekuuḍa ongaḷe kaaṇoom.

KANNAPPAN: oru pustagam eẓudureen, illeyaa? adunaale veele konjam adigam. veḷiye pooradulle.

MADHIVANAN: pustagam eẓudurade patti romba magiẓcci. onga oẓeppe paaraaṭṭaṇum.

KANNAPPAN: naan ongaḷukku paaraaṭṭu sollaṇum.

MADHIVANAN: edukku?

KANNAPPAN: ongaḷukku ilakkiya parisu keḍekka pooradukku. adukkudaanee naaḷekki paaraaṭṭu kuuṭṭam?

MADHIVANAN: onga paaraaṭṭukku nanri. naan perusaa oṇṇum seyyale. seyya veeṇḍiyadu innum evḷavoo irukku.

MADHIVANAN: *Come (in). I've not been able to see you for a long time. You were even absent from the meeting yesterday.* (lit: *Even at the meeting yesterday you were not to be seen*)

KANNAPPAN: *I'm writing a book, aren't I? For that reason I am rather busy. I don't go out.*

MADHIVANAN: *I'm very happy that you're writing a book. I must congratulate you on your hard work.*

KANNAPPAN: *I should congratulate you.*

MADHIVANAN: *For what?*

KANNAPPAN: *On your getting the literary award. Isn't the presentation meeting for that tomorrow?*

MADHIVANAN: *Thanks for your congratulations. I've done nothing great. There's still a lot that needs to be done.*

Vocabulary

kuuḍa	even	**kaaṇoom**	not to be found, missing
eẓudu	write		
adunaale	so, because of that	**veele**	work
		adigam	much
oẓeppu	hard work	**sollu**	say
ilakkiyam	literature	**parisu**	award, prize
naaḷekki	tomorrow	**nanri**	gratitude, thanks
seyyi	do	**innum/innom**	still, yet

paaraaṭṭu (verb) appreciate, congratulate, praise
paaraaṭṭu (noun) congratulation, appreciation
veeṇḍiyadu things needed, the necessary

Language points

Expression of appreciation

Expressions of appreciation (**paaraaṭṭu**) and of gratitude (**nanri**) belong to the domain of formal interaction. When the relation is informal and the conversation is casual, words like **sandooṣam** 'happiness', 'happy', **nalladu** 'good' express these sentiments respectively. No less often, the sentiment is not expressed verbally, but rather by facial expression. Bilingual Tamils may use the English words 'congratulations' and 'thanks'. The verbal expression of thanks is not heard in situations of monetary transaction, as in shops, or of civility, like somebody yielding you his place out of courtesy.

Tag questions

In English, there is a range of questions that can be tagged on at the end of an utterance to seek the listener's confirmation of what one has said; e.g. 'didn't you', 'can't he', 'won't they', 'hasn't she'. In colloquial Tamil, there is basically one form of tag question: **illeyaa** (**ille** 'not' + the interrogative suffix **-aa**). This can be compared to the situation that obtains with French 'n'est-ce pas' and German 'nicht wahr' (or even 'innit?' in some varieties of English). As an alternative for **illeyaa**, the abbreviated form **-le** with question intonation may also be used; this can also occur inside the sentence. So instead of '**oru pustagam eẓudureen, illeyaa?**' Kannappan could have said '**oru pustagam eẓudureen-le?**', with his voice going up at the end.

Emphasis

Tamil uses emphatic particles frequently for meanings such as 'only', 'just', 'also', 'even', 'indeed'. In previous dialogues **taan** 'only' and **-um** 'also' were used. In this dialogue **kuuḍa** 'even' is used.

Something missing: kaaɳoom

The verb form **kaaɳoom** is unusual in that it does not have a subject; it occurs with a noun or pronoun as its object, which has the ending **-e** that indicates the object of a sentence. It means the object (which can be a person) 'is missing', 'unavailable', 'not found', e.g. **en peenaave kaaɳoom** 'My pen is missing', 'I can't find my pen'; **en tambiye kaaɳoom** 'My brother is missing', 'I can't find my brother'. The time reference can be present or past. The precise English equivalent will vary depending on the context.

Habitual negative

In the explanations that followed Dialogue 1, there was some discussion of the negation of events taking place in past, present and future time. We now look at negation with regard to habitual acts, for which a different verb form from the ones so far discussed is used. The word **pooradulle** in Dialogue 2 illustrates this. Its composition is: **poo** 'go' + marker of present tense **-r-** + **-adu** (which, you may recall, makes a verb stem into a noun form) + **ille** 'not'; the last two components can produce either **-adulle** or **-adille**. That is to say that you will hear both and can use either. This form does not vary for person, number, or gender: **naan pooradulle** 'I don't (habitually/usually) go'; **avanga pooradulle** 'They don't (habitually/usually) go'. The future negative, discussed earlier in this unit (infinitive + **maaʈʈ-**) can also be used in a habitual sense, and the difference between the two forms is a subtle one. One might say that the future negative includes a stronger element of will or intention.

Habitual positive

The future tense was introduced earlier as having as one of its functions a statement about an action expected to take place in the future. Another important use is in the making of statements which are generally or habitually true:

apɖi solluvaanga.	So they say.
pasu paalu kuɖukkum.	Cows give milk.
Smith kaalele kaapi kuɖippaan.	Smith drinks coffee in the morning.

Unknown or unspecified entity: -oo

The suffix **-oo** indicates that the speaker is uncertain or doubtful. When it is added to question words, the words generally have the meaning of 'some': **yaaroo** 'someone', **engeyoo** 'somewhere', etc. **evḷavoo** in this dialogue means 'so much', indicating an unknown quantity. As a question marker, used in places where **-aa** can occur, **-oo** indicates doubt in the speaker's mind. Compare the following three examples: **avan varuvaanaa?** 'Will he come?'; **avan varuvaan-le?** 'He will come, won't he?'; **avan varuvaanoo?** 'Maybe he will come – I wonder'. When **-oo** is added to more than one word or sentence, it indicates alternatives (without excluding the possibility of both occurring): **avanoo avaḷoo varuvaanga** 'He or she will come.' Note here the plural ending (**-aanga**) on the verb. The same happens with **yaaru** 'who': **yaaru varuv*aanga*** 'Who's coming?'

Another postposition: patti

The dialogue contains another postposition, **patti** 'about', 'concerning'. This follows a noun in the accusative case (**-e**, the case used for the object of a sentence): **avane patti** 'about him'. In Dialogue 2 it occurs after a verbal noun, **ez̧uduradu** 'writing', to give **ez̧udurade patti** 'about (your) writing'.

Exercise 5 (Audio 1: 29)

Mala asks you about what Raja is doing or will do. He does not do any of the things she mentions, and you answer her accordingly.

Example: **Raajaa tuunguraanaa?** Is Raja sleeping?
ille, tuungale. No, he is not.

1 Raajaa paḍikkiraanaa?
2 Raajaa peesuvaanaa?
3 Raajaa varuvaanaa?
4 Raajaa varraanaa?
5 Raajaa viiṭṭule iruppaanaa?
6 Raajaa viiṭṭule irukkaanaa?

Exercise 6

Mala does not know what Raja is doing or will do. She wonders about a possibility and expresses it to you. You tell her that her suspicion is likely to be true.

Example: **Raajaa tuunguraanoo? tuungalaam.**

1 Raajaa paḍikkiraanoo?
2 Raajaa peesuvaanoo?
3 Raajaa varuvaanoo?
4 Raajaa varraanoo?
5 Raajaa viiṭṭule iruppaanoo?
6 Raajaa viiṭṭule irukkaanoo?

Exercise 7

Kumar did not get the names right and he repeats the questions with alternative names. You answer that neither is doing the thing in question, using the phrase **reṇḍupeerum** 'the two of them'.

Example: **Raajaa tuunguraanaa? Paaṣaa tuunguraanaa?**
Is Raja sleeping or Pasha?

reṇḍupeerum tuungale.
Neither of them is sleeping.

Exercise 8

In this exercise, give yourself some practice in forming and using verbal nouns, taking as a basis the sentences in Exercise 5. Combine two sentences into one by substituting a verbal noun (ending **-adu**) for the main verb of the first one. You are explaining that you are unaware of the action Raja is performing.

Example: **Raajaa tuunguraan; adu enakku teriyaadu.**
Raja is sleeping; I don't know that.

Raajaa tuunguradu enakku teriyaadu.
I don't know that Raja is sleeping.
or
I don't know of Raja's sleeping.

Dialogue 3 (Audio 1: 30)

Thanks for the house

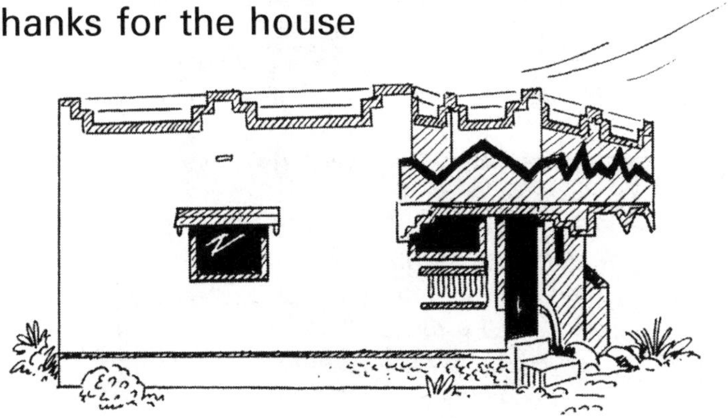

Murugan helps Smith in his negotiations with the agent to rent a house.

SMITH: naan Tamiʐnaaʈʈule aaru maasam tanga pooreen. ooʈʈalle irukka muɖiyaadu. vaaɖagekki oru viiɖu paakkaɳum.

MURUGAN: enakku oru viiʈʈu taragare teriyum. avarʈʈe poogalaam.

(*In the house*)

AGENT: inda viiʈʈule ellaa vasadiyum irukku. ongaɭukku viiɖu piɖikkidaa?

MURUGAN: taɳɳi eppavum varumaa?

AGENT: koʐaayle eppavum varaadu. aanaa pinnaale oru keɳaru irukku.

MURUGAN: ivarukku taɳɳi erekka teriyaadu. paravaayille. vaaɖage evɭavu?

AGENT: maasam reɳɖaayiram ruubaa. reɳɖu maasa vaaɖage munpaɳamaa kuɖukkaɳum.

MURUGAN: ongaɭukku sammadamaa?

SMITH: sammadam. naaɭekki paɳam kuɖukkireen.

(*Back in the hotel*)

SMITH: onga odavikki romba nanri. enakku taragar irukkiradu teriyaadu.

MURUGAN: idu enna periya odavi! varaʈʈumaa?

SMITH: *I'm going to stay in Tamil Nadu for six months. I can't be in the hotel. I must look for a house to rent.*

MURUGAN: *I know an estate agent. We can go to him.*

(In the house)

AGENT: *In this house there is every facility. Do you like the house?*

MURUGAN: *Is there water all the time?* (lit. *Does water come always?*)

AGENT: *There isn't always water in the pipes. But there is a well behind (the house).*

MURUGAN: *He doesn't know how to draw water. Never mind. How much is the rent?*

AGENT: *Two thousand rupees a month. You have to give two months rent in advance.*

MURUGAN: *Is that acceptable to you?*

SMITH: *Yes. I'll pay the money tomorrow.*

(Back in the hotel)

SMITH: *Many thanks for your help. I didn't know there were agents.*

MURUGAN: *Don't mention it.* (lit. *What sort of big help is this!*) *Bye!* (lit. *May I come?*)

Vocabulary

Tamiẓnaaḍu	the state of Tamil Nadu		
maasam	month	**tangu**	stay
vaaḍage	rent	**taragar**	agent, broker
ellaam	all	**vasadi**	convenience, facility
piḍi	like	**eppavum**	always
koẓaa(y)	tap, faucet	**keṇaru**	well
ere	draw (water)	**teri**	know
aayiram	thousand	**munpaṇam**	advance
odavi	help	**sammadam**	being agreeable, OK
periya	big		

Language points

Goodbye!

Let's start at the end of the dialogue, where Murugan takes leave. You may be surprised to see someone saying 'Goodbye' by using the verb **vaa** 'come'. You should therefore be aware that all parting expressions when leaving a person incorporate this verb: **varaṭṭumaa** 'May I come?', or **pooyiṭṭuvarreen** 'I shall go and come', or **varreen** 'I am coming', all of which are equivalent to 'Au revoir' in French or 'See you' in a number of varieties of modern English. It is considered inauspicious – and therefore impolite – to take leave saying **pooreen** 'I am going'/'Let me go'.

'Let it be'

The various parting expressions in the previous paragraph include a verb form ending in **-ṭṭum** (added to the infinitive of a verb). This, like **-laam**, is a permissive. Used with a third person subject, it has the sense of 'let' that person perform the action of the verb and expresses the idea that the speaker consents to the action. With a first person subject, it occurs only in the interrogative and seeks the hearer's approval of the action proposed:

ava varaṭṭum.	Let her come.
avan peesaṭṭum.	Let him speak.
naan varaṭṭumaa?	Shall I come?

Subject in the dative

Verbs of knowledge (like **teri** 'know', **puri** 'understand') and of mental state (like **piḍi** 'like', **mara** 'forget') normally occur with the neuter ending and with the subject in the dative case. Such verbs have in common that the action denoted is not through the agency of, or through the volition, of the subject. An example in Dialogue 3 is **ongaḷukku viiḍu piḍikkidaa?**

'All' and 'any'

To express the notion of 'all', **ellaarum** is added after human nouns and **ellaam** after non-human and human nouns. Alternatively, **ellaa** may occur before the noun and **-um** after the noun.

pustagam ellaam	all books
ellaa pustagamum	all books
payyanga ellaarum/ellaam	all boys
ellaa payyangaḷum	all boys

To express the notion of 'any', **-um** may be added to a question word, as in (1). If there is a noun in the phrase, there are two possibilities: firstly the question word + **-um** may occur after the noun, as in (2); or secondly, an interrogative adjective may precede the noun and **-um** follow it (3).

1	**eduvum**	anything
2	**pustagam eduvum**	any book
3	**enda pustagamum**	any book

This type of noun or phrase can be the subject of a negative sentence:

yaarum vara maaṭṭaanga. No one will come.

Exercise 9 (Audio 1: 31)

Give alternatives to the following phrases by placing **ellaa** after the noun, making necessary changes as exemplified in the preceding language point:

1 ellaa kaṇḍakṭargaḷum
2 ellaa kaaleejum
3 ellaa koẓaayum
4 ellaa taragargaḷum

Adjective

Attributive adjectives – adjectives that modify a noun – come before the noun and are invariable. Such adjectives are of various types. Any noun may modify another noun and make a nominal compound or phrase. Adjectives may be derived from nouns by adding **-aana**: **aʐagaana** 'beautiful' (**aʐagu** 'beauty' + **-aana**). Simple adjectives, of which the number is not large (though all are of frequent occurrence), generally end in **-a**: **nalla** 'good', **periya** 'big', **cinna** 'small', **pudiya** 'new', **paʐaya** 'old'. Adjectives that do not have this ending include **saadaa** 'ordinary' and **modal** 'first'. On **ellaarum/ellaam** 'all' as an exception to this rule, see the section immediately preceding this one.

Thousands

When used to indicate 'one thousand', **aayiram** is used without a preceding numeral. It can be added to all other numerals (with the dropping of the final **-u** from such numerals): **reɳɖaayiram** '2000', **pattaayiram** '10,000'. Some numerals in this set have an alternative form for the first element: **muuɳaayiram/muuvaayiram** '3000'; **anjaayiram/ayyaayiram** '5000'; **eʈʈaayiram/eɳɳaayiram** '8000'. You do not need to use these less regular alternative forms, but it might help to be able to recognise them.

Exercise 10

You disagree with my statements about some people as being generally or habitually true of them. How will you state your disagreement?

Example: **Raajaa kaalele kaapi kuɖippaan.**
Raja drinks coffee in the morning.

Raajaa kaalele kaapi kuɖikka maaʈʈaan.
Raja does not drink coffee in the morning.

1 bas denam varum. The bus comes daily.
2 Smith kaalele doose saapɖuvaan. Smith eats dosa in the morning.
3 Maalaa nallaa paaɖuvaa. Mala sings well.
4 Jaanukku Tamiʐ teriyum. John knows Tamil.
5 ellaarukkum iɖli pidikkum. Everyone likes idli.

Tamil script

Having looked, in the closing section of Unit 4, at the set of vowel letters and vowel signs, we turn now to consonants. These fall into two sets, a basic set and a supplementary one. The basic set goes back in its history to the beginnings of Tamil writing and is still entirely adequate for the modern written language as far as native Tamil words are concerned. However, throughout its history Tamil has accepted words from other languages and, where these are not fully assimilated to the sound pattern of the language, there are occasions when the pronunciation of the word is not clear from the spelling. To achieve a partial easing of the problem, a few additional letters were introduced into Tamil writing a few centuries ago. They were borrowed from Grantha, a writing system used in south India for Sanskrit.

In this unit, attention is restricted to the basic set. The consonants in this set total eighteen, which is considerably less than the number of consonants we have been using to represent colloquial Tamil. There are two reasons for this: (1) more are needed if the pronunciation of borrowed words is to be indicated; (2) a given consonant letter in the script represents more than one sound in Tamil words, depending on its position in the word.

The list of consonant letters follows in dictionary order. The letter forms are those with the 'inherent' vowel **a**. Each is followed by one of the standard transcriptions in Roman: க **ka**, ங **ŋa**, ச **ca**, ஞ **ña**, ட **ṭa**, ண **ṇa**, த **ta**, ந **na**, ப **pa**, ம **ma**, ய **ya**, ர **ra**, ல **la**, வ **va**, ழ **ẓa**, ள **ḷa**, ற **ṟa**, ன **ṉa**.

Some comments on these are needed. Firstly, there are two 'r's and two 'n's, which we look at in turn. The letters ர and ற share one environment, in that both occur between vowels in the middle of a word and in that position have the same pronunciation. They must, nevertheless, always be distinguished in writing. In older Tamil they represented different sounds (and still do in some dialects, such as Jaffna Tamil). The position is different in respect of ந and ன. The first of these occurs at the beginning of words and (as ந்) before த; ன occurs elsewhere.

Second, some letters – க, ச, ட, த, ப – are each associated with different sounds. In Tamil words, these are predictable from the position in the word. In the case of words borrowed from other languages, it is necessary to know the word. A few examples of Tamil words follow to illustrate this. Note that ங் represents the sound of 'ng' in English 'sing'.

க	கால்	**kaal**	leg	மகன்	**magan**	son
	பக்கம்	**pakkam**	side	அங்கே	**angee**	there
ச	சொல்	**sol**	say	பசி	**pasi**	hunger
	பச்சை	**paccai**	green	இஞ்சி	**inji**	ginger
ட	டீ	**ṭii**	tea	படி	**paḍi**	read
	பாட்டு	**paaṭṭu**	song	வண்டி	**vaṇḍi**	cart
த	தலை	**talai**	head	அது	**adu**	it
	பத்து	**pattu**	ten	இந்த	**inda**	this
ப	பத்து	**pattu**	ten	தபால்	**tabaal**	post
	இப்போது	**ippoodu**	now	பாம்பு	**paambu**	snake

If we set aside ச for the moment, and if we note that no native Tamil word begins with ட, we can say that the sounds **k**, **ṭ**, **t** and **p** occur (1) at the beginning of a word and (2) when the letter in question is doubled; **g**, **ḍ**, **d** and **b** occur (1) between vowels and (2) when preceded by a nasal consonant. The pattern for ச is slightly different. The examples show: **s** at the beginning of a word and between vowels; **c** (a similar sound to the 'ch' of English 'church') when the letter is doubled; and **j** when preceded by a nasal consonant. A further complication lies in the fact that at the beginning of a word ச may represent either **c** or **s**. Sometimes this depends on the word, and sometimes it depends on the grammatical context. Because the rules for deciding between the two are very complex, it is best to observe and then to imitate occurrences.

As you listen to a native speaker or to the tapes, you will observe that the sounds we have written as **g**, **ḍ**, **d** and **b** have a somewhat different sound from what the letters suggest when they occur between vowels. This point has already been made in the section on pronunciation in the Introduction, but we repeat it here as a reminder that this is a feature of the written language as well as of the spoken. Members of this set of consonants are sometimes described as being articulated more laxly in this position than when they follow a nasal consonant. This is particularly noticeable for **g** and **d**. Careful listeners, however, will notice that **ḍ** is a rapidly pronounced tap, and that **b** seems to lie somewhere between English 'b' and 'v'. In the case of **g**, some speakers use an 'h' sound, and others a sound similar to the Scottish pronunciation of 'ch' in 'loch'. Between vowels **d** is not unlike 'th' in English 'other'.

Exercise 11

Familiarise yourself with the importance of the distinction between single and double consonants by putting together closely similar pairs in the following list and then saying them aloud:

அம்மா mother; இலை leaf; புளி tamarind; மகள் daughter; கன்னம் cheek; பாட்டு song; மக்கள் children; இல்லை not; பாடு sing; குதி jump; ஆமா yes; புள்ளி dot; கனம் heaviness; குத்தி having punched

6 Mahaabalipuram poovamaa?

Shall we go to Mahabalipuram?

In this unit you will learn to:

- plan an outing
- talk about food
- refer to family members
- express likes and dislikes
- make emphatic statements
- offer alternatives
- say what day of the week it is

Dialogue 1 (Audio 1: 33)

Planning an outing

Three friends – Ani, Melli, and Sarah – plan a day's outing. They decide to visit the famous shore temples and rock carvings at Mahabalipuram.

ANI: naaḷekki nyaayittukkeẓame. engeyaavadu veḷiye poogalaamaa?

MELLI: Mahaabalipuram poovamaa?

SARAH: ange paakka enna irukku?

MELLI: ange aẓagaana kaḍalkare irukku. kaḍal ooramaa Pallavar kaala sirpangaḷ irukku.

SARAH: enakku sirpangaḷ paakka piḍikkum. angeyee poovoom.

ANI: en tangacciyeyum kuuṭṭikiṭṭuvaraṭṭumaa?

MELLI: taaraaḷamaa. Sarah, niinga onga akkaa Mary-eyum kuuṭṭikiṭṭuvaanga.

SARAH: epḍi pooroom? basleyaa?

Melli: ille. enga pakkattu viiʈʈukaararʈʈe oru væn irukku. avarʈʈe ade keekkireen.

Ani: saappaaʈʈukku enna seyradu?

Melli: ovvoruttar viʈʈulerundum edaavadu saappaaɖu konɖuvaruvoom.

Sarah: naan ooʈʈalle samekka muɖiyaadee. naan enna koɳɖuvara?

Melli: niinga oɳɳum koɳɖuvara veeɳɖaam. paʐam vaanguradukku paɳam kuɖunga, poodum.

Ani: naaɭekki ettane maɳikki keɭamburoom? enge ellaarum sandikkiroom?

Melli: kaalele pattu maɳikki keɭambuvoom. enga viiʈʈule sandippoom.

Ani: ellaarum veɭeyaaɖa naan ciiʈʈukkaʈʈu koɳɖuvaravaa? ellaarukkum puɭiyoodare piɖikkumaa? naan ade koɳɖuvaraʈʈumaa?

Melli: sari. naan puuri keʐangu koɳɖuvaravaa, alladu cappaatti kurumaa koɳɖuvaravaa?

Ani: puuri keʐangee koɳɖuvaa. kuuɖa medu vaɖeyaavadu masaalaa vaɖeyaavadu koɳɖuvaa. naan tayirccoorum uurugaayum kuuɖa koɳɖuvarreen.

Melli: ellaarum naalekki kaalele sariyaa pattu maɳikki enga viiʈʈule irukkaɳum. sariyaa?

Ani and Sarah: sari.

Ani: *Tomorrow's Sunday. Could we go out somewhere?*

Melli: *Shall we go to Mahabalipuram?*

Sarah: *What's there to see there?*

Melli: *There's a very fine beach there. Close to the sea there are sculptures from the Pallava period.*

Sarah: *I like looking at sculptures. Let's go there.*

Ani: *Can my younger sister come along too?*

Melli: *By all means. Sarah, bring your elder sister Mary along too.*

Sarah: *How shall we go? By bus?*

Melli: *No. Our next-door neighbour has a van. I'll ask him for it.*

Ani: *What shall we do about food?*

Melli: *Let's each bring some food from home.*

Sarah: *I can't cook in the hotel, can I? What should I bring?*

Melli: *You don't need to bring anything. If you give money for buying fruit, that will do.*

Ani: *At what time shall we set off tomorrow? Where shall we all meet?*

Melli: *Let's meet at ten in the morning. We'll meet at my house.*

Ani: *Shall I bring a pack of cards so that we can all play? Does everyone like tamarind rice? Should I bring that?*

Melli: *Fine. Am I to bring puri and potato, or chapati and kurma?*

Ani: *Bring puri and potato. Also bring some medu vadai or masala vadai. I'll bring curd rice and pickle.*

Melli: *Everybody must be at our house tomorrow at ten in the morning exactly. Right?*

Ani and Sarah: *Right.*

Vocabulary

nyaayittukeẓame	Sunday	**kaḍalkare**	beach, sea shore
veḷiye	out, outside	**ooramaa**	along, along the edge of
sirpam	sculpture	**tangacci**	younger sister
kuuṭṭikiṭṭuvaa	bring along	**akkaa**	elder sister
taaraaḷamaa	by all means, freely	**keeḷu**	ask, ask for
		væn	van
pakkattu viiṭṭukaararu	next-door neighbour	**saappaaḍu**	food, meal
		koṇḍuvaa	bring
ovvoruttaru	everyone	**same**	cook

oṇṇum	anything	**paẓam**	fruit
vaangu	buy	**paṇam**	money
keḷambu	start, set out	**sandi**	meet
veḷeyaaḍu	play	**ciiṭṭukkaṭṭu**	pack of playing cards
puḷiyoodare	rice cooked with tamarind powder or juice		
puuri	flat, unleavened wheat bread that is deep fried		
keẓangu	potato curry, root vegetable		
cappaatti	chapati, unleavened wheat bread that is fried over fire or on a flat pan		
kuruma	thick spiced sauce with potato and other vegetables or meat		
medu vaḍe	doughnut-like (but savoury, not sweet) snack made of black gram flour and deep fried		
masaalaa vaḍe	doughnut-like (but not sweet) snack made of yellow split pea flour and deep fried		
tayirccooru	rice mixed in yoghurt		
sooru/cooru	rice		
uurugaa(y)	pickle (made of lemon or any other vegetable cooked in oil with chilli powder and spices)		
sariyaa	exactly		

Mahabalipuram

Mahabalipuram, also known as Mamallapuram, is one of the major historical sites of Tamil Nadu. It is situated a short distance from Chennai on the shore of Bay of Bengal. It has rock cut temples and sculptures created by early Pallava kings, who ruled the northern part of the Tamil country from the fourth to the ninth century.

Language points

Very few new grammatical points are included in this unit. Make use of it to revise the grammatical forms and constructions introduced in Units 1–5, in particular personal pronouns and the verb forms that go with them.

Exercise 1 (Audio 1: 34)

Give a few possible answers to Ani's question **naaḷekki ettane maɳikki keḷamburoom?** Use **kaalele** for times in the morning and **madyaanam** for times in the afternoon: 9.30 a.m.; 11 a.m.; 2.45 p.m.; 3.15 p.m.

Exercise 2

Based on the dialogue, tell us what each will bring to eat on the outing to Mahabalipuram.

Example: **Kalyaaɳi uppumaa koɳḍuvaruvaa.**

1 Ani (Aɳi) 2 Melli 3 Sarah

Days of the week (Audio 1: 35)

The seven days are named after the planets and their satellites. They are:

tingakkeẓame	Monday
sevvaakkeẓame	Tuesday
budankeẓame	Wednesday
viyaaẓakkeẓame	Thursday
veḷḷikkeẓame	Friday
sanikkeẓame	Saturday
nyaayittukkeẓame	Sunday

Their short forms are **tingaḷ** (Moon), **sevvaa(y)** (Mars), **budan** (Mercury), **viyaaẓan** (Jupiter), **veḷḷi** (Venus), **sani** (Saturn), **nyaayiru** (Sun).

Kinship terms (Audio 1: 36)

One aspect of social custom that has an impact on the terms that are used for family relationships is that cross-cousin marriage is permitted in Tamil society. Cross-cousin marriage is marriage to one's father's sister's child or to one's mother's brother's child. Children of one's father's brother and mother's sister are differentiated from cross cousins, and they are counted as brothers and sisters like one's own siblings. Father's brother and mother's sister are called 'elder' or 'younger father' (**periyappaa** or **cittappaa**) and 'elder' or 'younger mother' (**periyammaa** or **cinnammaa**) respectively, the choice of 'elder' or 'younger' depending on the age of the person in question relative to that of one's father or mother. The terms 'uncle' and 'aunt' (**maamaa** and **atte**) are restricted to mother's brother and father's sister. The other basic kin terms are: **appaa** 'father', **ammaa** 'mother', **aṇṇan** 'elder brother', **akkaa** 'elder sister', **tambi** 'younger brother', **tangacci** 'younger sister', **taattaa** 'grandfather', **paaṭṭi** 'grandmother' (the older different terms for paternal and maternal grandparents have been standardised), **magan/payyan** 'son', **maga(ḷ)/poṇṇu** 'daughter', **peeran** 'grandson', **peetti** 'granddaughter'.

Exercise 3

Study this family tree and then answer the questions that follow. You will need to keep in mind the fact that **peeru** has two meanings – 'name' and 'person'. In (9) and (10), **enna veeṇum** is an idiomatic (and frequently used) way of asking how X is related to Y. An alternative, using the word **more** 'relationship', is **enna more aagaṇum? kuuḍaperandavanga(ḷ)** = 'siblings'.

Example: **Kriṣṇanooḍa tambi yaaru?**
Kriṣṇanooḍa tambi Murugan.

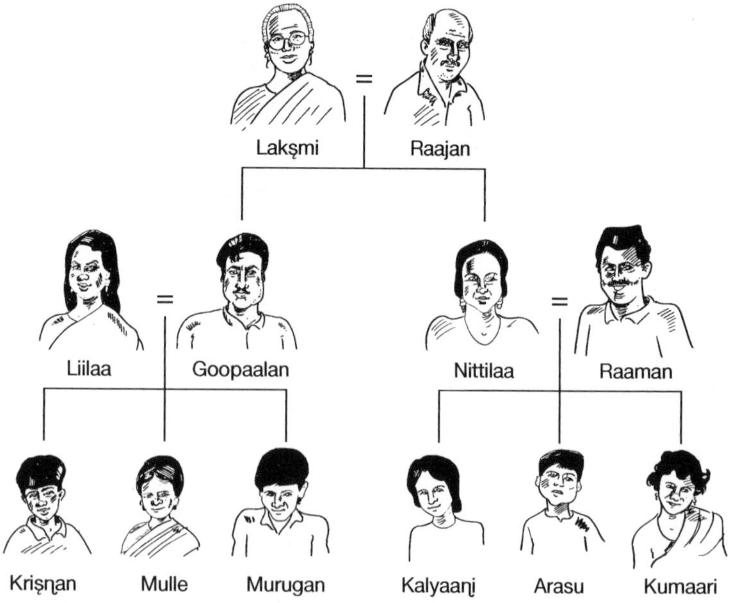

1 Goopaalanooḍa manevi yaaru?
2 Nittilaavooḍa ammaa yaaru?
3 Raamanukku ettane piḷḷega?
4 ettane aaṇu? ettane poṇṇu?
5 Goopaalanooḍa maga peeru enna?
6 Raajanooḍa peettiga peeru enna?
7 Arasu kuuḍaperandavanga ettane peeru?
8 Krişṇan, Murugan reṇḍu peerule yaaru muuttavan?
9 Kumaarikki Lakşmi enna veeṇum?
10 Mullekki Nittilaa enna veeṇum?
11 Arasu Goopaalane epḍi kuupḍuvaan?
12 Raaman Raajane epḍi kuupḍuvaan?

Permissive forms: alternatives

You have learnt two ways of giving or asking permission: adding **-laam** or **-ṭṭum** to the infinitive of a verb: **nii varalaam** 'You may come'; **avan varaṭṭum** 'He may come', 'Let him come'. If the sentence is a question, then (a) a verbal noun ending in **-adu** may be used instead of the first: **enna seyradu** (= **enna seyyalaam**) 'What may one do', 'What's to be done?'; and (b) a simple infinitive may be used instead of the second: **enna seyya** (= **enna seyyaṭṭum**) 'What may one do', 'What to do?' Thus, Sarah says **naan enna koṇḍuvara?** 'What am I to bring?' 'What may I bring?'

Two uses of -aavadu

Some endings or suffixes may have different meanings, depending on what type of words they are added to. One of these is **-aavadu**. When added to question words it has the meaning of 'some': **edaavadu** 'something', **engeyaavadu** 'somewhere'. Second, when added to more than one word, it has the meaning of 'or' (and so in this sense is equivalent to **-oo**): **puuriyaavadu cappaattiyaavadu** 'puri or chapati?' It is used when the tense of the verb is future. Remember the further alternative for 'or', namely **alladu**. This is used before the last word in enumeration or before every word except the first word in enumeration: **cooru** (**alladu**) **puuri alladu cappaatti** 'rice (or) puri or chapati'.

More on -um = *'any'*

In Unit 3 you saw that to express 'any', **-um** may be added to a question word. It has the same meaning when added to **oṉṉu** 'one', in combination with which it means 'anything': **niinga oṉṉum koṇḍuvara veeṇḍaam** 'You don't need to bring anything.'

A special case of emphatic -ee

We have seen that **-ee**, when added to a noun or other words excludes others of the same kind and means 'alone', 'just'. At the end of a sentence, it excludes other possibilities and implies that the action in question is unlikely: **naan samekka muḍiyaadee** 'I can't cook, can I?'

Two different meanings for -aa

You may have noticed that in Melli's last utterance in Dialogue 2 **sariyaa** occurs twice. It is not, however, the same **-aa** that is added to **sari** in each case. In the first occurrence, **-aa** makes **sari** into an adverb, to give the meaning 'precise*ly*' or 'exact*ly*'. In the second, it is the 'interrogative' **-aa**, which produces a 'yes/no' question.

Exercise 4

Pair each of your family members on the left with an appropriate verb from the right.

1 cittappaa	a vandaan
2 tangacci	b vandaaru
3 paaṭṭi	c vandaa
4 appaa	d vandaanga
5 periyammaa	
6 aṇṇan	
7 tambi	
8 maamaa	

Dialogue 2 (Audio 1: 37)

Don't like it

Melli discusses the presentation of a prize to one of their friends.

MELLI: onakku viʂayam teriyumaa?
ANI: enakku oɳɳum teriyaadu. enna viʂayam?
MELLI: Aruɳukku parisu kuɖukka pooraanga.
ANI: edukku parisu?
MELLI: denam sariyaana neerattukku veelekki varradukku.
ANI: eɳɳekki kuɖukka pooraanga?
MELLI: naaɭekki. onakku anda kuuʈʈattukku vara muɖiyumaa?
ANI: ennaale muɖiyaadu. enakku Aruɳe piɖikkaadu.
MELLI: summaa peerukku vaa.
ANI: ille. enakku naaɭekki veere veele irukku. maamaa viiʈʈukku oru viseeʂattukku poogaɳum.
MELLI: enakku keʈʈikaarangaɭe paaraaʈʈaɳum. naan Aruɳukku paaraaʈʈu solla pooreen.
ANI: enakku yaarukkum paaraaʈʈu solradukku iʂʈam ille.

MELLI: *Have you heard the news?*
ANI: *I don't know anything. What news?*
MELLI: *They're going to give Arun a prize.*
ANI: *A prize for what?*
MELLI: *For coming to work at the correct time each day.*
ANI: *On what day are they going to present it?*
MELLI: *Tomorrow. Can you come to the meeting?*
ANI: *I can't. I don't like Arun.*
MELLI: *Just come.*
ANI: *No. I have other work tomorrow. I have to go to a special function at uncle's house.*
MELLI: *I must congratulate successful people. I'm going to offer congratulations to Arun.*
ANI: *I don't like congratulating anyone.*

Vocabulary

viʂayam	news, matter	**denam**	daily
maamaa	uncle	**sariyaana**	correct, appropriate
keʈʈikkaaran	clever person	**viseeʂam**	special event, function

Language points

Dative with temporal nouns

When nouns are used to locate an event in time, the dative case suffix **-kku** (which, you will recall, varies with **-kki**) is sometimes used. Examples in the dialogue are: **neerattukku** 'on time', and **eṇṇekki** 'on what day', 'when'. The first of these is the dative of **neeram**. (We have noted earlier that nouns ending in **-am** change this to **-attu** before a case ending is added.) In Unit 4, following Dialogue 1, you learnt that 'at' a particular time of day is expressed by the dative too: **aaru maṇikki** 'at six o'clock'. The instances where the dative is used to indicate location in time should be learnt individually, since the locative **-le** is also used to place an event in time, as **kaalele** in the next paragraph shows.

Dative with 'must'

The use of the infinitive of a verb + **-ṇum**, with a noun or pronoun in the nominative, has been shown in Unit 3 to indicate an obligation to do something. Dative instead of nominative in a sentence with infinitive + **-ṇum** means that doing the action of the infinitive is a 'must' for the person denoted by the noun in the dative: **enakku kaalele kaapi kuḍikkaṇum** 'I *must* drink coffee in the morning.'

Exercise 5

Here are some verbs of motion. Give their meanings. Pair types of movements that contrast. You are given the meaning of the first.

naḍa (walk)

poo eeru vaa ooḍu erangu

Exercise 6

Give the names of ten food items people eat in Tamil Nadu. Then imagine saying to a friend about each in turn, 'Let's eat . . .' Describe each of them, saying whether it is hot (**kaaramaa**), sweet (**inippaa**), sour (**puḷippaa**), soft (**meduvaa**), or hard (**valuvaa**). You can also say that some food was neither hot nor sweet, neither soft nor hard, if that is your experience.

Example: **vaḍe saapḍuvoom; adu kaaramaa irukkum.**
Let's eat vada; it'll be hot.

Dialogue 3 (Audio 1: 39)

Going out of town

Melli and Ani discuss Ani's proposed trip out of town the following day.

MELLI: nii naaḷekkaa uurukku poore?
ANI: aamaa, naaḷekkidaan.
MELLI: naanum varaṭṭumaa?
ANI: nii maṭṭumaa?
MELLI: aamaa, naan maṭṭumdaan.
ANI: ivan on reṇḍaavadu tambi Kiraṇdaane?
MELLI: aamaa, avaneedaan.
ANI: ivane maṭṭumaavadu kuuṭṭikiṭṭuvaralaamee?
MELLI: ille, ivanukku neettudaan paricce aarambam.
ANI: naaḷekki kaaleleyee keḷambalaam, illeyaa?
MELLI: aaru maṇikkee keḷambalaam. appadaan modal basse piḍikka muḍiyum.

MELLI: *Are you going out of town tomorrow?*
ANI: *Yes, tomorrow.*
MELLI: *May I come too?*
ANI: *Just you?*
MELLI: *Yes, just me.*
ANI: *Is this your second younger brother Kiran?*
MELLI: *Yes, it's him.*
ANI: *Can't you at least bring him along?*
MELLI: *No, it was the beginning of his exams yesterday.*
ANI: *We can set off in the morning tomorrow, can't we?*
MELLI: *We can set off at six o'clock. Then we can catch the first bus.*

Vocabulary

uuru	village or town, home town	**paricce**	examination
piɖi	catch	**aarambam**	beginning

Exercise 7

Plan another outing to Vandalur (**Vaɳɖaluur**) where there is a zoological garden (**mirugakkaacci saale**). The animals there include **singam** 'lion', **puli** 'tiger', **karaɖi** 'bear', **yaane** 'elephant', **maan** 'deer', **korangu** 'monkey'. (The domestic animals **naayi** 'dog', **puune** 'cat', **aaɖu** 'goat' and **maaɖu** 'cow', 'bull', **kudire** 'horse' can be seen in the streets of Chennai (Madras)!)

Exercise 8

1 List the above animals in order of their height.
2 Which of them eat the flesh of other animals?
3 **kuʈʈi** is 'young one of animals'. Make the above animals into young ones. (Note that there is no **maaʈʈukkuʈʈi** (calf of cow); it is **kaɳɳukkuʈʈi**).

Exercise 9

Say what you typically do on each day. Translate your sentences.

Example: **veɭɭikkeʐame naan kooyilukku pooveen.**
On Fridays, I go to the temple.

Exercise 10

The following are the words for different times of the day and related expressions:

kaale	morning (from sunrise to noon)
madyaanam	afternoon (from noon to around four)
saayangaalam	late afternoon, evening (from around four to sunset)
raatri	night (from sunset to sunrise)
pagalu	day (from sunrise to sunset)

neettu	yesterday
iṉṉekki	today
naaḷekki	tomorrow
mundaanaaḷu	day before yesterday
naaḷekkaẓiccu	day after tomorrow
reṇḍu naaḷekki munnaale	two days before/ago
reṇḍu naaḷekki peragu	two days after (later)
naaḷu	day (24 hours)
vaaram	week
maasam	month
varuṣam	year

1 Arrange the following sequentially from morning to night.

saayangaalam, kaalele, raatri, madyaanam

2 Arrange the following from the largest period of time to the smallest.

maasam, vaaram, varuṣam, naaḷu

3 How would you say the following in Tamil?

five days ago, one day earlier, after ten days,
one and a half days later

4 You can combine day sequence with part of the day to make complex expressions of time. Make five such expressions.

Example: **iṉṉekki raatri** tonight

5 You can similarly combine parts of the day with hours. Make five such phrases.

Example: **raatri pattu maṇikki** at ten o'clock at night

Exercise 11

Convert the following conversation about going to a film into Tamil.

a: Shall we go to a film tonight?
b: I have some work today. Shall we go tomorrow?
a: Let's go on Sunday. There is no work on that day.
b: Which film shall we go to?
a: You decide (You say!)
b: Do you like Tamil films or Hindi films?
a: I see only Tamil films.

b: A good Tamil film is running in Sun Theatre.
a: We will go to that (emphasis).

Tamil script

We turn now to the set of supplementary consonant letters – the 'Grantha' letters that were added to the Tamil writing system to make it easier to indicate the pronunciation of words borrowed from Sanskrit. These letters do not occur in classical Tamil texts, and a few modern writers try to avoid them. They are, however, to be seen frequently – in newspapers and on signs, for instance. There are four single consonants (ஜ **ja**, ஷ **ṣa**, ஸ **sa**, ஹ **ha**) and one symbol representing a sequence of two sounds (க்ஷ **kṣa**). In addition, there is the special symbol ஸ்ரீ **śrii**. This is used as a title prefixed to the names of deities or great men. It has also been used in the sense of 'Mr', but திரு (**tiru**) is now more common in this usage.

Whenever you see one of these symbols, you can be sure that the word has been borrowed from another language. When the same sound occurs in a Tamil word, a letter from the basic form of the script is used. Thus **j** and **s** are both represented by ச in Tamil words, as explained in Unit 5. A few examples of Grantha letters follow:

ஜுரம்	**juram**	fever
ஜூலை	**juulai**	July
ரிஷி	**riṣi**	rishi
கஷ்டம்	**kaṣṭam**	trouble
ஸ்தானம்	**staanam**	place, position
புஸ்தகம்	**pustakam**	book
ஹிந்தி	**hindi**	Hindi language
ஹோட்டல்	**hooṭṭal**	hotel
க்ஷேமம்	**kṣeemam**	well being

Lexicographers differ as to where they place these letters in ordering entries. A recent dictionary of contemporary (written) Tamil places them after all other consonants, in the order of the words listed above; i.e. ஜ, (ஸ்ரீ), ஷ, ஸ, ஹ, க்ஷ.

Exercise 12

Grantha letters are often used in newspapers when foreign (and some Indian) place names are written in Tamil script. Try to work out what places the following represent:

வாஷிங்டன், ஜப்பான், ஸ்பெயின், பீஜிங், அஸாம், மாஸ்கோ.

Exercise 13

After working out the Tamil pronunciation, decide which Tamil letters will be used to write the following English words in Tamil script: ‘bus’, ‘June’, ‘shoes’. Remember that the Tamil writing system does not distinguish between **p** and **b**.

Certain principles are generally followed in writing, among which are the following: (1) when a letter begins with a loop, that is the starting point, (2) otherwise one starts at the top left-hand corner; (3) a given consonant or vowel symbol is written continuously without lifting pen from paper, even though this may mean going over a part of the line twice; (4) except where a vowel sign precedes the consonant (ெ, ே, ை), the whole of the consonant is completed before the vowel sign is added. Appendix 2 on the Tamil script presents a representative set of letters in larger type to give a clearer idea of their shapes.

7 niinga enge pooriinga

Where are you going?

In this unit you will learn to:

- talk about things that happened in the past
- express purpose
- indicate possession
- use more negative forms of verbs
- understand and use compound verbs

Dialogue 1 (Audio 1: 40)

A train journey

Martin has a conversation with a fellow passenger on the train going from Chennai to Madurai.

PASSENGER: niinga enge pooriinga? Madurekkaa?
MARTIN: aamaa. niinga?
PASSENGER: naanum Madurekkidaan. niinga Amerikkaavaa?
MARTIN: ille. enakku Ingilaandu. Indiyaave sutti paakka vandeen.
PASSENGER: Tamiẓnaaṭṭule endenda uurukku pooniinga? enda uuru piḍiccudu?
MARTIN: neettudaan Meḍraasule eranguneen. Madurekkaararu oruttaru Lanḍanle ennooḍa veele paakkiraaru. avaru modalle Madurekki pooga connaaru. pooreen.

PASSENGER: *Where are you going? To Madurai?*
MARTIN: *Yes. You?*
PASSENGER: *I'm also going to Madurai. Are you from America?*

MARTIN:	*No. I'm from England. I've come to look around India.*
PASSENGER:	*What are the places you have been to in Tamil Nadu? Which place did you like?*
MARTIN:	*Yesterday I arrived in* (lit. *got down in*) *Madras. A man from Madurai works with me in London. He told me to go to Madurai first. I'm going there.*

Vocabulary

suttipaaru	sightsee, see around
veele paaru	work, do a job (not usually a manual one)

Language points

enda/endenda

Some question words, such as **enda** 'which' and **enge** 'where' can be duplicated to give a different shade of meaning. The duplication involves the dropping of the final vowel in the first of the pair: **endenda**, **engenge**. In some varieties of English, including Indian English, the corresponding forms are 'which all' and 'where all'. That is to say that, whereas the use of **enda** seeks to know 'which one(s)' of a larger set, in using **endenda** one is asking to be informed about the whole set. In answering a question containing **enge**, one might appropriately mention just one place, whereas a person asking **engenge** would expect a more comprehensive answer. This is illustrated in the dialogue by a sequence of two questions which Martin's fellow passenger asks him: **endenda uurukku pooniinga? enda uuru piḍiccudu?** 'What are *all* the place*s* you have gone to? Which place (in particular) did you like?'

Reporting commands that someone has given

Notice from this dialogue how to report an instruction given by one person to another. The commonest way is by the use of the verb **sollu** (sometimes pronounced **collu**) 'say', 'tell', preceded by an infinitive, the noun or pronoun representing the person receiving the order/instruction/advice being in the accusative case:

avaru enne Madurekki pooga connaaru.
He told me to go to Madurai.

Exercise 1 (Audio 1: 41)

Report that Raja told you to do certain things:

Example: Study Tamil:
Raajaa enne Tamiẓ padḍikka connaan.

1 Go to Chennai.
2 Go to America.
3 Read the professor's book.
4 Get off in Madurai.

Exercise 2

Report that you told Raja to do these things.

Example: **naan Raajaave Tamiẓ paḍikka conneen.**

Dialogue 2 (Audio 1: 42)

Need for dollars

Mohan asks his friend Mark to help him out with a few American dollars.

MOHAN: neettu niinga sinimaavukku pooniingaḷaa?
MARK: aamaa, ongaḷukku yaaru sonnaanga?
MOHAN: onga manevi sonnaanga. paḍam epḍi irundudu?
MARK: naḍippu nallaa irundudu. kade avḷavu nallaa ille.
MOHAN: ongagiṭṭe oru odavi keekka vandeen.
MARK: enna odavi? niinga yaarṭṭeyum odavikki poogamaaṭṭiingaḷee?
MOHAN: veere oṇṇum ille. en tangacci bi. ii. paḍiccaa, illeyaa? avaḷukku Amerikkaavule paḍikka aase.
MARK: ippadaan payyangaḷum poṇṇugaḷum nereya pooraangaḷee.
MOHAN: avaḷukku appḷikeeṣanooḍa anuppa konjam ḍaalar teeve.
MARK: idukkaa ivḷavu tayanguniinga? oṇṇum kaṣṭamee ille. naan innoru payyanukku cekku kuḍutteen. adee maadiri onga tangaccikkum kuḍukkireen.

MOHAN: *Did you go to the cinema yesterday?*
MARK: *Yes; who told you?*
MOHAN: *Your wife told me. How was the film?*
MARK: *The acting was good. The story was not so good.*
MOHAN: *I've come to ask a favour of you.*
MARK: *What favour? You won't ask favours of anyone, will you?*
MOHAN: *It's not a big thing. My younger sister studied for a B.E., didn't she? She wants to study in America.*
MARK: *Now lots of young men and women go, don't they?*
MOHAN: *She needs a few dollars to send with the application.*
MARK: *Why did you hesitate to ask for this?* (lit. *Did you hesitate so much for this?*) *There's no problem. I gave a cheque to another young man. In the same way I'll give one to your sister.*

Vocabulary

naḍippu	acting
avḷavu	that much, so much
veere oṉṉum ille	not any big thing
paḍi	read, study
Amerikkaa	USA
nereya	in plenty, in great numbers
ḍaalar	US dollar
tayangu	hesitate
cekku	cheque
kade	story
odavi	help
veere	different, some other (thing)
bi ii	B(achelor of) E(ngineering)
aase	desire
appḷikeeṣan	application
anuppu	send
teeve	need
kaṣṭam	difficulty
adee maadiri	likewise, in the same manner

Language points

Past tense

The range of suffixes that indicate past tense is considerably larger than that for present and future. The suffixes for past tense are **-n-**, **-tt-**, **-cc-**, **-nd-**, **-nj-**, **-d-**, **-ṭṭ-**, **-ṇḍ-**, **-ṇṇ-**. The first four suffixes are introduced in this dialogue. The choice of a particular suffix depends on the verb. It can be predicted to some extent by the form of the verb, but it is better to memorise each one separately. We have seen that in the present and future tenses, there are two suffixes for each tense, namely **-r-** and **-kkir-** for the present, and **-v-** and **-pp-** for the future. The verbs that take **-r-** and **-v-** are called 'weak' verbs and the verbs that take **-kkir-** and **-pp-** are 'strong' verbs. The strong verbs have **-kka** added to their stem to form an infinitive; weak verbs take just **-a**. Of the first four past tense suffixes listed above, **-n-** occurs with weak verbs, **-nd** occurs with weak and strong verbs, and **-tt-** and **-cc-** occur with strong verbs. Final consonant **r**, **-l**, **-ḷ**, or **-y** of a strong verb disappears before the past tense suffix or becomes the same as the consonant of the past tense suffix. From now on, the past tense suffix for each verb that occurs will be given in the vocabulary lists. Remember that the first entry for a verb in such lists is the singular imperative. When you come across a new verb, you may find that it helps to fix it in your mind if you repeat a few times both the imperative and the first person singular of the past. Thus, for an entry such as

vaa (**vand-**) come

repeat both **vaa** 'Come!' and **vandeen** 'I came'.

Examples of the different classes of verb follow:

a Verbs that take **-n-** (all are 'weak' verbs):

ooḍu, **paaḍu**, **erangu**, **eeru**, **keḷambu**, **tayangu**, **anuppu**, **sollu**, **poo** (e.g. **ooḍunaan** 'He ran', **sonnaan** 'He said').

b Verbs that take **-nd-**:

weak verb **vaa**, strong verb **iru**
(e.g. **vandaan** 'He came', **irundaan** 'He was').

c Verbs that take **-tt-** (all are 'strong' verbs)

kuḍu, **paaru** (e.g. **kuḍuttaan** 'He gave', **paattaan** 'He saw').

d Verbs that take **-cc-** (all are 'strong' verbs):

paḍi, **naḍi** (e.g. **paḍiccaan** 'He read').

(Verbs in this set end in **-i**, **-e** or **-y** (**-yi**).)

Exercise 3 (Audio 1: 43)

Here is a person speaking of things that happened in the past as if they are happening in the present or will happen in the future. Correct him and say them in the past.

Example: **Raajaa iṉṉekki kaaleejle ooḍraan.**
Raja runs in the college today.

ille, Raajaa neettu kaaleejle ooḍunaan.
No, Raja ran in the college yesterday.

1 Maalaa iṉṉekki kaaleejle paaḍraa.
(Mala sings in the college today.)

2 Saaraa ippa solla tayanguraanga.
(Sarah now hesitates to say.)

3 Jaan inge baslerundu eranguraan.
(John gets down from the bus here.)

4 Murugan naaḷekki uurukku pooraan.
(Murugan goes to his home town tomorrow.)

5 paaṭṭi naaḷekki kade solluvaanga.
(Grandmother will tell stories tomorrow.)

6 Raajaa naaḷekki viiṭṭukku varraan.
(Raja comes home tomorrow.)

7 Maalaa inda viiṭṭule irukkaanga.
(Mala is in this house.)

8 Saaraa inge ukkaaruvaanga
(Sarah will sit here.)

9 ellaarum iṉṉekki raatri sinimaa paappaanga.
(Everyone will see a movie tonight.)

10 ellaarum raatri enge paḍukkiraanga?
Where will everyone sleep tonight?

11 yaaru yaaru inda paḍattule naḍikkiraanga?
Who are all those who will act in this picture?

Exercise 4

Use the appropriate form of the verb in brackets:

1 naan neettu (ooḍu)
2 Raaman naaḷekki (naḍa)
3 ava Raamane neettu (paaru)
4 niinga neettu (sollu)
5 Lakṣmi naaḷekki (paḍi)

Purposive

The dative case suffix **-kku**, which most commonly is the equivalent of English 'to', also has the sense of 'for', 'for the purpose of'. An alternative form used specifically in this sense is **-kkaaga**; e.g. **odavikki** or **odavikkaaga** 'for help'. This sense is common for both these suffixes in action nouns (that is, nouns made from verbs by the addition of **-adu**); e.g. **paḍikkiradukku**, **paḍikkiradukkaaga** 'for studying', 'in order to study'. In addition, **-kkaaga** also has the sense of 'for the sake of'.

More on -ooḍa

The suffix -**ooḍa** has been introduced earlier as indicating possession, in such phrases as **avanooḍa pustagam** 'his book' (where there is the alternative of the unsuffixed form **avan**). Another use of **-ooḍa** is to give the meaning 'with', 'along with', as in **iḍliyooḍa caṭni** 'idli with chutney'; **Jaan Saaraavooḍa sinimaavukku poonaan** 'John went to the cinema with Sarah'. Because it relates to the association of one thing with another or the joining of one thing with another, **-ooḍa**, when occurring in such contexts is sometimes referred as the 'sociative' or 'conjunctive' case. These examples are to be compared with **iḍliyum caṭniyum** 'idli and chutney', and **Jaanum Saaraavum** 'John and Sarah', in which both items are equally primary.

We take this opportunity of recapitulating other ways of indicating possession – in sentences, rather than in phrases where English might have apostrophe + 's'. You will recall that the noun with **-kku** or **-ʈʈe** gives the sense of possession with the verb **iru** 'be': e.g. **enakku veele irukku** 'I have work'; **engiʈʈe paɳam irukku** 'I have money'. The same sense may be found without this verb when no need is felt to indicate tense or time: e.g. **enakku paɳam teeve** 'I have need for money', 'I need money'; **enakku paɖikka aase** 'I have a desire to study', 'I desire to study'. The verb **iru** 'be' occurs in such sentences when the tense is expressed: **enakku paɳam teeve irukku** 'I *have* need for money', 'I need money'; **enakku paɳam teeve irundudu** 'I *had* need for money', 'I needed money'.

Exercise 5

Don't be repetitive. Make your sentences shorter by combining them. Remember to use the correct ending of the verb. This will be different from the one in either of the original sentences. (The principle is the same as in English, if a little more complicated: I *am* going, She *is* going, She and I *are* going.) Remember, too, that if **-um** is used in the sense of 'and', it is added to each word in the sequence.

Example: **Raajaa paaɖunaan; Maalaa paaɖunaa.**
Raajaavum Maalaavum paaɖunaanga.

1 Jaan sinimaavukku poonaaru;
Saaraa sinimaavukku poonaanga.
2 Maalaa Madurele irundaa; Saaraa Madurele irundaanga.
3 naan eʈʈu maɳikkee paɖutteen;
Raajaa eʈʈu maɳikkee paɖuttaan.
4 nii Tamiẓ paɖicce; naan Tamiẓ paɖicceen.
5 nii nidaanamaa vande; ava nidaanamaa vandaa.

Exercise 6

In the following sentences, use the 'sociative' ending **-ooɖa** to rephrase the nouns joined together by **-um ... -um**. Remember to make an appropriate change to the verb.

Example: **Raajaavum Maalaavum paaɖunaanga.**
Raajaa Maalaavooɖa paaɖunaan.

1 Jaanum Saaraavum Madurekki vandaanga.
2 Jaanum Saaraavum Tamiʐ paɖiccaanga.
3 naanum niiyum inda kaaleejle paɖiccoom.
4 niiyum avaɭum enge pooniinga?
5 Maalaa Tamiʐ paaʈʈum Hindi paaʈʈum paaɖunaa.

Exercise 7

The action nouns – nouns made from verb stems + **-adu** – are in the present tense in the following sentences. Make them past and translate them.

Example: **Tamiʐ paɖikkiradu nalladu.**
Learning Tamil is good; it is good to learn Tamil.

Tamiʐ paɖiccadu nalladu.
To have learnt Tamil is good;
it is good to have learnt Tamil.

1 nii Madurele irukkiradu enakku teriyaadu.
2 Kumaar viiʈʈukku varradu enakku piɖikkale.
3 Maalaa paaɖrade yaarum enakku sollale.
4 nii ade solla tayanguradu saridaan.

Dialogue 3 (Audio 1: 44)

A bad dream

Mohan tells Mark of a frightening dream that turned him into a vegetarian.

MARK: iɳɳekki Maariyamman tiruviʐaa aaccee. viiʈʈule enna saapʈiinga?
MOHAN: mattavanga aaʈʈukkari saapʈaanga, naan saivam aaccee, vaʐakkamaana saappaaɖudaan.
MARK: niinga epɖi saivam aaniinga?
MOHAN: romba varuʂattukku munnaale Maariyamman tiruviʐaavukku enga viiʈʈuleyee oru aaʈʈe koɳɳaanga.
MARK: anda paʐakkam uɳɖaa?
MOHAN: uɳɖu. ippavum kiraamangaɭɭe uɳɖu . . . naan romba aʐudeen. aɳɳekki raatri oru kanavu kaɳɖeen.
MARK: kanavule enna vandudu?

MOHAN:	bayangaramaa oru alaral keeṭṭudu. oru aaḍu tale illaama ooḍuccu. adooḍa tale en kaalu munnaale uruṇḍudu.
MARK:	niinga enna senjiinga?
MOHAN:	naan taleye eḍukka kuninjeen. tale maayamaa marenjudu.
MARK:	bayangaramaana kanavudaan.
MOHAN:	adulerundu kari saapḍaama irukkeen.
MARK:	*Today is Mariyamman Festival, isn't it? What did you eat at home?*
MOHAN:	*The others ate mutton; but I'm a vegetarian, aren't I, (so) the usual food.*
MARK:	*How did you become a vegetarian?*
MOHAN:	*Many years ago they killed a goat in our house for Mariyamman Festival.*
MARK:	*Does that custom exist?*
MOHAN:	*It does. It exists in villages even now . . . I cried a lot. That night I had a dream.*
MARK:	*What happened in the dream?*
MOHAN:	*There was a terrible scream. A goat was running without a head. Its head rolled in front of my feet.*
MARK:	*What did you do?*
MOHAN:	*I bent down to pick up the head. The head disappeared without a trace.*
MARK:	*A terrible dream indeed.*
MOHAN:	*From then on I have not eaten meat.*

Vocabulary

Maariyamman	goddess of rain	**tiruviẓaa**	festival
aaccee	is it not (equivalent to the tag question form **illeyaa**)		
mattavanga(ḷ)	others	**kari**	meat
aaḍu	goat, sheep	**saivam**	vegetarian, vegetarianism
aa(gu) (-n-)	become, be		
vaẓakkamaana	usual	**kollu (-ṇṇ-)**	kill
paẓakkam	custom, practice	**uṇḍu**	be (with no tense difference)
kiraamam	village		
aẓu (-d-)	cry	**kanavu**	dream
kaaṇ (kaṇḍ-)	see (restricted to a few object nouns like **kanavu**)		
kanavu kaaṇ	have a dream	**bayangaram**	something terrible
alaral	scream	**keeḷu (-ṭṭ-)**	hear, listen

illaama	without	**uruḷu**	roll
seyyi (-nj-)	do	**kuni**	bend down
maayamaa	without a trace	**mare (-nj-)**	disappear

Language points

Pronunciation tip

If you listen to the tape carefully, you will notice that the final vowel of the neuter ending of the verb **-ccu** is pronounced as a sound that is between **u** and **i**. No special letter is needed for this, as the sound is associated with a **u** that is preceded by **cc**.

Past tense

As you have seen, past tense forms of verbs are much more varied than present or future forms. A number of the consonants and consonant sequences that indicate past are illustrated in what follows. Though, as you will see, it is possible to state some rules for these past tense forms, these rules are a little complicated, and you may prefer to remember the forms through usage and practice.

A number of verbs take **-ṭṭ-** as an indicator of past tense. Verbs in this set have roots (generally the form that is used for the singular imperative) that end in **-ḍu** or **-ḷu**. Among the common verbs in this set are: **saapḍu** 'eat', **pooḍu** 'put down', **viḍu** 'let go' (all weak verbs), and **keeḷu** 'hear', 'listen', 'ask' (strong verb); e.g. **saapṭaan** 'He ate', **keeṭṭaan** 'He heard/asked'. Note that in verbs where the past tense is indicated by **-ṭṭ**, the **-ḍu** or **-ḷu** of the verb root disappears.

All the following past tense suffixes occur with weak verbs. With the exception of **-nj-**, each of these occurs with only a small set of verbs.

1 Verbs that take **-nj-**: **mare** 'disappear', **seyyi** 'do' (**-yyi** disappears): e.g. **marenjaan**, **senjaan**. These verbs end in **-i**, **-e** or **-y** (**-yi**).
2 Verbs that take **-d-**: **aẓu** 'weep': e.g. **aẓudaan**. In the present tense the stem of this verb is **aẓuvu**.
3 Verbs that take **-ḍ-**: **kaaṇ** 'see': e.g. **kaṇḍaan**. These verbs end in **-ṇ**. Note that in the past tense the stem of **kaaṇ** becomes **kaṇ**.

4 Verbs that take **-ṇḍ-**: **uruḷu** 'roll' (**-ḷu** disappears): e.g. **uruṇḍaan**. These verbs end in **-ḷ(u)**.
5 Verbs that take **-ṇṇ-**: **kollu** 'kill' (**-llu** disappears): e.g. **koṇṇaan**.

'Without doing'

The suffix **-aama(l)** (sometimes referred to as the 'negative adverbial participle') added to a verb stem gives the meaning 'without (doing something or other)'. With nouns **illaama(l)** is added: **paṇam illaama** 'without money', **paṇam varaama** 'without money coming (to my hands)', **paṇam kuḍukkaama** 'without giving money'. A verb + **-aama** + **iru** may mean habitually not doing or being without doing: **saapḍaama irukkeen** 'I don't eat'; **poogaama irukkeen** 'I shan't be going'. As you can see, the bracketed (**l**) is not pronounced in the examples. It comes as a linking sound, however, if a suffix such as emphatic **-ee** is added.

Exercise 8

Using the verb in parentheses, fill in the blanks with the appropriate **-aama** (negative participle) form – that is to say, to give the meaning 'without (doing something)'. Give the meaning of the sentences you produce.

Example: **Raajaa —— kaaleejukku poonaan (paḍi).**
Raajaa paḍikkaama kaaleejukku poonaan.
Raja went to college without studying.

1 Raajaa —— veele senjaan (peesu).
2 Maalaa —— viiṭṭukku vandaa (sollu).
3 nii —— peesu (tayangu).
4 appaa kaalelerundu —— irukkaaru (saapḍu)
5 naan onakkaaga —— irundeen (tuungu).
6 niinga yaarum —— naan poogale (vaa).
7 naan veele —— irukkale (seyyi).
8 Kumaar enakku —— sinimaavukku poonaan (teri).

Neuter ending in past tense

As with present and past tense verbs, no distinction of singular and plural is made in the neuter in the past. There are two neuter suffixes: **-udu** and **-uccu**. The second of these, **-(u)ccu**, occurs routinely with verbs that take **-n-** as the past tense suffix. However, this suffix (**-n-**) is absent in the neuter: compare the neuter forms **ooḍuccu** and **pooccu** with the masculine forms **ooḍunaan** and **poonaan**. The ending **-uccu** occurs as an alternative for **-udu** with other verbs: **vandudu/vanduccu**; **paattudu/paattuccu**.

Adverbial modifier of noun

Adjectives are formed, as explained earlier, by adding **-aana** to a noun: **bayangaramaana** (**bayangaram** + **-aana**) **alaral** 'frightening scream'. Adverbs formed of noun + **-aa** may also modify a noun: **bayangaramaa oru alaral** 'a scream that was frightening; a frightening scream'. Notice the position of **oru** in such cases.

Exercise 9

Change the following sentences with adverbs (ending in **-aa**) into sentences with adjectives. Give the meaning of the sentences you make. Pay attention to word order.

Example: **enakku nalladaa oru peenaa vaangu.**
enakku oru nalla peenaa vaangu.
Buy me a good pen.

1 Kumaar perusaa (big) oru viiḍu vaangunaan.
2 aẕagaa (beautiful) oru poṇṇu kaaleejukku vandaa.
3 ammaa meduvaa (soft) reṇḍu iḍli kuḍuttaanga.
4 suuḍaa (hot) kaapi kuḍu.

Nouns derived from verbs

Nouns can be seen to be derived from verbs by the use of different derivational suffixes. We have already noted **-kaaran** and its gender/number variations; these suffixes can be used freely and productively. Many instances of nouns derived from verbs, however, have to be learnt individually. Some examples are: **paaḍu** 'sing' – **paaṭṭu** 'song'; **saapḍu** 'eat' – **saappaaḍu** 'food', 'meal'; **peesu** 'speak' – **peeccu** 'speech'; **paḍi** 'study' – **paḍippu** 'education', 'learning'; **kuuḍu** 'gather' – **kuuṭṭam** 'gathering', 'meeting'; **ooḍu** 'run' – **ooṭṭam** 'run'; **alaru** 'scream' – **alaral** 'scream'.

Compound verbs

Compound verbs may be created by adding 'auxiliary' verbs to nouns. One such auxiliary verb is **-paḍu** 'experience', 'undergo': **kaṣṭam** 'suffering' + **paḍu** → **kaṣṭappaḍu** 'suffer'; **koobam** 'anger' + **paḍu** → **koobappaḍu** 'get angry'. The transitive form of this auxiliary verb is **paḍuttu** 'cause to experience' and this, used with some of the verbs that take **paḍu**: **kaṣṭappaḍuttu** 'make (someone) suffer'; **koobappaḍuttu** 'make someone get angry'.

The verb **paṇṇu** 'do', 'make', used as a main verb with a direct object in such constructions as **tappu paṇṇu** 'make a mistake' and **doose paṇṇu** 'make dosa', is added to nouns to make compound verbs, as in **kalyaaṇam** 'marriage' + **paṇṇu** → **kalyaaṇam paṇṇu** 'marry'. An alternative to **paṇṇu** is **seyyi** 'do', but this is less common in spoken than in written Tamil. A very common type of compound in the speech of bilinguals consists of an English verb stem followed by **paṇṇu**: e.g. ***try*-paṇṇu** 'try', ***reserve*-paṇṇu** 'reserve', ***miss*-paṇṇu** 'miss (someone)'. You will learn more of this later.

Also of frequent occurrence in noun-verb compounds is **pooḍu** 'put': **saṇḍe** 'fight' + **pooḍu** = 'fight', **sattam** 'noise' + **pooḍu** = 'make a noise', 'shout', 'shout at'. This, like **paṇṇu**, also functions as a main verb with a direct object: **sooru** 'rice' + **pooḍu** = 'serve rice', **paḍam** 'picture' + **pooḍu** = 'draw a picture', **saṭṭe** 'shirt' + **pooḍu** = 'put on a shirt'.

Exercise 10

Make verbs from the nouns given by adding **-paḍu**. Give the meaning of the verbs.

Example: **kaṣṭam** **kaṣṭappaḍu** suffer

1 koobam
2 aase
3 teeve
4 kavale (sorrow, concern)
5 erakkam (pity, sympathy)

Tamil script

In the modern version of the Tamil script, the sign for a given vowel when it follows a consonant is in most cases identical for each occurrence of that vowel. The signs for **i** and **ii** vary slightly, depending on the shape of the preceding consonant letter, but they are easily recognisable. This is apparent from a look at the full set of consonant-vowel letters in the alphabet section (Appendix 1, p. 225). The signs for **u** and **uu**, however, have a number of different realisations, with those for the long vowel being more variable than those for the short. In the table that follows, the consonants are grouped together on the basis of the nature of the sign used for **u**. Examples are given only when they can be found in common words or words you already know. Notice the Tamil letters that represent more than one sound: **k/g**, **c/s**, **ṭ/ḍ**, **t/d**, **p/b**.

	Consonant		*Cons. + u*	*Cons. + uu*		
1	க்	**k**	கு	கூ	குடம் கூட்டம்	**kuḍam** pot **kuuṭṭam** crowd
	ட்	**ṭ**	டு	டூ	பாடு	**paaḍu** sing
	ம்	**m**	மு	மூ	முகம் மூச்சு	**mugam** face **muuccu** breath
	ர்	**r**	ரு	ரூ	ஒரு ரூபாய்	**oru** one **ruubaay** rupee
	ழ்	**ẓ**	ழு	ழூ	விழு	**viẓu** fall
	ள்	**ḷ**	ளு	ளூ	அவளும்	**avaḷum** she too
2	ங்	**ŋ**	ஙு	ஙூ		
	ச்	**c**	சு	சூ	கொசு சூடு	**kosu** mosquito **suuḍu** warmth
	ப்	**p**	பு	பூ	புலி பூ	**puli** tiger **puu** flower
	ய்	**y**	யு	யூ	மெல்லியும்	**melliyum** Melli also
	வ்	**v**	வு	வூ	ராஜாவும்	**raajaavum** Raja also

	Consonant		*Cons. + u*	*Cons. + uu*		
3	ஞ்	**ñ**	ஞு	ஞூ		
	ண்	**ṇ**	ணு	ணூ	கண்ணும்	**kaṇṇum** the eye also
	த்	**t**	து	தூ	துணி	**tuṇi** cloth
					தூக்கம்	**tuukkam** sleep
	ந்	**n**	நு	நூ	நுங்கு	**nungu***
					நூல்	**nuul** thread
	ல்	**l**	லு	லூ	புல்லும்	**pullum** grass also
	ற்	**ṟ**	று	றூ	மாறு	**maaṟu** change
	ன்	**ṉ**	னு	னூ	அவனும்	**avaṉum** he also
4	ஜ்	**j**	ஜு	ஜூ	ஜுரம்	**juram** fever
					ஜூன்	**juun** June
	ஷ்	**ṣ**	ஷு	ஷூ		
	ஸ்	**s**	ஸு	ஸூ	பஸ்ஸும்	**bassum** bus also
	ஹ்	**h**	ஹு	ஹூ		

* **nungu** (colloquial **nongu**) is the kernel of a tender palmyra fruit. Its soft flesh and juice are delicious.

Exercise 11

Put the following words in dictionary order:

1 பாடு	2 நாம்	3 தபால்	4 வீடு
5 டீ	6 யார்	7 காடு	8 மணி
9 அந்த	10 புலி		

8 niinga eppa Indiyaavukku vandiinga?

When did you come to India?

In this unit you will learn to talk about:

- business dealings
- bureaucracy
- sequences of actions
- continuous actions
- completed actions
- reflexive actions

Dialogue 1 (Audio 2: 1)

Business tour

Stephen discusses his business plans with Shankar.

SHANKAR:	aḍa, niinga eppa Indiyaavukku vandiinga?
STEPHEN:	naan vandu oru vaaram aagudu. naan ongaḷe paattu reṇḍu varuṣam aaccule?
SHANKAR:	aamaa. Laṇḍanle paḍippe muḍiccu inge vandu oru marundu kampenile seendu veele paakkireen. Ingilaandulerundu marundu erakkumadi senji vikkiroom.
STEPHEN:	romba sandooṣam. naan *Edinburgh*-vukku pooyi oru tuṇi kampeni aarambiccu naḍattikiṭṭurukkeen.
SHANKAR:	vyaabaara viṣayamaa inge vandiingaḷaa?
STEPHEN:	Tamiẓnaaṭṭule ḍras tayaariccu Ingilaandule vittu paṇampaṇṇa oru tiṭṭampooṭṭu vandeen.
SHANKAR:	nalla tiṭṭandaan.

SHANKAR:	*Hello! When did you come to India?*
STEPHEN:	*It's a week since I came. It's two years since I saw you, isn't it?*
SHANKAR:	*Yes. On coming here after finishing my studies in London, I took a job with a pharmaceuticals company. We import medicines from England and sell them.*
STEPHEN:	*I'm very pleased* (*to hear about it*). *I went to Edinburgh and set up a clothing company which I run.*
SHANKAR:	*Did you come here on business?*
STEPHEN:	*I came with* (lit. *after making*) *a plan to make money by producing clothing in Tamil Nadu and selling it in England.*
SHANKAR:	(*That's*) *a good plan.*

Vocabulary

aḍa	expression of surprise	**Indiyaa**	India
marundu	medicine, pharmaceuticals	**muḍi (-cc-)**	finish
Ingilaandu	England	**kampeni**	company, firm
tuṇi	cloth, clothes, garments	**seeru (-nd-)**	join
		erakkumadi	import (noun)
		erakkumadi seyyi (-nj-)	import (verb)

aarambi (-cc-)	begin, start	**naḍattu (-n-)**	run, conduct
vyaabaaram	business		
tiṭṭam	plan (noun)		
tayaari (-cc-)	prepare, produce, manufacture		
ḍras	garment, dress, clothing		
tiṭṭampooḍu (-ṭṭ-)	plan, draw up a plan		

Language points

Actions in sequence

In English, two or more sentences can be strung together with 'and' to form compound sentences ('I came, I saw, and I conquered'). In what can be regarded as the equivalent in Tamil, all but the last verb in the sequence will have the form of a 'verbal participle', rather as if one were to say 'Having come, having seen, I conquered'. A verbal participle is a verb with a tense suffix but without the person-number-gender suffix. The tense suffix is that of the past tense. With one important exception, the consonant or consonants that indicate past tense are followed by **-u** (the pronunciation of which is a little like **i** if the consonants are **-cc-** or **-nj-**). The exception to this rule concerns verbs for which the marker of past tense is **-(u)n-** or **-nn-**. The verbal participle of these is formed by replacing the final **-u** of the verb root with **-i**; the participle of **poo** (**pooyi**) is a variant of this. The most common use of the verbal participle is to indicate that the action performed by the verb precedes the action of the next verb.

One special use of a 'verbal participle' is with a following expression which indicates a period of time – as in the case of **oru vaaram** 'a week' in the above dialogue. Then the meaning of the participle is that it is a week (or whatever the period in question) since the action indicated by the participle was performed.

A few examples of verbal participles follow:

Verb		*Past tense*	*Participle*
paḍi	read	**paḍiccaan**	**paḍiccu**
seyyi	do	**senjaan**	**senju**
kuḍu	give	**kuḍuttaan**	**kuḍuttu**
vaa	come	**vandaan**	**vandu**

pooɖu	put	**pooʈʈaan**	**pooʈʈu**
villu	sell	**vittaan**	**vittu**
vaangu	buy	**vaangunaan**	**vaangi**
sollu	say	**sonnaan**	**solli**
poo	go	**poonaan**	**pooyi**

Compare the Tamil and English constructions in the following, where English has two verbs linked by 'and', while Tamil has a participle ('having done something') followed by a main verb. Notice that English has the same tense form for both verbs, whereas in Tamil the first verb has the same participle form, whatever the tense of the verb at the end of the sentence.

avan ooʈʈalukku pooyi ooyvu eɖuttaan.
He went to the hotel and took a rest.

avan ooʈʈalukku pooyi ooyvu eɖuppaan.
He will go to the hotel and take a rest.

As you will see from the dialogue, there is no upper limit on the number of participles in the sequence that precedes the main verb (any more than there is a limit on the number of a sequence of verbs linked by 'and' in English).

Exercise 1

Pick out the verbal participles in Dialogue 1. What verbs are these derived from?

Example: **vandu** **vaa**

Exercise 2 (Audio 2: 2)

Kumar did two things. Can you combine them into one sentence? Give the meaning of the resulting joined sentences.

Example: **Kumaar baslerundu erangunaan; viiʈʈukku naɖandaan.**

Kumaar baslerundu erangi viiʈʈukku naɖandaan.
Kumar got down from the bus and walked home.

1 Kumaar kaɖele doose vaangunaan; viiʈʈule saapʈaan.
2 Kumaar kaaleejukku poonaan; peeraasiriyare paattaan.
3 Kumaar viiʈʈukku vandaan; ennooɖa peesunaan.

4 Kumaar pattu ruubaa kuḍuttaan; inda peenaave vaangunaan.
5 Kumaar paaṭṭu paaḍunaan; ellaareyum sandooṣappaḍuttunaan.
6 Kumaar kaṣṭappaṭṭaan; paḍiccaan; paas paṇṇunaan. (pass)

Progressive forms of verbs

This verb form, in contrast with the simple tense, indicates that the action or state continues or is in progress over a period of time. The meaning is somewhat similar to that given when a verb in English is preceded by 'be' and followed by '-ing', as in 'She is eating', or 'He was working'. The indicator of progressive action in Tamil is **-kiṭṭuru** (**-kiṭṭu** + **iru**) added to the verbal participle. An example in Dialogue 1 is **naḍattikiṭṭurukkeen** 'I am running' (in the sense of 'managing'). This progressive form of a verb may have any of the three tenses:

Raaman tuungikiṭṭurukkaan.	Raman is sleeping.
Melli paaḍikiṭṭurundaa.	Melli was singing.
appaa saapṭukiṭṭuruppaaru.	Father will be eating.

One point to be aware of with regard to progressive forms in the present tense is that in some contexts English has a progressive where Tamil has a simple present; and sometimes the reverse is the case. This point is illustrated by the translation of **naḍatti-kiṭṭurukkeen** in the dialogue. One important instance of a 'progressive' form in English where a Tamil progressive is not possible is in reference to a future event. Thus in English such utterances as 'She *is* com*ing* tomorrow' are common, while in such instances, only a simple tense form is possible in Tamil: **naaḷekki varraa**.

Exercise 3

Fill in the blanks with the progressive form of the verb in parentheses and give the meaning of both sentences.

Example: **naan Kumaar viiṭṭukku pooneen;**
appa avan —— (saapḍu).

naan Kumaar viiṭṭukku pooneen;
appa avan saapṭukiṭṭurundaan.
I went to Kumar's house; he was eating then.

1 naan kaaleejukku pooneen; appa Kumaar veḷiye —— (past) (vaa).
2 neettu Maalaa paaḍunaa; appa Kumaar veḷiye —— (past) (nillu).
3 ammaa kaalele doose paṇṇuvaanga; appa nii —— (future) (tuungu).
4 innum oru varuṣattule Kumaar kampenile veele —— (future) (paaru).
5 Maalaa paaḍraa; nii —— (present) (peesu).
6 Kumaar onne paaraaṭṭuraan; nii veḷiye —— (present) (paaru).
7 raatri maṇi pattu aagudu; bas innum —— (present) (ooḍu).

Dialogue 2 (Audio 2: 4)

Business contract

Stephen tells Shankar how his negotiations went at the factory.

SHANKAR: onga tiṭṭappaḍi ellaa veeleyeyum muḍiccuṭṭiingaḷaa?
STEPHEN: paadi veele muḍinjirukku. ḍras kampenikaarangaḷe paattu peesiṭṭeen. avanga renḍu maasattule sarakku anuppa ottukkiṭṭaanga.
SHANKAR: munpaṇam kuḍutturukkiingaḷaa?
STEPHEN: ille. sarakke anuppiṭṭu bille anuppuvaanga. naan paṇatte kaṭṭi sarakke eḍukkaṇum.
SHANKAR: adudaan nalladu. moosamaana sarakke tiruppi vaangikiḍuvaangaḷḷe?
STEPHEN: aamaa, apḍidaan oppandam. tirumba vangikiṭṭu kaṇakkule kaẓiccuruvaanga.
SHANKAR: ide ellaam eẓudi vaangikkanga. appadaan pinnaale piraccane eduvum varaadu.
STEPHEN: apḍidaan senjirukkeen.

SHANKAR: *Did you finish all the work in accordance with your plan?*
STEPHEN: *Half the work is finished. I've seen and spoken to the people at the clothing factory. They agreed to send the goods in two months.*
SHANKAR: *Have you given an advance payment?*

STEPHEN: *No. They'll send the goods and (then) send the invoice. I have to pay the money and pick up the goods.*

SHANKAR: *That's good. They'll take back poor quality goods, won't they?*

STEPHEN: *Yes, That's the agreement. After taking them back, they'll deduct from the account.*

SHANKAR: *Get all this in writing. Then there won't be any problems later.*

STEPHEN: *That's what I've done.*

Vocabulary

paḍi	according to, as	**tiṭṭappaḍi**	according to plan
paadi	half	**muḍi (-nj-)**	be over
ottukkiḍu (-ṭṭ-)	agree, accept	**sarakku**	goods, commodity
kaṭṭu (-n-)	pay	**moosamaana**	bad, of poor quality
tiruppi	back, in return	**tirumba**	back, again
oppandam	contract, agreement	**kaṇakku**	account
kaẓi (-cc-)	subtract	**piraccane**	problem

Language points

Compound forms of verbs

In addition to the past, present, and future tense forms of verbs, there are more complex forms which add a meaning in addition to that of tense. These include, in addition to the progressive already mentioned, completive, perfect, and reflexive forms. All of these are formed by adding a suffix to the past participle of a verb (introduced earlier in this unit). Each of the complex forms can appear in each of the three tenses.

Completive

What is often called the completive aspect of a Tamil verb indicates, as the label is intended to suggest, that the action referred to in the verb is, or definitely will be, accomplished or completed.

In English the same sense (if explicitly indicated at all) is conveyed in different ways. Compare, for instance, the different meanings in the following pairs: ‘eat’ and ‘eat up’; ‘finish’ and ‘finish off’. Sometimes, as examples given below (including those in Exercise 4) show, the most convenient English equivalent of a Tamil completive is an adverb. The completive suffixes – which follow an adverbial participle and are themselves followed by the usual personal endings – are **-ṭṭ-** (past), **-rr-** (present) and **-ruv-** (future). For a singular imperative (used when one wants to ask or request someone to do something), **-ru** is added, and for a plural imperative **-riinga**. As with simple tenses, third person verbs for which the subject is non-human follow a different pattern, as will be clear from the following examples of the verb **vaa** ‘come’.

vanduru.	Do come.
vanduṭṭaan.	He (really) came.
vanduruccu.	It (really) came.
vanduruvaan.	He will (definitely) come.
vandurum.	It will (definitely) come.
vandurraan.	He’s coming (surely).
vandurudu.	It’s coming (surely).
vanduṭṭu.	Having come.

An example in Dialogue 2 is **kaẓiccuruvaanga**.

You may hear an alternative form for the third person neuter (‘it’) past. This, for **vaa**, is **vanduṭṭudu** – which self-evidently is more ‘regular’ in that it follows the pattern of such forms as **vanduṭṭaan** where the subject is human. This alternative for neuter past forms is not available for verbs which have **-n-** to indicate past tense. Thus **ooḍiruccu** is the only possibility for ‘It ran off’.

Exercise 4 (Audio 2: 5)

The given sentences here represent the narration of events as simple occurrences. Change them to indicate that the events referred to were completed or will be completed, or that some result was accomplished. Suggested English translations of the given sentence and of the aimed-for sentence will give you some idea of these added meanings that you are aiming to convey by the changes you make.

Example: **Kumaar neettu vandaan.**
Kumar came yesterday.

Kumaar neettee vanduṭṭaan.
Kumar came yesterday itself.

1 Raajaa kaaleejukku poonaan.
(Raja went to college → Raja has already gone to college *or* Raja went away to college.)

2 appaa pattu maṇikki paḍuttaaru.
(Father lay down at 10 o'clock → Father went to bed at 10 o'clock.)

3 kaḍekkaaran kadave muuḍunaan.
(The shopkeeper closed the door → The shopkeeper closed down the door (for the day).)

4 ḍaakṭar palle piḍungunaaru.
(The doctor pulled the tooth → The doctor pulled out the tooth.)

5 paappaa kiiẓe viẓundudu.
(The baby fell down → The baby fell down (suddenly).)

6 enakku paṇam keḍeccudu.
(I got money → I got the money (I was looking for).)

Perfect

The so-called perfect or perfective of a verb is closely similar in meaning to English 'perfect' (as in 'he has done'), though perhaps more widely used. It indicates the relevance of a completed action to another action, as in English 'When I came, he *had* already done it', where 'had (already)' indicates his doing something was completed at the time of my coming. The forms of the perfect are those of the verb **iru** 'be' when added to participles ending in **-i**; in the case of participles ending in **-u**, the initial **i-** of **iru** is dropped:

vandurundaan.	He had come.
vandurukkaan.	He has come.
vanduruppaan.	He will have come.
vaangiyirundaan.	He had bought.
vaangiyirukkaan.	He has bought.
vaangiyiruppaan.	He will have bought.

Note that with the verb **ukkaaru** 'sit (down)', the meaning of the perfect is different.

ukkaandurundaan.	He was sitting.
ukkaandurukkaan.	He is sitting.
ukkaanduruppaan.	He will be sitting.

Examples in Dialogue 2 are **kuḍutturukkiinga** and **senjirukkeen**.

Exercise 5

When a past event has relevance to the present, the verb describing this past event is in the present perfect. Add the appropriate marker of the perfect to the verb of the first sentence in the context of the second sentence. Translate both sentences.

Example: **Kumaar viiṭṭukku vandaan.**
Kumar came to (our) house.

ṭi vi paappaan.
He will watch TV.

Kumaar viiṭṭukku vandurukkaan; ṭi vi paappaan.
Kumar has come to our house; he will watch TV.

1 appaa Laṇḍanukku poonaaru.
aḍutta vaaram tirumbi varuvaaru.

2 naan nallaa paḍicceen.
nalla maark vaanguveen.

3 naan appaaṭṭe onakku paṇam kuḍukka sonneen.
pooyi vaangikka.

4 ivan aaru maṇi neeram veele paattaan.
kuuḍa paṇam kuḍutturu.

5 naan sinna vayasule sigareṭṭu kuḍicceen.
ippa viṭṭuṭṭeen.

6 niinga Laṇḍan pooniingaḷaa?
ille, poonadulle.

Reflexive

A reflexive verb form indicates that an action has some effect on the subject of the sentence. Normally, but not necessarily, the subject and the object of a transitive verb are identical when a reflexive form is used. The reflexive often translates in English as 'self' when the verb is transitive. The reflexive also occurs with intransitive verbs, when it indicates that the action of the verb has some effect on the subject. The forms of the reflexive are: **-kka** in the imperative, **-kiṭṭ-** in the past tense, **-kiḍr-** in the present, and **-kiḍuv-** in the future (with appropriate personal endings being added, of course, for the three tensed forms):

aḍiccukiṭṭaan.	He hit himself.
aḍiccukiḍuvaan.	He will hit himself.
aḍiccukiḍraan.	He hits himself. (Note that with the present tense suffix the sense is not present time, i.e. not 'He is hitting himself').
aḍiccukiḍuccu.	It hit itself. (When the reference is to a non-human, you will also hear the alternative form **aḍiccukkiṭṭudu** for the past tense, though this is less common.)
oḷinjikiṭṭaan.	He hid himself.
paḍuttukiṭṭaan.	He lay down (snugly).

In Dialogue 2, the force of the reflexive in **vaangikkanga** is 'Get (this) for yourself.'

'As', 'according to'

The form **paḍi** occurs frequently in the sense of 'as', 'according to', 'in accordance with'. It may follow either a noun (as in **tiṭṭappaḍi** in Dialogue 2) or a verbal form – the relative participle, about which you will learn more in Unit 9. It often indicates the source or director of an action:

en solpaḍi Tamiẓ paḍi.	Study Tamil as per my word/advice.
naan solrapaḍi Tamiẓ paḍi.	Study Tamil as I say.

'Isn't it?'

You may be puzzled by the ending of **vaangikiḍuvaangaḷḷe** in Dialogue 2. The last two sounds are a variant of **-le**, the short form of **ille** or **illeyaa**. This, as you may recall from Unit 5, is a 'tag question'. Apart from possible abbreviations, this has one form in Tamil, but has a different equivalent in English depending on the context. Here the appropriate translation is 'Won't they?' The change of **-le** to **-ḷe** is through the influence of the final sound of the plural ending **-ga(ḷ)**.

Exercise 6

One of the uses of the perfect form of verbs is in relation to an event in the past which has not been observed directly, but which is deduced from some evidence in the present. If the evidence suggests that the assumed event was probable, the future tense of the perfect is used; otherwise the present tense is selected. Change the verbs in the sentences given below to the present or future perfect, choosing whichever is appropriate in the context of the second sentence that follows. Translate the new sentences. Where the speaker takes the event to have been probable, an English translation may well include the words 'must have'.

Example: **viiṭṭukkuḷḷe yaaroo vandaanga.**
Someone came into the house.

kadavu terandurukku.
The door is open.

viiṭṭukkuḷḷe yaaroo vandurukkaanga; kadavu terandurukku.
Someone has come into the house; the door is open.

1 neettu raatri maẕe penjudu; tare iiramaa irukku.

2 Maalaa aẕudaa; ava kaṇṇu sevappaa irukku.

3 Raajaa edoo tappu paṇṇunaan;
reṇḍu naaḷaa enne paakka varale.

4 Kumaar veḷeyaaḍa poonaan; avan pande kaaṇoom.

5 Kumaar nallaa paḍiccaan;
alladu veḷeyaaḍa pooyirukkamaaṭṭaan.

Dialogue 3 (Audio 2: 6)

Chasing papers

Stephen tells Shankar of his experiences with bureaucracy.

SHANKAR: ḍras eettumadikki arasaangattooḍa anumadi keḍeccuruccaa?
STEPHEN: adukkudaan alenjikiṭṭurukkeen.
SHANKAR: idu Tamiẓnaaṭṭu kampenikaaranga veele, illeyaa?
STEPHEN: avanga veeledaan. avangadaan senjukiṭṭurukkaanga. aanaa veele veegamaa naḍakkale. naan mandiriye kuuḍa paattuṭṭeen.
SHANKAR: arasaanga kaṭṭuppaaḍu innum muẓusaa poogale. ovvoru aafiisaraa fayil pooradukku oru maasam kuuḍa aayirum. adukkuḷḷe onga porume pooyirum.
STEPHEN: inda veelekkaaga Indiyaavukku vandaaccu. epḍiyaavadu muḍiccuṭṭudaane pooganum?
SHANKAR: adu uṇmedaan. onga oḍambe paattukkanga. maẓe kaalam aarambiccuruccu.

SHANKAR: *Have you got government permission for clothing exports?*
STEPHEN: *I'm running around for that very thing.*
SHANKAR: *This is the Tamil Nadu company people's job, isn't it?*
STEPHEN: *It is their job. They are doing it. But the work isn't happening quickly. I even saw the minister.*
SHANKAR: *Government control still hasn't completely gone. Even for the file to go to each officer will take a month. By then your patience will be exhausted.*
STEPHEN: *It was for this job that I came to India. Somehow I have to complete it, don't I?*
SHANKAR: *That's true. Take care of your health. The rainy season has begun.*

Vocabulary

eettumadi	export	**arasaangam**	government
anumadi	approval, permission	**ale (-nj-)**	run around
mandiri	minister	**kaṭṭuppaaḍu**	control
muẓusaa	completely	**aafiisar**	officer
fayil	file	**porume**	patience

oḍambu	body, health
paattukka	take care, look after
maẓe kaalam	rainy season, monsoon

Language points

Another meaning of the 'progressive'

As indicated earlier in this unit, the progressive or durative form of a verb (**kiṭṭuru**) has to do with duration; it indicates that an action or a state of affairs continues or is in progress over a period of time. It can also indicate an event that takes place repeatedly over a period.

viiṭṭukku vandukiṭṭurukkaan.	He is coming to the house.
denam vandukiṭṭurukkaan.	He comes every day.

Simultaneous action

While the completive form of the verbal participle (**-ṭṭu**) indicates that the events are thought of as entirely separate, the progressive form of the verbal participle (**-kiṭṭu**) indicates that the events are simultaneous. The emphatic marker **-ee** is commonly added to the latter in the simultaneous sense.

ennooḍa peesikiṭṭu vandaan.
He came while talking to me.

ennooḍa peesikiṭṭee saapṭaan.
He ate while talking with me.

Exercise 7

Change the first sentences in the pairs below to fit the context of the following sentences. That is to say, show that the first eventwas taking place when the second happened. Translate the sentences.

Example: **naan paḍicceen.**
naan paḍiccukiṭṭurundeen; appa karaṇṭ pooyiruccu.
(**karaṇṭ** = electricity, power)

1 Kumaar saapṭaan; appa Umaa vandaa.
2 Kumaar viiṭṭukku poonaan; vaẓile Umaave paattaan.
3 appaa pattu maṇikki tuunguvaaru; appa naama ṭi vi paakkalaam.

Exercise 8

Change the given sentences of separate events into sentences of simultaneous events. Translate both sentences.

Example: **appaa peesiṭṭu saapṭaaru.**
Father spoke and then ate.
appaa peesikiṭṭee saapṭaaru.
Father ate while talking.

1 Kumaar kaapi kuḍiccuṭṭu veḷiye vandaan.
2 maamaa irumiṭṭu peesa aarambiccaaru (irumu 'cough').
3 ammaa tuungiṭṭu ṭi vi paakkiraanga.
4 nii paḍiccuṭṭu veele paaru.
5 Madurele irunduṭṭu *John* Tamiẓ peesa kaṣṭappaḍraaru.

Exercise 9

Fill in the gaps with an appropriate verb form. Keep in mind such questions as to whether actions are continuous, completed, successive, and so on. Translate the passage.

Moohan sinimaavukku —— (poo). vaẓile Raajaave —— (paaru). avan bassukkaaga —— (kaa 'wait'). avanooḍa avan tambi Kumaarum —— (nillu). Kumaare Moohan oru taḍave kaaleejule —— (paaru). Moohan sinimaavukku reṇḍu ṭikkeṭ —— (vaangu). Raajaaveyum sinimaavukku —— (kuupḍu). Raajaa tambiye basle viiṭṭukku —— (anuppu) sinimaavukku vara —— (ottukkiḍu). reṇḍu bassu nikkaama —— (poo). sinimaavukku neeram —— (aagu). Raajaa tambi kayyile pattu ruubaa —— (kuḍu) basle pooga —— (sollu) Moohanooḍa —— (keḷambu). tambi paṇatte —— (vayyi) bassukkaaga —— (nillu). Moohanum Raajaavum veegamaa —— (naḍa). sariyaana neerattukku sinimaavukku —— (poo).

Tamil script

As your knowledge of Tamil improves, you may wish to look at a newspaper (பத்திரிகை **pattirigai**, colloquial **patrikke**). Here are the names of some of the more widely circulated ones in South India: தினமணி, தினத்தந்தி, தினமலர், தினகரன். Try reading these out and transcribing them. You will hear the initial consonant in each case pronounced as **t** or **d**. The first two syllables are from the word தினம் **dinam** 'day' (also used adverbially to mean 'daily'). One of the meanings of மணி is 'bell' – and so a possible translation of தினமணி is 'Daily Clarion'. தந்தி may mean 'wire', giving us 'Daily Telegraph' for தினத்தந்தி. There is no obvious English equivalent of தினமலர்; two common meanings of மலர் are 'blossom' and 'issue of a journal or paper'. For தினகரன் we have simply 'The Sun'. Weekly journals that have a wide circulation are குங்குமம், குமுதம் and ஆனந்த விகடன்.

Exercise 10

Translate these newspaper headlines:

1 தமிழ் நாட்டில் மார்ச் மாதம் தேர்தல்
2 அசாமில் பயங்கர ரயில் விபத்து
3 கிரிக்கெட் போட்டியில் இந்தியா வெற்றி

(அசாம் Assam; தேர்தல் election; பயங்கர terrible; போட்டி contest; மாதம் month; விபத்து accident; வெற்றி victory, win. Words borrowed from English are omitted from this list!)

9 niinga pooṭṭurukkira caṭṭe

The shirt you are wearing

In this unit you will learn to:

- talk about current affairs
- report things you have heard
- use relative clauses
- make nouns from verbs

Dialogue 1 (Audio 2: 9)

Tailor-made clothes

Stephen and Shankar talk about having clothes made to measure by a tailor.

SHANKAR: niinga pooṭṭurukkira caṭṭe ongaḷukku ḍras anupra kaḍele vaangunadaa?

STEPHEN: ille. oru ṭeylarṭṭe aḷavu kuḍuttu taccukiṭṭeen.

SHANKAR: aḍe. niinga vikkira ḍrasse niingaḷee pooḍa maaṭṭiingaḷaa?

STEPHEN: apḍi ille. naan indiyaavukku vandadunaale taccukiṭṭeen. enakku terinja tayyakaararu oruttaru inge irukkaaru. avaru taccukuḍuttaaru.

SHANKAR: summaa veḷeyaaṭṭukku sonneen . . . aḷavu saṭṭe kuḍuttiingaḷaa?

STEPHEN: ille. en paẓaya saṭṭe ellaam konjam piḍikkidu. saṭṭe, pæṇṭs, kooṭṭu ellaattukkum pudusaa ṭeylar aḷavu eḍuttaaru. saṭṭe evḷavu poruttamaa irukku, paarunga.

SHANKAR: aamaa. onga naaṭṭule pudusaa vandurukkira sṭaylleyum irukku.

SHANKAR: *Was the shirt you are wearing bought at the shop that supplies you with clothes?*

STEPHEN: *No. I gave the measurements and had it sewn at a tailor's.*

SHANKAR: *Oh. Don't you want to wear the clothes you sell?*

STEPHEN: *It's not like that. I had it sewn because I came to India. There's a tailor I know here. He stitched it for me.*

SHANKAR: *I was only joking . . . Did you give a shirt as a model?*

STEPHEN: *No. All my old shirts are a bit tight. For the shirt, trousers, jacket – everything – the tailor took measurements afresh. See what a good fit the shirt is.*

SHANKAR: *Yes. It's in a style that's recently come into fashion in your country.*

Vocabulary

ṭeylar	tailor	**aḷavu**	measurement
tayyi (tacc-)	stitch, sew, get stitched/sewn	**tayyakaararu**	tailor
		piḍi (-cc-)	be tight
poruttam	being a good fit	**sṭayl**	style
aḷavu saṭṭe	model shirt (for measurement)	**velayaaḍu**	fun, game

Language points

Pronunciation

The usual pronunciation of the second word in the dialogue, **pooṭṭurukkira**, is more like **pooṭrukra**. This is because the vowels **u** and **i** in the middle of words tend to be dropped. This has already been mentioned in Unit 2 in connection with the general reduction of the present tense marker **-kkir-** to **-kr-**. The fuller spelling of the word is given here so that you may more readily recognise the separate grammatical parts – to be discussed in the following paragraph.

Relative participle

The relative participle is a verbal form that modifies a noun. In common with adjectives, it precedes the noun it modifies. For this reason it is also called the 'adjectival participle'. As the phrase 'relative participle' is intended to indicate, it occurs in clauses of which the most usual equivalent in English is a relative clause, i.e. a clause of the sort that commonly begins with words such as 'who', 'whose', 'which', 'that'. This class of word – namely, a relative pronoun – is not found in Tamil.

A relative participle is formed by the addition of the ending **-a** to the present or past tense stem of a verb. A future relative participle is found in the written language, but this is very rare in relative clauses in the colloquial language, the present form being used to convey both present and future meaning. This future form (verb + **-um**) will be introduced in a later unit in connection with 'time' clauses. The formation of the past and present relative participles is seen in the third column in the following examples; the first column contains past or present tense forms with the masculine singular ending **-aan**. A hyphen is inserted in the first column to show where the stem, mentioned above, ends.

vand-aan	he came	**vanda**
varr-aan	he comes	**varra**
kuḍutt-aan	he gave	**kuḍutta**
kuḍukkir-aan	he gives	**kuḍukkira**
sonn-aan	he said	**sonna**
solr-aan	he says	**solra**
saapṭ-aan	he ate	**saapṭa**
saapḍr-aan	he eats	**saapḍra**

In Dialogue 1, look again at the instances: **pooṭṭurukkira**, **anupra**, **vikkira**, **terinja**, **vandurukkira**.

Here are some more examples of relative clauses:

vanda payyan.	The boy who came.
varra payyan.	The boy who is coming.

sooru saapṭa payyan. The boy who ate rice.
payyan saapṭa sooru. The rice that the boy ate.

The last pair of examples illustrates one of the difficulties that you will experience at first in using this construction: the noun that follows the relative participle may be either the subject or object of the verb in question (or, indeed, in yet some other relationship with it). In some cases, such as this, common sense tells you that only **payyan** can be the subject, and so **sooru** must be the object, whatever its position. Sometimes, as in the case of nouns referring to animals or human beings, the accusative case ending **-e** on the first noun (the one preceding the relative participle) shows that this is the object, and therefore that the one following is the subject. Compare these two:

eliye koṉṉa naayi. The dog that killed the rat.
naayi koṉṉa eli. The rat that the dog killed.

Nouns can be in other relationships with the relative participle than subject and object. The listener is able to grasp the relationship through common sense alone, as no case ending can be added to indicate the meaning. Thus compare the locative ending **-le** in the sentence **naan basle vandeen** 'I came by bus' with its absence in **naan vanda bas** 'the bus *in* which I came'. This is not to say that a case ending cannot be added to **bas** in such an example – but the ending is determined by the function of **bas** in the main clause: **naan vanda basse paattiingaḷaa** 'Did you see the bus I came in?'

Exercise 1 (Audio 2: 10)

In English, if I saw an exhibition, I can refer to this as 'the exhibition that I saw', that is to say by using a relative clause. Practise doing this in Tamil by inserting the appropriate relative participle in the gaps below. Translate both the original sentence and the relative clause.

Example: **naan paḍam paatteen; naan paatta paḍam.**
I saw a film; the film that I saw.

1 ṭaaksi varudu; —— ṭaaksi.
2 neettu Raaman patrikke paḍiccaan; Raaman neettu —— patrikke.

3 Lakṣmi basle vandaa; Lakṣmi —— bas.
4 naan Goovindanukku paṇam kuḍutteen; naan Goovindanukku —— paṇam.

Exercise 2

Find the odd one out in these groups of words:

1 kooẓi kaakkaa paambu kiḷi parundu
2 meḷagaa maambaẓam vengaayam veṇḍakkaa uruḷekkeẓangu
3 puune naayi kudire aaḍu nari
4 arisi vaḍe puuri iḍli doose
5 kuṭṭi paaru sollu keḷambu kuḍi

Dialogue 2 (Audio 2: 11)

Profit from traditional knowledge

Shankar and Stephen discuss the problems that arise when foreign companies register rights internationally to plants that have long been used in indigenous medicine.

SHANKAR: enga marundu kampeni veeppamarattulerundu pudusaa oru marundu tayaariccurukku.

STEPHEN: olagam muẓusum ippa veeppamarattooḍa perumeye purinjukiṭṭurukkaanga.

SHANKAR: enga pudu marunde vikkiradule oru periya piraccane irukku.

STEPHEN: enna piraccane?

SHANKAR: veeppamarattulerundu marundu tayaarikkira urimeye oru Amerikka kampeni vaangiyirukkaam. veere yaarum anda marunde tayaarikka kuuḍaadaam.

STEPHEN: idu enna aniyaayamaa irukku. veeppamarattooḍa nanmeye modalle terinjukiṭṭavanga inda naaṭṭukaaranga daane.

SHANKAR: adu maṭṭum ille. poona maasam naan paḍicca viṣayam oṇṇu solreen. veeppa elelerundu eḍutta marundu anda kaalattule ingerundu veḷinaaṭṭukkukuuḍa pooccaam.

STEPHEN: vaḷarra naaḍugaḷḷe irukkira inda maadiriyaana arivooḍa balan anda naaṭṭu makkaḷukku keḍekkira maadiri seyyaṉum.

SHANKAR: *Our pharmaceutical company has recently prepared a drug from the neem tree.*

STEPHEN: *Now the whole world is getting to understand the greatness of the neem tree.*

SHANKAR: *In selling our new drug, there is a big problem.*

STEPHEN: *What problem?*

SHANKAR: *It seems that an American company has obtained the rights for preparing drugs from the neem tree. It seems that nobody else is allowed to prepare drugs from the neem tree.*

STEPHEN: *How unjust this is! Those who first understood the benefits (to be derived from) the neem tree were people from this country.*

SHANKAR: *Not only that. I'll tell you about the thing I read last month. It seems that at that time medicine extracted from neem leaves went from here to foreign countries.*

STEPHEN: *We should make it that the benefit of this sort of knowledge that exists in developing countries goes to the people of those countries.*

Vocabulary

veeppamaram	neem tree	**olagam**	world
muẓusum	whole, all	**perume**	greatness
piraccane	problem	**urime**	right
veere	other, different	**aniyaayam**	unfairness, injustice
nanme	goodness, benefit		
vaḷaru (-nd-)	develop, grow up	**balan**	benefit
arivu	knowledge		

Exercise 3

The use of the adverbial participle (Unit 8) to combine a sequence of simple sentences into a complex sentence is very common in both speech and writing. Give yourself a little more practice by combining sequences in this way. Translate your sentences also.

Example: **Kumaar kaḍekki poonaan; oru pustagam vaangunaan.**

Kumaar kaḍekki pooyi oru pustagam vaangunaan.
Kumar went to the shop and bought a book.

1 Kumaar viiṭṭukku vandaan; pustagam keeṭṭaan.
2 Sundar pudu saṭṭe pooṭṭukiṭṭaan; veḷiye keḷambunaan.
3 Raajaa peenaave toleccuṭṭaan; aẓudaan.
4 naan keeḷvi keeṭṭeen; avan padil sollale.
5 Umaa naaḷekki kaaleejukku varuvaa; ange onne paappaa.
6 Murugan kaṇṇe muuḍikiḍraan; epḍi kaare ooṭraan?

Exercise 4

The following sentences are simple and meant for children. Can you make them into one sentence by using relative participles? Translate your sentences.

Example: **naan oru yoosane solreen; keeḷu.**
naan solra yoosaneye keeḷu.
Listen to the suggestion I give (tell) you.

1 neettu oru kade paḍicceen; romba nallaa irundudu.
2 neettu oru pustagam vaanguneen; romba vele.
3 naan paṇam eḍuttukiṭṭeen; adu enga appaa paṇam.

4 naan oru kaaleejule paḍikkireen; adu romba duurattule (distant) irukku.
5 naan oru paaḍam paḍiccukiṭṭurukkeen; adu kaṣṭamaa irukku.
6 naan oru veele sonneen; ade senjiṭṭiyaa?
7 naan oru veele solreen; ade siikram seyyi.
8 naan oru odavi keeppeen; ade nii kaṭṭaayam seyyaṇum.

Language points

Participial noun

Endings that show gender and number (but not person) may be added to a relative participle to produce a noun which is often referred to as a participial noun. It generally translates as 'one who/which . . .' The human plural marker may give a more general sense – rather like 'the' + past participle in English, as in 'the educated'. Like the relative participle, the participial noun has past and present tense forms. Participial nouns, like simple nouns, may take case endings.

paḍikkiravan	one who is studying
paḍiccavan	one who studied/he who is educated/ an educated (male) person
paḍiccava	one who studied/she who is educated/ an educated (female) person
paḍiccavanga	they who are educated/the educated
paḍiccadu	that which is educated
Madurele ennooḍa paḍiccavanukku	to him who studied with me in Madurai
Madurele ennooḍa paḍikkiravanukku	to him who is studying with me in Madurai

Exercise 5

The following sentences describe specific persons and things. Make them more general by using a participial noun. Translate both sentences.

Example: **ennooḍa veele paakkira poṇṇuga keṭṭikkaaranga.**
The girls who work with me are clever.

ennooḍa veele paakkiravanga keṭṭikkaaranga.
Those who work with me are clever.

1 engiṭṭe Laṇḍanle Tamiẓ paḍicca Ingliṣkaaranga Indiyaavukku vandurukkaanga.
2 engiṭṭe Tamiẓ paḍicca Jim Amerikkaavule irukkaaru.
3 bas-sṭaaple nikkira poṇṇe engeyoo paatturukkeen.
4 enakku piḍicca saappaaṭṭe inge saapḍa muḍiyale.

Verbal noun

When the neuter singular marker **-adu** is added to the relative participle, the resulting noun may be a participial noun denoting the agent of the action, or a verbal noun denoting the action itself (which is equivalent to verb + 'ing' in English, as in 'the awakening').

ooḍunadu	that which ran *or* running (in the past)
ooḍradu	that which is running *or* running (in the present)
ooḍunadu puune	the thing that ran is a cat
ooḍradu puune	the thing that is running is a cat
ooḍunadu nallaa irukku	(Someone) feels good with the running (he or she did) (lit. The having run is good.)
ooḍradu nalladu	Running is good.

Exercise 6

Combine the following pairs of sentences into single sentences as shown in the example (i.e. by using a verbal noun to replace the verb in the first sentence). Translate your sentences.

Example: **naan Tamiẓ paḍicceen; adu yaarukkum piḍikkale.**
I studied Tamil; no one liked it.

naan Tamiẓ paḍiccadu yaarukkum piḍikkale.
No one liked my studying Tamil/that I studied Tamil.

1 naan kaaleejukku basle pooneen; adu kaṣṭamaa irundudu.
2 naan kaaleejukku kaarle pooreen; adu nallaa irukku.
3 naan nalla maark vaanguneen; ade aasiriyar paaraaṭṭunaaru.
4 naan uurukku pooreen; adukku aasiriyar anumadi kuḍuttuṭṭaaru.
5 naan onne patti aasiriyarṭṭe sonneen; adule enna tappu?
6 naan paṇatte tiruppi keeṭṭeen; adunaale avanukku koobam.

'As' and 'as if'

If **maadiri** is added to the relative participle (in the past or present tense) it conveys the meaning 'like', 'as', 'as if' (the action). An alternative to **maadiri** in this sense is **-paḍi** (with the alternative pronunciation **-baḍi** when preceded by **m**). When it is added to the relative participle in the future tense (as in the last two examples below), it provides an alternative form to the infinitive in some of its functions. Its range of meanings includes 'in such a way as'.

naan sonna maadiri seyyi/naan sonna paḍi seyyi.
Do as I said.

naan solra maadiri seyyi/naan solra paḍi seyyi.
Do as I say.

avan ellaam terinja maadiri peesuraan.
He speaks as if he knows everything.

yaaroo varra maadiri irukku.
It looks as if someone is coming.

naan avane mudugu viingura maadiri/viingumbaḍi aḍicceen.
I hit him in such a way that his back swelled.

avane nallaa paḍikkumbaḍi sonneen.
I told him to study well.

Reportive

When reporting an event or a state of things from another source, one may add **-aam** at the end of it. This will be intended to imply that the speaker is non-committal with regard to the truth of the statement made. The indefinite 'They say' in English carries a similar sense.

avan poy sonnaan.
He told a lie.

avan poy sonnaanaam.
He told a lie, it is said/it seems.

avan poy sonnaanaamaa?
Is it said that he told a lie?

nii poy solluviyaam.
It is said that you tell lies/You are reported to tell lies.

Exercise 7 (Audio 2: 12)

You don't want to vouch for the statements you report, as they were made by others, inferred by you, or disapproved of by you. Or you don't want to specify the source of your report. How will you make the statements where you cannot use quotation marks? Translate both sentences.

Example: **naaḷekki maẓe peyyum.**
It will rain tomorrow.

naaḷekki maẓe peyyumaam.
They say that it will rain tomorrow.

1 tambikki vayiru valikkidu.
2 raajaa amerikkaavukku pooraan.
3 inda veelekki irubadu ruubaa aagum.
4 inda pustagam irunuuru ruubaa.
5 naan senjadu tappu.
6 Moohan Ingilaandulerundu vandurukkaan.
7 nii niccayam parisu vaanguve.
8 puunekki pasikkidu.
9 Kumaar appaaṯṯe enne patti enna sonnaan?

Exercise 8

Fill in the blanks with an appropriate form of the verb in parentheses that follows. Sometimes you will use an infinitive, sometimes a relative participle, sometimes a participial noun or a verbal noun with an appropriate case marker, and so on. Translate the passage.

Raajaa ——— (paɖi) vaguppuledaan Raaɳiyum paɖiccaa. maark ——— (vaangu) reɳɖu peerukkum pooʈʈi. Tamiʐ aasiriyarʈʈe nuuttukku arubadu maarkkukku meele ——— (vaangu) romba kaʂʈam. avaru Tamiʐ ilakkiyam nereya ——— (paɖi). ilakkiya varigaɭe apɖiyee kaʈʈurele ——— (eʐudu) avarukku romba piɖikkum. Raajaavum Raaɳiyum kaʂʈappaʈʈu paɖiccaanga. ——— (tuungu) neeram tavira matta neeram ellaam ——— (paɖi) selavaʐiccaanga. adu ——— (teri) Tamiʐ aasiriyar avangaɭe romba paaraaʈʈunaaru. vaguppule ——— (iru) ellaareyum avanga ——— (paɖi) maadiri kaʂʈappaʈʈu paɖikka sonnaaru.

Tamil script

In Unit 4 we imagined taking a bus journey. We look here at a few of the words you may read when you do this in Chennai. The bus shelters there are set up by the Chennai Corporation: சென்னை மாநகராட்சி (நகர் 'town'; மாநகர் 'city' ('big town'); ஆட்சி 'government'). At bus stops you may see சென்னை மாநகராட்சி பேருந்து நிறுத்தம். Here பேருந்து is an alternative in the written style for பஸ் 'bus', and நிறுத்தம் is 'stop'. At the entrance to the bus you will see ஏறும் வழி ('getting-on way'), and at the exit இறங்கும் வழி ('getting-down way'). As you ride or walk around town, you will be able to pick out police vehicles by the word காவல் and police stations by the sign காவல் நிலையம். Vehicles for hire – taxis and autorickshaws – will display the word வாடகை 'rent'.

Exercise 9

Identify the compound words in the second set in which the words in the first set occur. Suggest a meaning for the compounds.

1 மருந்து medicine	2 துணி cloth
3 சோறு rice	4 பணம் money
a சோற்றுப்பருக்கை	b பணப்பெட்டி
c பட்டுத்துணி	d மருந்துச்சீட்டு

(பருக்கை grain பெட்டி box பட்டு silk சீட்டு note, ship)

10 neettu oru kalyaaɳattukku pooyirundeen

Yesterday I went to a wedding

In this unit you will learn to:

- talk about social issues
- talk about attempting to do something
- use pronouns to refer to people or things
- refer back to things you have already mentioned

Dialogue 1 (Audio 2: 13)

Arranging marriage

Stephen tells Shankar about a wedding he attended. The two of them discuss the pros and cons of arranged marriages.

STEPHEN: neettu oru kalyaaɳattukku pooyirundeen. Indiya vaaʐkkeye patti sila viʂayangaɭ terinjikiʈʈeen.

SHANKAR: pudusaa enna terinjikiʈʈiinga?

STEPHEN: kalyaaɳattukku munnaale payyanum poɳɳum peesunadee illeyaamee? oruttare oruttar paakkiradu maʈʈum kalyaaɳattukku poodumaa?

SHANKAR: ambadu varuʂattukku munnaale paakkiradukuuɖa ille.

STEPHEN: peesi paʐagaama epɖi oruttare oruttar purinjikiɖuvaanga? seendu kuɖumbam naɖattuvaanga?

SHANKAR: purinjikiḍradu kalyaaṉattukku peragu aarambikkidu. adule periya piraccane varaama irukkiradukku oree maadiri kuḍumba suuẕnelele reṉḍu peerum vaḷandadu oru kaaraṉamaa irukkalaam.

STEPHEN: pettavanga kuḍumbatte paattu naḍattivakkira kalyaṉattule ellaam piraccane varaama irukkaa?

SHANKAR: adu epḍi varaama poogum? piraccanegaḷe samaaḷikkiradukku vaḷanda vedam, kuḍumba aadaravu ellaam odavi seyyidu.

STEPHEN: *Yesterday I went to a wedding. I got to know a few things about Indian life.*

SHANKAR: *What did you learn that's new?*

STEPHEN: *It seems that before the marriage, the bride and groom don't speak at all, do they? Is it enough for marriage that they only see each other?*

SHANKAR: *Fifty years ago they didn't even see each other.*

STEPHEN: *Without speaking and getting used to each other, how do they understand each other? How do they manage family life together?*

SHANKAR: *Understanding each other begins after marriage. A reason for there being no great problem in that may be that both were brought up in the same family background.*

Stephen: *Are all marriages that parents arrange after checking the family (background) free of problems?*

Shankar: *How could it be so? The way one is brought up, family support – all these help in dealing with problems.*

Vocabulary

kalyaaṇam	marriage, marriage function, married life
oruttar + oruttar	each other (the first **oruttar** takes case marker)
paẓagu (-n-)	be used to, be accustomed
naḍattivay (-cc-)	conduct (something for it to stay on)
Indiya	Indian
seendu	together, jointly
suuẓnele	background, environment
vaḷa (-nd-)	grow, develop
vedam	manner, way
vaaẓkke	life
kuḍumbam	family
pettavanga	parents
samaaḷi (-cc-)	manage, handle
aadaravu	support

Language points

Reciprocals

When an action is reciprocal, that is to say when there is mutual interaction, the form **oruttar** ('one person') is repeated, with appropriate case endings on each instance. An example in Dialogue 1 is **epḍi oruttare oruttar purinjikiḍuvaanga?** 'How do they understand one another?' – or more closely 'How do they understand one (nominative case) the other (accusative)'. Note the use of the reflexive form of the verb (**-kiḍu-**) with reciprocals (see the explanation that follows Dialogue 2 in Unit 8).

Exercise 1

Answer in Tamil the following questions about the dialogue.

1 Who went to a wedding?
2 Did the bride and groom speak to each other before the wedding?
3 What was the situation fifty years ago?
4 What factor might explain the comparative lack of problems in an arranged marriage?

Exercise 2

Tell Shankar that:

1 The bride and groom saw each other before the marriage.
2 They spoke to each other before the marriage.
3 John and Raja each gave a book to the other.

Dialogue 2 (Audio 2: 14)

Happy marriage

Stephen and Shankar continue their discussion of the relative merits of different marriage customs.

STEPHEN: neettu naama peesuna kalyaaɳa viṣayatte patti yoosiccu paatteen. innum teriya veeɳɖiya viṣayam nereya irukku.

SHANKAR: toɖandu ade patti peesalaamee. niinga innum enna terinjikiɖaɳum?

STEPHEN: Indiyaavule vivaagarattu koreyaa irukkiradukku peɳɳukkoo payyanukkoo kalyaaɳatte patti tanippaʈʈa karuttu eduvum illaama irukkiradu oru kaaraɳamaa?

SHANKAR: irukkalaam. aanaa sandooṣamaa irukkira kuɖumbam ellaa naaʈʈuleyum kiʈʈattaʈʈa oree aɭavudaan irukkum. Indiyaavule vivaagarattukku eduraa irukkira samuuga manappaanme oru mukkiyamaana kaaraɳam.

STEPHEN: appa kaɳavanum maneviyum veera vaẓi illaama manasukku piɖikkaama irukkira kalyaaɳatte poruttukiʈʈurukkaangaɭaa?

SHANKAR: aamaa. ade maatta muɖiyale. adunaale eettukiɖraanga. idule peɳɳu romba viʈʈukuɖukkiraa.

STEPHEN: peɳgaɭ sudandiram illaama irukkiradu avanga poruttupooradukku oru kaaraɳam, illeyaa?

SHANKAR: aamaa. peɳgaɭsudandiratte aaɳgaɭ ottukiɖradum avasiyam. appa kuɖumbam oɖeyaama irukkum.

STEPHEN: *I've been trying to think about the subject of marriage that we spoke of yesterday. There are lots of things that I still need to know.*

SHANKAR: *We can go on talking about it, can't we. What else do you want to know?*

Stephen: *Is a reason for there being little divorce in India the fact that neither the woman nor the man have any particular opinion about marriage?*

Shankar: *It could be. But in all countries there will be happy families to the same extent. In India an important reason is the social attitude that exists against divorce.*

Stephen: *Then do husband and wife put up with a marriage they don't like with the attitude that there is no other choice?*

Shankar: *Yes. They can't change it. Therefore they accept it. In this, women give up a lot.*

Stephen: *A reason for women putting up with it is that they have no freedom, isn't it?*

Shankar: *Yes. There's a need for men to accept women's freedom. Then families will not break up.*

Vocabulary

yoosi (-cc-)	think	**toḍandu**	continuously
vivaagarattu	divorce	**tanippaṭṭa**	individual, particular
karuttu	opinion		
kiṭṭattaṭṭa	about, nearly	**eduraa**	against
samuuga	social (**samuugam** society)		
manappaanme	attitude	**kaṇavan**	husband
manevi	wife	**poru (-tt-)**	bear with, put up with
maattu (-n-)	change		
viṭṭukuḍu (-tt-)	concede, give up	**eettukiḍu (-ṭṭ-)**	accept
peṇ	woman (**peṇgaḷ** women) (cf. **poṇṇu** girl, bride)		
sudandiram	freedom, independence		
aaṇ	man (**aaṇgaḷ** men)		
avasiyam	necessity, essential		
oḍe (-nj-)	break		

Language points

Reference back

Reference back to a noun occurring in a previous sentence or to a noun in the same sentence is in many languages achieved by one or another pronoun. The pronouns used for this purpose in Tamil are the remote demonstrative pronouns, i.e. those that begin with **a-** (as opposed to the 'proximate' **i-**; see the section on 'Distance from speaker' in Unit 1). You will recall that these, which you may also find referred to as general pronouns, are **avan** 'he', **avaru** 'he' (polite form), **ava(ḷ)** 'she', **avanga(ḷ)** 'they' and **adu** 'it'. If the noun referred to by a pronoun from this set is in the same sentence, the noun cannot be the subject; reference back to the subject – very often in a possessive phrase – will be by a reflexive pronoun, e.g. **tan** (possessive singular) or **tanga** (possessive plural); these pronouns are discussed later in this unit. The noun in question generally precedes the pronoun, though (as in English) this rule is not absolute. Example:

Kumaar Umaaṭṭe ava pustagatte kuḍuttaan.
Kumar gave Uma her book.

Kumaar Umaaṭṭe tan pustagatte kuḍuttaan.
Kumar gave Uma his book.

Such pronouns, general or reflexive, can be more readily omitted than in English:

Kumaar Umaave viiṭṭukku saapḍa kuupṭaan.
Kumar invited Uma to eat in (his) house.

Kumaar Umaave viiṭṭukku kuupṭu saappaaḍu pooṭṭaan.
Kumar invited Uma to (his) house and gave (her) food.

Trying to do something

An attempt to do something is typically expressed by the auxiliary verb **paaru** preceded by a verbal participle. Used as a full verb, **paaru** has the sense of 'see'. Preceded by a verb in its verbal participial form, it means 'try (performing the action of the verb)' to find out whether it can be done, what it is, etc.

naan kadave terandu paatteen; muḍiyale.
I tried to open the door; I couldn't.

naan oyine kuḍiccu paatteen; kasandudu.
I tried to drink the wine; it was bitter.

The verb **paaru** has a different sense when preceded by an infinitive. Then it means to try to do something without actually doing it; it is equivalent to 'be about to do something'. In some contexts, an infinitive + **poo** 'go' can be used with a similar meaning.

naan kadave terakka paatteen; nalla veeḷe, terakkale.
I was about to open the door; thank God, I didn't.

naan oyine kuḍikka paatteen; nalla veeḷe, kuḍikkale.
I was about to drink the wine; thank God, I didn't.

naan kiiẓe viẓa paatteen.
I was about to fall down/I tried to fall down.

naan kiiẓe viẓa pooneen.
I was about to fall down/I was going to fall down.

Exercise 3

Match the second sentences that are most appropriate to follow the first sentences. Translate the sentences you have matched.

Example:
i **naan Raajaaṭṭe paṇam keeṭṭu paatteen.**
ii **naan Raajaaṭṭe paṇam keekka paatteen.**

A **aanaa kuuccamaa irundudu.**
B **avan kuḍukkale.**

i B I tried to ask Raja for money; but he didn't give it.
ii A I tried to ask Raja for money; but I was shy.

1 i naan puunekki paal kuḍuttu paatteen.
ii naan puunekki paal kuḍukka paatteen.

A neeram ille.
B adu kuḍikkale.

2 i naan inda naavale paḍiccu paatteen.
ii naan inda naavale paḍikka paatteen.

A nallaa ille.
B ammaa viḍale.

3 i naan Maalaavukku puttimadi solli paatteen.
ii naan Maalaavukku puttimadi solla paatteen.

A ava keḍekkale.
B ava keekkale.

4 i naayi sovarle eeri paattudu.
ii naayi sovarle eera paattudu.

A naan iẓuttukiṭṭu vanduṭṭeen.
B muḍiyale. vaẓukki viẓunduruccu.

5 i Kumaar oyine kuḍiccu paakkiraan.
ii Kumaar oyine kuḍikka paakkiraan.

A muḍiyale.
B bayamaavum irukku.

Dialogue 3 (Audio 2: 16)

Joining a new family

Stephen and Shankar discuss the dowry system.

STEPHEN: niinga neettu sonnade yoosiccu paatteen. adu sariyaa paḍudu. aaṉ peṉ reṇḍu peerum kuḍumbattukkaaga tangaḷooḍa sonda viruppu veruppugaḷe konjam viṭṭukuḍukkiradu romba avasiyam. aanaa reṇḍu peerum samamaa irukkiradukku varadaccane oẓiyaṉum, illeyaa?
SHANKAR: niccayamaa. varadaccaneyaale romba kudumbanga keṭṭupooyirukku.
STEPHEN: varadaccanekkaaga peṇṇe koḍumepaḍutturade patti patrikkele paḍiccurukkeen. idu maarumaa?
SHANKAR: maaraṉum. aanaa romba paḍiccavangaḷee varadaccane keekkiraanga.
STEPHEN: ide oẓikkiradukku enna vaẓi?
SHANKAR: peṇgaḷ paḍiccu veelekki poogaṉum. varadaccane kuḍuttu kalyaaṇam paṇradukku padil kalyaaṇam paṇṇaamalee irukka tayaaraa irukkaṉum.
STEPHEN: apḍi oru kaalam varumaa?
SHANKAR: varaṉum. varum.

STEPHEN: *I've been thinking about what you said yesterday. It sounds right. It is very necessary that for the sake of their families both man and woman should give up their likes and dislikes a little. But for both of them to be equal, the dowry has to be eliminated, doesn't it?*

SHANKAR:	*Certainly. Many families are ruined by the dowry system.*
STEPHEN:	*I've read in the newspaper how women are made to suffer for the sake of a dowry. Will this change?*
SHANKAR:	*It must change. But even many educated people claim dowry.*
STEPHEN:	*What's the way to eradicate this?*
SHANKAR:	*Girls must study and go to work. Instead of giving dowry and marrying, they must be ready to remain unmarried.*
STEPHEN:	*Will a time like that come?*
SHANKAR:	*It must come. It will come.*

Vocabulary

paḍu (-ṭṭ-)	sound, occur	**sonda**	own, native (place)
viruppu veruppu	likes and dislikes	**samam**	equality, equity
		varadaccane	dowry
oẓi (-nj-)	be eradicated	**oẓi (-cc-)**	eradicate
niccayam	certainty	**keṭṭupoo (-n-)**	be ruined
koḍumepaḍuttu (-n-)	ill-treat, make suffer		

Language points

Reflexive pronoun: 'self'

The reflexive pronoun is used to refer to a third person subject in the sentence. When there is a reflexive pronoun in the sentence, the auxiliary verb **-kiḍu** may occur with the predicate. It is not however obligatory. The forms of the reflexive pronoun are **taan** 'self (sg)' and **taanga(ḷ)** 'self (pl)'. When case markers are added to them they have the 'non-subject' forms **tan** and **tanga(ḷ)** respectively. As mentioned earlier, the reflexive pronoun may be omitted.

Kumaar tanne tiṭṭikiṭṭaan.
Kumar scolded himself.

Kumaar tan tambiye tiṭṭunaan.
Kumar scolded his brother.

Kumaar tanakku oru pustagam vaangikiṭṭaan.
Kumar bought a book for himself.

Kumaar tan tambikki oru pustagam vaangikiṭṭaan.
Kumar bought a book for his brother.

Exercise 4

Fill in the right pronoun (e.g. general or reflexive) in the gaps in the following passage. The case ending that should occur with the pronoun is given in parentheses; where a possessive (genitive) would be indicated by the lack of any ending, this is indicated by '(gen)'. Translate the completed passage.

Raajaa —— (ooḍa) paḍicca Maalaave kalyaaṇam paṇṇikiḍa aasepaṭṭaan. aanaa —— (ooḍa) appaa —— (kku) ottukiḍale. —— paatturukkira poṇṇe kalyaaṇam paṇṇikiḍa sonnaaru. Raajaa —— (gen) ammaaṭṭe —— (gen) aaseye sonnaan. —— (kku) Maalaave piḍikkum. —— (gen) appaaṭṭe paṇam romba ille; aanaa —— (ooḍa) kuḍumbam romba nalla kuḍumbam. adunaale —— (kku) —— (e) piḍikkum. maganooḍa aaseye appaaṭṭe solli —— (e) ottukiḍa vaccaanga. Raajaavukku. oree sandooṣam.

Exercise 5 (Audio 2: 17)

Describe, in Tamil, how you got married – or how you want to get married.

Exercise 6 (Audio 2: 18)

Describe, in Tamil, why you think there are unhappy marriages.

Tamil script

If you go to the beach in Chennai, you will see a number of statues in the gardens between the beach and the road. All are important figures in Tamil literature or in the study of the Tamil language. Among them are: கண்ணகி, திருவள்ளுவர், ஜி. யூ. போப்பு and அவ்வையார். Kaṇṇagi is the heroine of the earliest Tamil epic poem சிலப்பதிகாரம் 'The lay of the anklet'. Tiruvaḷḷuvar is the author of the most famous poetic work in Tamil, திருக்குறள் (which features in Unit 16). Revd G.U. Pope (1820–1908) was one of the great western authorities on Tamil language and literature. Avvaiyaar, who lived perhaps 2000 years ago, was one of the earliest Tamil women poets.

Exercise 7

You will have observed in the previous paragraph that the inscription on Revd Pope's statue indicates in Tamil script the sound of his initials. What English letters are represented by the following Tamil syllables?

1 பி	2 சி	3 என்	4 ஆர்	5 எம்
6 ஈ	7 எஸ்	8 டி	9 ஜே	10 ஏ

11 nii enne paakka varakkuuɖaadaa

Shouldn't you come to see me?

In this unit you will learn to:

- mix English words in Tamil conversation
- make a short speech
- express uncertainty
- talk about repeated actions

Dialogue 1 (Audio 2: 19)

Turn on the music

Mamta and Mumtaj, both of whom speak English fluently, use lots of English words when they converse with each other.

Mamta: naandaan vandu vandu onne paakkaɳumaa? nii enne paakkavarakkuuɖaadaa?

Mumtaj: on *room*-ukku vara evɭavoo *try*-paɳɳuneen. muɖiyale. oree *busy*.

Mamta: apɖi enna *busy*, *friend*-e kuuɖa paakka muɖiyaama?

Mumtaj: periya periya *officers inspection*-ukkaaga *headquarters*-lerundu vandurukkaanga enga *office*-ukku. avanga keeɭvigaɭukku *answers ready*-paɳɳi vaccuʈʈu viiʈʈukku vara *night* pattu, padinooru maɳi aaccu. *one week* idee maadiridaan.

Mamta: onakku on veeleye viʈʈaa veere olagamee keɖeyaadu. sari. *stereo*-e *on*-paɳɳu. Rahmaanooɖa *latest music* keeppoom.

MAMTA: *Do I have to keep coming to see you? Couldn't you come to see me?*

MUMTAJ: *I've tried so much to come to your room. I couldn't manage it. I was really busy.*

MAMTA: *What's all this about being busy? Couldn't you even come to see a friend?*

MUMTAJ: *Top level officers have come to our office from headquarters for an inspection. Getting answers ready for their questions has meant that we got home at night at ten or eleven o'clock. It's been like this for a week.*

MAMTA: *Apart from your work you have no other world. Fine. Turn on the stereo. Let's hear Rahman's latest album.*

Language points

Using English words when speaking Tamil

You will already have observed that in modern spoken Tamil there is a considerable admixture of loanwords from English. Such words (e.g. **bas** and **hooṭṭal**) are as much a part of the language as, say, 'café' and 'garage' in English. Rather different from this is the mixing of English words in a Tamil conversation that is common among the educated. Though the mixing is relatively free, there are some constraints, which are left to be learnt by experience. In the dialogues in this unit, the two styles are differentiated by the fact that words not considered to have been assimilated into the language are given in their English spelling. In most cases, English words are used in this way not because Tamil equivalents are unavailable, but to convey a social meaning like identity with the educated class. English words are also used when there is no Tamil word for a new object or concept – in which case the chances are that the word in question will be gradually assimilated – or when the Tamil word is taboo or otherwise stigmatised.

When an English word is used as a verb (whether the word in English is a verb, noun, adjective, or preposition), the various Tamil suffixes, such as those marking tense or person, are not added directly. Instead, the verb **paṇṇu** 'do' is first added, and then the appropriate endings are added to this in a regular fashion.

When the meaning of the verb resulting from this process is intransitive, **aagu** 'be', 'get to be' is added instead of **paṇṇu**.

***light*-e *on*-paṇṇu.**	Turn on the light.
***light on*-aagale.**	The light did not turn on.

Words used other than as verbs are treated as Tamil words, in the sense that case endings, adverbial suffixes, and so on, are added directly – as in the accusative case form (**-e**) in ***light*-e** above. Similarly, ***late*-aa vandaan** 'He arrived late' (where **-aa** marks the word as an adverb).

It will already be apparent that an English word may be used as a different part of speech or word class when introduced into Tamil conversation. For instance in Dialogue 1, in the phrase **oree *busy***, 'busy' is a noun, in the sense that the appropriate Tamil word in the context would be the noun **veele** 'work'. Similarly 'night' is used as an adverb in the phrase ***night* pattu maṇi** 'ten o'clock at night'.

Exercise 1 (Audio 2: 20)

Imagine that Chezhian (செழியன்) and Anban (அன்பன்) have the above conversation. They are purists and do not mix English words into their speech. Enact the conversation as they would do. Identify any English word for which there is no commonly used Tamil equivalent.

Reduplication

Except when it is subject of a clause or the main verb, any word may be duplicated to indicate multiples of a thing or the repetition or intensity of an action.

periya periya pustagam	many big books
vandu vandu sonnaan.	He came and said (it) again and again.
kayye kayye tuukkunaan.	He raised his hand many times.
veega veegamaa vandaan.	He came very fast.
ooḍi ooḍi vandaan.	He came running fast/ He came running many times.

'Other than'

viṭṭaa(l) added to the accusative noun means 'other than', 'besides'; literally it means 'if you leave X out'. It is an equivalent of **tavira** 'besides' when the verb is negative.

Exercise 2

Mamta prefers to use **tavira** but you like to use the other form. Make the following sentences by Mamta into your own and translate them.

Example: **enakku Tamiẓe tavira veere oṇṇum teriyaadu.**
enakku Tamiẓe viṭṭaa veere oṇṇum teriyaadu.

1 naan paale tavira veere oṇṇum kuḍikka maaṭṭeen.
2 Maalaavukku Kamalaave tavira veere yaareyum piḍikkaadu.
3 en tambi iḍliye tavira veere eduvum saapḍamaaṭṭaan.
4 enga ammaa Madureye tavira veere enda uurukkum poonadulle.
5 mannippu keekkirade tavira veere vaẓi ille.

Exercise 3

You think the following are understatements and feel that Raja did the things many times over but to no avail. Correct these statements and translate them.

Example: **Raajaa Kumaarṭṭe pooyi connaan; avan keekkale.**
Raajaa Kumaarṭṭe pooyi pooyi connaan; avan keekkale.

1 Raajaa Kumaarṭṭe solli paattaan; avan keekkale.
2 Raajaa kadave terandu paattaan; muḍiyale.
3 Raajaa paṇatte tiruppi kuḍuttaan; Kumaar vaangale.

Dialogue 2 (Audio 2: 21)

What's the score?

Two keen cricket fans discuss the match that has just concluded between England and Sri Lanka.

JESUDAS: *Sri Lanka*-vukkum *England*-ukkum naḍanda *one day match*-ile yaaru *win*-paṇṇunaanga?

RAMADAS: *Sri Lanka*. anda *team* piramaadamaa aaḍuccu. *Superb bowling.*

JESUDAS: *Score* enna?

RAMADAS: *One seventy-seven for seven.*

JESUDAS: yaaru *maximum run* eḍuttadu?

RAMADAS: Jayasuuriyaa. *easy*-aa *century* pooṭṭaan.

JESUDAS: nii *match*-e *TV*-le paattiyaa?

RAMADAS: ille. iṇṇekki pagal puuraavum *power cut*. koobam koobamaa vandudu. enna seyradu? *transistor*-le *running commentary* keeṭṭeen.

JESUDAS: niiyaavadu paravaayille. naan vanda *train five hours late*. naan *taxi* piḍiccu viiṭṭukku varradukkuḷḷe *match* muḍinjupooccu.

RAMADAS: naama edukku romba aasepaḍramoo adu keḍekkaadu.

JESUDAS: *Who won the one-day match between Sri Lanka and England?*
RAMADAS: *Sri Lanka. The team played splendidly. Superb bowling.*
JESUDAS: *What was the score?*
RAMADAS: *One seventy-seven for seven.*
JESUDAS: *Who got the most runs?*
RAMADAS: *Jayasuriya. He easily made a century.*
JESUDAS: *Did you see the match on TV?*
RAMADAS: *No. The whole morning today there was a power cut. I was really angry. What to do? I listened to the running commentary on the radio.*
JESUDAS: *Never mind you. The train I came in was five hours late. Before I got home by taxi the match was over.*
RAMADAS: *Whatever we really want we don't get.*

Vocabulary

piramaadam	excellent, splendid
aaḍu (-n-)	play
puuraavum	entire, whole
aasepaḍu (-paṭṭ-)	desire

Language points

More on mixing

When English words are mixed, their pronunciation is not Tamilised as in loanwords. Compare 'Sri Lanka' and '**Ilange**'; England and **Ingilaandu**. Notice also that there is no change in the form of an English noun when case endings are added: ***time*-ukku**, not **ṭayattukku**. With this can be compared what happens in the case of **paaram** (or **faaram** – borrowed from English 'form'), of which the dative form is **paarattukku**.

Whole phrases, clauses and sentences of English are also mixed into Tamil speech. This dialogue is to caution you on what you may encounter in a conversation with an educated Tamil speaker and to help you identify and comprehend such mixing. Don't resort to extensive mixing yourself if you want to learn Tamil by practice!

Exercise 4 (Audio 2: 22)

Converse with a friend on soccer.

yaaru ***and verb forms***

To ask 'who' did something, **yaaru** is used with a verb ending in **-aanga**, that is to say the ending that indicates human plural: **yaaru vandaanga** 'Who came?' However, in Dialogue 2, Jesudas asks **yaaru** ***maximum run*** **eḍuttadu?** The effect of using the neuter ending **-adu** is to give the sense 'Who was it that . . .' rather than just 'Who . . .'

Co-relative clauses

You will sometimes hear an alternative to the type of relative clause that was introduced in Unit 9, though that one is the more frequently used type. The alternative is sometimes referred to by the slightly technical label 'co-relative'. A co-relative is formed with an interrogative word (generally beginning with **e-**, but also including **yaaru** 'who') in the dependent clause and a demonstrative word (beginning with **a-**) in the main clause; the two clauses are linked by the addition of **-oo** at the end of the first. See the last sentence in the dialogue. It is rather as if one were to say in English, 'What we want very much, that we don't get.' It is enough if you can learn to recognise such sentence types if you hear them.

One thing happening before another

One way of expressing the fact that one event preceded another involves the use of **uḷḷe** 'inside'/'within'. This is exemplified by the word **varr-adu-kk-uḷḷe** in Dialogue 2. The hyphens inserted in the previous sentence show how this is made up. First there is the 'verbal noun' (see Unit 5) made up of the present tense stem of the verb **vaa** + **-adu**. To this is added the dative case marker **-kku**, after which follows **uḷḷe**. Remember that these forms are the same, whatever the subject. Thus **naan viiṭṭukku varradukkuḷḷe** means 'Before I came home'. As Jesudas is speaking of an event that has already happened, he could equally well have used the past tense:

vandadukkuḷḷe. Notice, however, that the reverse is not possible; that is, if the reference is to a present or future happening, this past tense form is not used: **naan viiṭṭukku varradukkuḷḷe *match* muḍinjupoogum** 'Before I get home, the match will be finished.'

Exercise 5

Show that the event in the first part of the sentence took place, or will take place, before the event in the second part. Use **-uḷḷe** with the appropriate form of the verb in brackets.

Example: **nii viiṭṭukku —— (vaa), naan pooyiruveen.**
nii viiṭṭukku varradukkuḷḷe, naan pooyiruveen.
I shall go before you come home.

1 naan viiṭṭukku —— (vaa), avan pooyṭṭaan.
2 appaa aapiisukku —— (poo), avarooḍa peesuveen.
3 naan keeḷviye —— (keeṭṭu muḍi), ava padil solliṭṭaa.
4 naan naaye —— (kaṭṭi vayyi), tabaalkaararu uḷḷe vanduṭṭaaru.

(Note: **muḍi** preceded by a verbal participle means 'finish (doing something)' (3); **vayyi** preceded by a verbal participle indicates that the action is performed with a subsequent action in mind (4).)

Exercise 6

Someone is asking about things on the assumption that they are happening in the present. Correct him by saying that they have already happened.

Example: **Raajaa saapḍraanaa.** **ille, Raajaa saapṭaan.**

1 Maalaa kaṣṭappaḍraaḷaa?
2 ammaa paaṭṭu keekkiraangaḷaa?
3 suuriyan (sun) mareyidaa?
4 tambi veele seyraanaa?
5 cakkaram (wheel) veegamaa uruḷudaa?
6 puli maane kolludaa?
7 maaḍu teruvule ooḍudaa?

Exercise 7 (Audio 2: 23)

Answer these questions in the positive.

Example: **niinga sinimaavukku pooniingaḷaa?**
aamaa, pooneen.

1. niinga sinimaa paattiingaḷaa?
2. niinga Tamiẓ paḍicciingaḷaa?
3. niinga kaaleejukku naḍandiingaḷaa?
4. niinga Madurele veele senjiingaḷaa?
5. niinga kaalele doose saapṭiingaḷaa?
6. niinga neettu raatri paaṭṭu keeṭṭiingaḷaa?
7. niinga sinimaavule aẓudiingaḷaa?
8. niinga enne patti kanavu kaṇḍiingaḷaa?
9. niinga kooyil (temple) munnaale uruṇḍiingaḷaa?
10. niinga puliye koṇṇiingaḷaa?

Tamil script

English words are mixed with Tamil not only in speech but also in the written language, as for instance on notices you will see in town centres. Here are a few examples:

பாங்க் ஆப் இந்தியா	**baank aap indiyaa**	Bank of India
சாப்பாடு ரெடி	**saappaaḍu reḍi**	meals ready
டிபன் ரெடி	**ṭipaṉ reḍi**	tiffin (snacks) ready
டிபன் கிடைக்கும்	**ṭipaṉ kiṭaikkum**	tiffin available
சாப்பாடு ஹோட்டல்	**saappaaḍu hooṭṭal**	restaurant (food hotel)
கூல் கியொஸ்க்	**kuul kiyosk**	cool kiosk (for the sale of cool drinks)
லாட்ஜ்	**laaḍj**	lodge (a modest hotel)
ராணி ஜராக்ஸ்	**raaṇi jaraaks**	Rani xerox
நோட்டீஸ் ஒட்டாதே	**nooṭṭiis oṭṭaadee**	Stick no bills

Sometimes instead of ரெடி 'ready' in the above examples you will see தயார் (a borrowing from Hindi-Urdu). Occasionally, extreme use of English in Tamil script will be found:

நட்ஸ் 'ன்' ஸ்பைஸஸ்	**naṭs 'ṉ' spaisas**	'nuts 'n' spices'

Finally, a wholly Tamil example: குடி நீர் **kudi niir** 'drinking water'.

Exercise 8

Translate these notices:

1. லக்ஷ்மி லாட்ஜ்
2. சாப்பாடு தயார்
3. ராஜா ஹோட்டல்
4. பிட்ஸா கார்னர்

12 en̲d̲e uuru Yaaʐppaaɳam

I'm from Jaffna

In this unit you will learn to:

- understand some of the differences between Indian and Sri Lankan Tamil
- compare things
- report what someone has said
- say where someone comes from
- express uncertainty
- cite titles or names
- express a condition

Dialogue 1 (Audio 2: 24)

Someone from Jaffna

Ramesh (a male student) and Rama (a female student) meet a visitor from Jaffna. They discuss with him the difference between various dialects of Tamil.

RAMESH: Ramaa, ivaru namma kaaleejule inda varuṣam seendurukkaaru.

RAMA: apḍiyaa? ittane naaɭaa paakkaleyee? onga peeru enna?

SINGAM: Taɭayasingam. en̲d̲e uur Yaaʐppaaɳam.

RAMESH: ange ippa *university function* paɳɳaleyoo?

SINGAM: *function* paɳr̲adu. aanaa paḍippikkir̲adile kana piraccinai.

RAMA: ivaru Tamiʐ konjam vittiyaasamaa irukku-le?

RAMESH: namme viḍa suttamaa peesuramaadiri irukku.

SINGAM: peeccil taan vittiyaasam. eʐuttil cila collukaɭ taan vittiyaasam.

RAMA:	onga peeccu Tamiẓnaaṭṭule puriyidaa?
SINGAM:	leesaa puriyidu. cilar enne Malayaḷi-n̲d̲u colr̲aangaḷ.
RAMESH:	*Singapore*, *Malaysia*-vule irukkiravanga peeccule romba vittiyaasam ille.
SINGAM:	niingaḷ colgir̲adu cari taan. Yaaẓppaaṇa Tamiẓ taan vittiyaasam.

RAMESH:	*Rama, he's joined our college this year.*
RAMA:	*Is that so? I haven't seen you so far, have I? What's your name?*
SINGAM:	*Talayasingam. I'm from Jaffna.*
RAMESH:	*Isn't the university there functioning now?*
SINGAM:	*It's functioning. But there (are) many problems in teaching.*
RAMA:	*His Tamil's a bit different, isn't it?*
RAMESH:	*Maybe his way of speaking is purer than ours.*
SINGAM:	*The difference is only in speech. In writing just a few words are different.*
RAMA:	*Is what you say understood in Tamil Nadu?*
SINGAM:	*They understand vaguely. Some say I'm a Malayali.*
RAMESH:	*There's not much difference in the speech of those who live in Singapore or Malaysia.*
SINGAM:	*What you say is true. It's Jaffna Tamil that's different.*

Vocabulary

paḍippi (-cc-)	teach	**kana**	a lot of, many
piraccinai	problem	**vittiyaasam**	difference
suttam	purity, cleanliness	**eẓuttu**	writing, letter
leesaa	slightly		

Language points

Jaffna Tamil

As is clear from the dialogue, in which Singam is a Sri Lankan, Tamil as spoken in Jaffna differs in a number of respects from that spoken in India. In Jaffna Tamil, for instance, there is in general less deletion of vowels and consonants that are found in written Tamil; compare **vittiyaasam** in colloquial Jaffna Tamil with **vityaasam** in Indian Tamil, or **colgir̲adu** with **solr̲adu**. There are some variations in the way that words are made up also; that is to say that suffixes added to nouns and verbs may have a different form. Thus Singam says **eṉḏe uur** for ‘my town’/‘my place’, where some one from India would say **en uuru** (with possessive or genitive expressed by the lack of any ending) or **ennooḍa uuru**. Sometimes, as in the case of British and American English, different words are used in the two dialects to refer to the same thing. You will have observed that the set of symbols we have been using for Indian Tamil lacks letters that we need for some of the sounds in Jaffna Tamil. In the Introduction to the book, it was noted that the letter **d** represents a ‘dental’ sound and the letter **ḍ** a ‘retroflex’ sound. Jaffna Tamil has a sound intermediate between these two which is rather like English ‘d’ (which phoneticians label ‘alveolar’, because the tip of the tongue touches the alveolar ridge behind the upper front teeth). This is indicated in the dialogue by an underlined **ḏ**. Underlined **ṟ** represents a trilled sound, somewhat like ‘r’ in Italian or in Scots English. Other differences between the dialects are shown by the pronunciation of **ḷ** at the end of a word in Jaffna Tamil. At the beginning of words, Jaffna Tamil has **c** (approximately like English ‘ch’) where there is alternation between **s** and **c** in Indian Tamil.

‘Where are you from?’

One way of asking where a person comes from is: **onga (sonda) uuru edu** (or with **enda uuru** instead of **edu**) ‘Your (native) place is which place?’ – to which a possible answer (in Indian Tamil) would be **enga uuru Laṇḍan** ‘I’m from London’. This is common if you are referring to your town or village (and notice that in this context the exclusive plural **enga** is more likely to be heard than the singular **en**). There is a further alternative way of asking the question by using the dative form of the pronoun: **ongaḷukku enda uuru**. If you wish to refer to your country or your nationality, it is more usual to use other expressions. These are introduced in Unit 13.

Exercise 1 (Audio 2: 25)

Guess what the following persons might answer if you asked them where they are from: (1) Raman; (2) Dwight; (3) Bandaranaike; (4) Nigel; (5) Nair; (6) Brigitte; (7) Sumiko.

Comparatives

Where comparisons may be made in English by the use of comparative forms of adjectives or adverbs (as in 'bigger (than)'), other processes are used in Tamil, in which adjectives and adverbs do not have such variant forms. The entity to which something is compared is in the accusative case and followed by **viḍa**, as in **namme viḍa suttamaa** 'more purely than us'. Here is another example: **avan viiḍu en viiṭṭe viḍa perusaa irukku** 'His house is bigger than my house.'

'Maybe'

When Rama says of Singam's way of speaking Tamil, **namme viḍa suttamaa peesuramaadiri irukku**, she is providing an explanation of which she is not absolutely certain. If she had been absolutely sure that this was the nature of the difference between his Tamil and hers, she might have said, **namme viḍa suttamaa peesuraaru** 'He speaks more purely than us' (where 'purely' means closer to the written or classical style). Notice the difference in the constructions. In a confident statement of fact, the present tense of the verb with a personal ending is used: **peesuraaru**. If one wishes to hedge or to imply that one is not so sure, this is replaced by the relative participle (see Unit 9) **peesura** followed by **maadiri**, which is in turn followed by the neuter of the present tense of the verb 'be' (**irukku**).

Exercise 2

Ramesh is confident about what he says, but Rama is not so sure. Change Ramesh's sentences into ones that Rama would say. Suggest translations for the utterances you provide for Rama.

Example: Ramesh: **appaa varraaru.**
Rama: **appaa varra maadiri irukku.**

1 enakku pasikkidu.
2 veḷiye maẓe peyyidu.
3 pakkattu viiṭṭule yaaroo paaḍraanga.
4 raatri maẓe penjidu.
5 appaa kaarle vandaaru.

Reported speech

Reported speech in Indian Tamil will be discussed further in Unit 15. Meantime, we introduce the notion of a quotative. A quotative is a form that is added at the end of an utterance that someone is reported to have made. It often happens that what precedes the quotative is the precise words that were used, but this is not necessarily the case, the difference between direct and indirect reported speech being less clear-cut than in English. The sequence of sounds that we are referring to as a quotative (which historically comes from the verbal participle of a verb meaning 'say') is followed by a verb of saying – taken in a very broad sense, as it includes such notions as 'asking' and 'thinking'. The quotative in Jaffna Tamil has the form **-ṉḏu**, as in **cilar enne Malayaḷi-ṉḏu colṟaangaḷ** 'Some say I am a Malayali'. A widely used form in Indian Tamil is **-(n)nu**, which occurs three times in Dialogue 2 (**enna peesa pooreen-nu**, **paappeen-nu** and **muḍiyum-nu**).

Exercise 3

Though both are sometimes translated by an adjective in English, we have described a noun + the ending **-aana** as an adjective, and a noun + the ending **-aa** as an adverb. This is because the first is usually followed by a noun and the second by a verb. With this in mind, pair off each word in the first column with the appropriate one in the second. Translate the phrases that result.

Example: I **suttamaana** A **peesu**
II **suttamaa** B **peeccu**
I, B 'pure speech'
II, A 'speak purely'

1 veegamaa	a padil
2 veegamaana	b paaḍu
3 aẓagaa	c naḍe
4 aẓagaana	d naḍa
5 sariyaa	e paaṭṭu
6 sariyaana	f padil sollu

Dialogue 2 (Audio 2: 26)

You will win

Rama and Ramesh discuss a speaking competition that is to take place in their college. Rama asks Ramesh for his views on what she has prepared.

RAMESH: namma kaaleejule oru peeccu pooʈʈi irukku. 'naan ɖaakʈar aanaa'-ngradu talappu. nii kalandukiɖriyaa?

RAMA: niccayamaa. enakku parisu vandaalum sari varaaʈʈaalum sari, peesa pooreen.

RAMESH: nii kalandukiʈʈaa veere yaarukku parisu kedekka poogudu? nii kalandukiɖradunaale mattavanga velagikiɖraangaɭoo ennamoo.

RAMA: adu epɖi solre? naan kalandukiɖradunaale raajaa niccayam pooʈʈikki varuvaan.

RAMESH: enna peesa poore-nnu peesi kaaʈʈu paappoom.

RAMA: ɖaakʈar toʐil makkaɭukku seeve seyra toʐil. adu ippa viyaabaaramaa aagikiʈʈurukku. ɖaakʈar paɳam paɳɳa kuuɖaadu-nnu sollale. paɳatte eɖuttuvaccaadaan vayttiyam paappeen-nu solla kuuɖaadu.

ippa pudu pudu viyaadi ellaam varudu. ade patti evɭavoo aaraaycci naɖakkudu. ade paɖiccu terinjikiʈʈaa pudu viyaadigaɭe muʐusaa purinjikiɖa muɖiyum; pudu sigicce moregaɭe payanapaɖutta muɖiyum-nu nenekkireen. adukku ɖaakʈar neeram odukkaɳum; muyarci eɖukkaɳum.

viyaadiye koɳapaɖutta enda maruttuva morele nalla vaʐi irundaalum ade eɖuttukiɖaɳum . . .

RAMESH: poodum. piramaadam. inda maadiriyee peesune-nnaa parisu onakkudaan.

RAMESH: *In our college there's a speaking competition. The title is 'If I were a doctor'. Are you taking part?*

RAMA: *Certainly. No matter whether I get the prize or not, I'm going to speak.*

RAMESH: *If you take part, who else is going to get the prize? Because you are taking part, maybe the others will withdraw.*

RAMA: *How can you say that? If I take part, Raja will certainly take part in the competition.*

RAMESH: *Show us what you're going to say, and we'll see.*

RAMA: *A doctor's profession is one of serving people. It's now becoming commercialised. I don't say doctors shouldn't make money. One shouldn't say, I'll give the treatment only if I've been paid.*

Now all sorts of new diseases are coming. So much research is being done on them. If we study them, we can get a full understanding of the new diseases; we can make use of the new methods of treatment. For that a doctor must set aside time, must make an effort.

Whatever new treatment there is in any medical system to cure diseases, one must take it up.

RAMESH: *That'll do. Splendid. If you speak like this, the prize is yours.*

Vocabulary

ḍaaktar	doctor
talappu	caption, title
kalandukiḍu (-ṭṭ-)	take part
velagu (-n-)	withdraw, stay out
toẓil	profession, vocation
makkaḷ	people
seeve	service
viyaabaaram	business
vayttiyam	medical treatment
viyaadi	disease
aaraaycci	research
sigicce	clinical treatment
koṇapaḍuttu (-n-)	cure, treat
more	system
payanpaḍuttu (-n-)	use
odukku (-n-)	set aside, allocate
muyarci	effort
maruttuvam	medical practice, medical treatment

Exercise 4

With very few exceptions indeed, any formal speech from a public platform is in formal Tamil and not in colloquial Tamil as in the dialogue. With this colloquial version compare the one in formal Tamil given in the Key, and note the differences.

Language points

Reported speech

In preparation for the fuller discussion in Unit 15, Dialogue 2 contains further examples of reported speech. The participants in the conversation are from Tamil Nadu, and you will see that, where Singam from Sri Lanka used the 'quotative' **-ṉḏu**, Ramesh uses **-(n)nu**. Look again at the places where this occurs: **pooreen-nu**, **kuuḍaadu-nnu**, **paappeen-nu**, **muḍiyum-nu**.

Expressing uncertainty

To indicate the possibility of an occurrence about which one is uncertain, the suffix **-oo** (one use of which is to express doubt) may be added at the end of a sentence, the suffix itself being followed by **ennamoo**. An example of this usage is found in Dialogue 5: **mattavanga velagikiḍraangaḷoo ennamoo** 'Maybe the others will withdraw (or something)'.

Demonstrating the possibility of something

In Unit 10 we saw that **paaru** used as an auxiliary verb expresses an attempt by the speaker to do something. In a similar way a verbal participle followed by the verb **kaaṭṭu** 'show' is used to demonstrate the possibility or the value of the action concerned to the listener.

inda pustagatte paḍiccu paatteen.
(I) read this book (to see if I can, if it is good etc.).

inda pustagatte paḍiccu kaaṭṭuneen.
(I) read out this book (to show that I can do it, for the listener to see if he can understand it, if he finds it good, etc.).

Quoting

When one wishes to state that something has a certain name or title, the title may be given followed by the form **-ngradu**. This is related to the 'quotative' referred to earlier in this unit, but it makes the phrase it concludes into a noun. So **naan ḍaakṭar aanaa-ngradu talappu** means 'the title (is) "If I were a doctor"'.

Conditionals

Dialogue 2 contains clauses that express conditions: **nii kalan-dukiṭṭaa** 'if you took part'; **paṇatte eḍuttuvaccaa** 'if (I) get money'; **peesune-nnaa** 'if you speak'. All of these have in common the final **-aa**. The reason for splitting off the sequence **-nnaa** in the third example will be apparent later.

The suffix **-aa** is added to the past tense stem of a verb, and the form that results remains the same whatever the subject:

vand- + **aa** → **vandaa** if (someone) came/comes

In the case of a negative condition, **-aaṭṭaa** is added to the infinitive form of the verb (without the suffix **-a**):

var(a) + **aaṭṭaa** → **varaaṭṭaa** if (someone) did/does not come

When the predicate of a conditional clause is not a verb marked for tense and person (e.g. a verb with the ending **-aṇum** and expressing obligation, or a noun), **-(n)naa** is added to the predicate form itself (the doubling of **n** occurs when the preceding sound is a vowel):

avan varaṇum-naa if he must come
adu tappu-nnaa if it is a mistake

In such cases as these, **-(n)naa** is the only possibility. Where the verb is marked for tense, **-(n)naa** can be used optionally. In such cases, the verb form complete with personal ending is used unchanged. Some of the possibilities are illustrated below:

avan vand-aa	**avan vandaan-naa**	if he comes
naan vand-aa	**naan vandeen-naa**	if I come
avan var-aaṭṭaa	**avan varale-nnaa**	if he does not come

Exercise 5

In the examples that follow, the second event is conditional on the first having happened, but they have been stated as independent events. Connect them so that the condition is explicit. Translate the connected sentence.

Example: **maẓe peyyum. naan kaaleejukku pooga maaṭṭeen.**
maẓe penjaa naan kaaleejukku pooga maaṭṭeen.
If it rains I will not go to college.

1 naaḷekki kaaleej irukkum. Kumaar Umaa viiṭṭukku pooga maaṭṭaan.
2 Maalaa sinimaavukku varuvaa. Raajaa sinimaavukku varuvaan.
3 appaa Madurekki poovaaru. appaa tavaraama kooyilukku poovaaru.

(Hint: If both sentences have the same noun, the one in the subordinate clause is not repeated.)

4 Rameeṣ nalla maark vaanganum. Rameeṣ kaṣṭappaṭṭu paḍikkaṇum.
5 naan sonnadu tappu. enne manniccuru.

Exercise 6

Do the same thing again when the condition relates to an event that will not happen.

Example: **maẓe peyyaadu. naan kaaleejukku pooveen.**
maẓe peyyaaṭṭaa, naan kaaleejukku pooveen.

or **maẓe peyyale-nnaa, naan kaaleejukku pooveen.**
I will go to college if it does not rain.

1 naaḷekki kaaleej ille. Kumaar Umaa viiṭṭukku poovaan.
2 Maalaa sinimaavukku vara maaṭṭaa. Raajaa sinimaavukku varuvaan.

(Hint: A verb in the future form becomes present in the conditional; e.g., **varamaaṭṭaa** becomes **varale-nnaa**.)

3 appaa Madurekki pooga maaṭṭaaru. appaa kooyilukku pooga muḍiyaadu.
4 Rameeṣ nalla maark vaanga veeṇḍaam. Rameeṣ enda neeramum veḻeyaaḍikkiṭṭurukkalaam.
5 naan sonnadu sari ille. enne manniccuru.

Concessives

Concessives, which can generally be translated as 'even if' or 'although', have **-aalum** where conditionals have **-aa(l)** (the final **-l** of the conditional is essential in the written language but is rarely pronounced in the colloquial).

avan vand-aalum	even if he comes
avan varaaṭṭ-aalum	even if he does not come
avan varaṇum-naalum	even if he must come
adu taapu-nnaalum	even if it is a mistake

Exercise 7

In the examples that follow, the first event will have no effect in producing the second. Connect them so that this is explicit. Translate the connected sentence.

Example:
maẓe peyyaadu. naan kaaleejukku pooga maaṭṭeen.
maẓe peyyaaṭṭaalum naan kaaleejukku pooga maaṭṭeen.
Even if it doesn't rain I won't go to college.

1 naaḻekki kaaleej irukkaadu. Kumaar Umaa viiṭṭukku pooga maaṭṭaan.
2 Maalaa sinimaavukku varuvaa. Raajaa sinimaavukku vara maaṭṭaan.
3 appaa Madurekki poovaaru. appaa tavaraama kooyilukku pooga maaṭṭaaru.
4 Rameeṣ nalla maark vaanganum. Rameeṣ kaṣṭappaṭṭu paḍikka maaṭṭaan.

13 inda eɖattukku epɖi pooradu?

How do I get to this place?

In this unit you will learn to:

- understand and give directions for finding the way
- consult a doctor
- compare things
- use more ways of saying where someone comes from

Dialogue 1 (Audio 2: 27)

Asking the way

Lebègue asks one passer-by and then another about the best way to get to his destination.

LEBÈGUE: haloo. Aɳɳaanagar naalaavadu kurukku teru enge irukku?

PEDESTRIAN 1: naan uurukku pudusu. enakku teriyaadu.

LEBÈGUE: haloo. (*Showing an address slip*) inda eɖattukku epɖi pooradu?

PEDESTRIAN 2: romba duuram ille. naɖandu pooriingaɭaa? basle pooriingaɭaa?

LEBÈGUE: naɖandee pooreen.

PEDESTRIAN 2: adudaan nalladu. anda eɖattukku oru maɳi neerattukku oru basdaan irukku. bassukku kaattrukkirade viɖa nadandu siikkiram pooyiralaam.

LEBEGUE:	*Excuse me. Where is 4th Cross Street in Anna Nagar?*
PEDESTRIAN 1:	*I'm new to town. I don't know.*
LEBEGUE:	*Excuse me.* (Showing an address slip) *How does one get to this place?*
PEDESTRIAN 2:	*It's not far. Will you walk or go by bus?*
LEBEGUE:	*I'll walk.*
PEDESTRIAN 2:	*That's good. A bus goes there every hour. One can get there more quickly walking than waiting for the bus.*

Vocabulary

haloo	hello
kurukku teru	cross street

Language points

Nouns from verbs

In Unit 9 you learnt to make nouns from verbs for the purpose of talking about a particular action. This involved adding the 'neuter' ending **-adu** to a present or past tense stem. This often corresponds to the addition of '-ing' to a verb in English – as in 'his coming'. This sort of verbal noun is useful in Tamil when one does not wish to be specific about the subject of a sentence. An example is **pooradu** in Dialogue 2: **epḍi pooradu** has the sense of English 'How does one go?' or 'How to go?'; similarly **enna seyradu** 'What to do?' or 'What should one do?' (These forms were first mentioned in the paragraph on 'Permissive forms: alternatives' in Unit 6.)

Getting around town

Anna Nagar is an area (relatively new) of Chennai. In recent years, when a new suburb is constructed in the city (and in other towns in the state), streets at right angles to the main streets, which are named, are numbered as 'Cross Streets'.

Comparative

The common way of comparing one thing with another was touched on in Unit 12, where **viḍa** was seen to be the equivalent of English 'than'. Note that the order of items in a comparison is different. Tamil starts with the thing to which something else is being compared, whereas this comes second in English:

ade viḍa idu nalladu. This is better than that.

Nominalised sentences, using the forms mentioned in the previous section, can be compared in the same way:

ṭi vi paakkirade viḍa pustagam paḍikkiradu nalladu.
It's better to read a book than to watch TV.

Exercise 1

Match the sentences in the first set (a–e) with those in the second set (i–v) that mean the same. Translate both in each case.

Example: **Laṇḍan Cenneye viḍa periya uuru.**
Cenne Laṇḍane viḍa sinna uuru.
London is a bigger town than Chennai.
Chennai is a smaller town than London.

a puune naaye viḍa sirusu.
b en tambi enne viḍa vaḷatti.
c enga viiḍu onga viiṭṭe viḍa kaaleejukku pakkam.
d Tamiẓe viḍa Ingliṣ kaṣṭam.
e ellaareyum viḍa naan keṭṭikkaaran.

i Ingliṣe viḍa Tamiẓ leesu.
ii naayi puuneye viḍa perusu.
iii enne viḍa yaarum keṭṭikkaaranga ille.
iv naan en tambiye viḍa kuṭṭe.
v onga viiḍu enga viiṭṭe viḍa kaaleejukku duuram.

Exercise 2

In the same way, pair off sentences in the two sets below.

Example: **naan paaḍrade viḍa Maalaa nallaa paaḍuvaa.**
enne viḍa Maalaa nallaa paaḍuvaa.

a naan peesurade viḍa *Sarah* nallaa Tamiẓ peesuvaanga.
b nii paḍiccurukkirade viḍa avan romba paḍiccurukkaan.
c enakku teriyirade viḍa enga appaavukku Madureye patti innum teriyum.
d Madurele peyrade viḍa Koḍekaanalle maẓe adigam peyyum.
e naan solrade viḍavum nii solrade viḍavum enga ammaa aẓagaa kade solluvaanga.

i enne viḍa enga appaavukku Madureye patti innum teriyum.
ii Madureye viḍa Koḍekaanalle maẓe adigam peyyum.
iii onne viḍa avan romba paḍiccurukkaan.
iv enneyum onneyum viḍa enga ammaa aẓagaa kade solluvaanga.
v enne viḍa *Sarah* nallaa Tamiẓ peesuvaanga.

Exercise 3

Look at the picture below and make a comparison of any aspect of the things marked with the same number using demonstratives (**inda** and **anda**) or descriptive terms (e.g. **ooṭṭu viiḍu** 'tiled house' and **maaḍi viiḍu** 'storeyed house').

Dialogue 2 (Audio 2: 28)

Seeking directions

Lebègue asks a passer-by to direct him to the Anbu Clinic.

PEDESTRIAN:	niinga Anbu klinikukku daanee poogaṇum?
LEBÈGUE:	aamaa.
PEDESTRIAN:	adoo oru laari nikkidee, ange eḍadu pakkam tirumbunga.
LEBÈGUE:	sari.
PEDESTRIAN:	tirumbi oru are kiloomiiṭṭar naḍandiinga-nnaa oru sinna kooyilu varum. ade viṭṭuṭṭu aḍutta teruvule valadu pakkam tirumbunga.
LEBÈGUE:	sari. klinik anda teruvule irukkaa?
PEDESTRIAN:	ille. adule konja duuram poonaa *right*-le oru *dead end street* varum. adule irukku inda klinik.
LEBÈGUE:	mikka nanri.
PEDESTRIAN:	Amerikkaavulerundu vandu nalla Tamiẓ peesuri-ingaḷee?
LEBÈGUE:	naan Frencukkaaran. Ingliṣ nallaa teriyaadu. inge Tamiẓle peesi peesi peeccu Tamiẓ paẓakkam aagikiṭṭu varudu.

PEDESTRIAN:	*So it's the Anbu Clinic you're going to?*
LEBÈGUE:	*Yes.*
PEDESTRIAN:	*There's a lorry standing over there. Turn left there.*
LEBÈGUE:	*Right.*
PEDESTRIAN:	*If you turn and walk for half a kilometre, (you'll come to) a small temple. Go past that and turn right at the next street.*
LEBÈGUE:	*Fine. Is the clinic in that street?*
PEDESTRIAN:	*No. If you follow it for a short distance you'll come to a dead-end street on the right. The clinic's in that (street).*
LEBÈGUE:	*Many thanks.*
PEDESTRIAN:	*You come from America and you speak good Tamil.*
LEBÈGUE:	*I'm French. I don't know English well. With continually speaking Tamil here, I'm getting used to spoken Tamil.*

Vocabulary

klinik	clinic (where one consults a doctor)
laari	lorry, truck
eḍadu	left
valadu	right (side)
Frencukkaaran	Frenchman

Language points

'Where are you from?'

In Unit 2 we saw that one way of asking where someone is from is **onga sonda uuru edu?** One could also ask, **engerundu varriinga?** – getting a reply, as shown in Dialogue 2, such as **Amerikkaavulerundu varreen** 'I come from America.' One can also state one's nationality by using the **-kaaran** forms introduced under the heading 'Derived nouns' in Unit 2. For stating most nationalities, the first part of the word will be borrowed from English. It may be either the name of the country or the (English) adjective for the nationality. Here are two examples of both types (the first and third speakers are men, the others are two women):

naan Frencukkaaran
naan Ingliṣkaari
naan Amerikkaakkaaran
naan Raṣyaakkaari

There are yet other ways of giving this sort of information. More common than the **-kaaran/-kaari** forms among educated speakers is the use of forms based on English adjectives; e.g. **ivan Amerikkan** 'He's American'; **ava Raṣyan** 'She's Russian'. Yet another way is by mentioning the name of the country or the town to which one belongs: **naan Amerikkaa** 'I'm from America'; **naan Madure** 'I'm from Madurai'.

Exercise 4

Tell us, in different ways, what the nationality of these people is, using an appropriate pronoun in each case:

Example: Robert is from Ottawa. **avan Kanaḍaa.**
avan Kanaḍaakkaaran.
avan Kaneeḍiyan.

1 Setsuko is from Kyoto.
2 Heinrich is from Leipzig.
3 Adriano is from Milan.
4 Cécile is from Versailles.
5 Jean is from Washington.
6 Jean is from Paris.
7 Mary is from Singapore.
8 Abdullah is from Kuala Lumpur.
9 David and Michael are from Edinburgh.

Getting somewhere

Note the use of the verb **vaa** in the giving of directions. Where in English one says 'You will come to a temple', in Tamil it is 'A temple will come up'.

Action in progress

Another use of the verb **vaa**, which it shares with **iru**, is to indicate 'an action in progress'. See **paẓakkam aagikiṭṭuvarudu** 'getting familiar with'.

'Yes'

Note that, for saying 'yes', **aamaa** is used in answer to a question (or a statement) in agreement and **sari** in response to an instruction (or a request or command).

Expressing thanks

As was mentioned in Unit 5, the expression of thanks is generally not verbalised. If it is, the common form is **romba** ***thanks***. In formal Tamil there is an expression, **mikka nanri**, which can be said to convey the same meaning. The expression **nalla Tamiẓ** 'good Tamil' refers to speaking in the formal style. To tell someone he speaks Tamil well, one would say **Tamiẓ nallaa peesuriinga**.

Exercise 5 (Audio 2: 29)

Look at the map. There is a post office, and a bus stop where you are waiting for a bus. A pedestrian, who does not know where the post office is, walks up to you and asks you how to get to the post office. Give him clear directions.

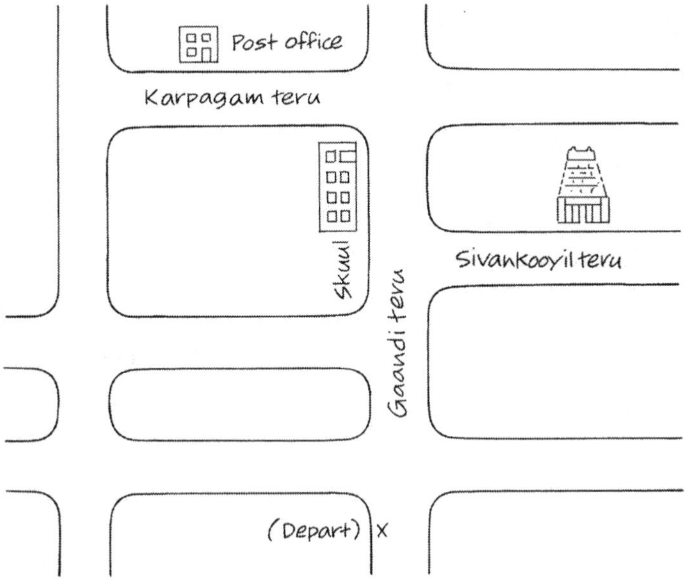

Exercise 6 (Audio 2: 30)

Imagine that you were going to the railway station but lost your way. Ask a passer-by how to get there by foot, or by bus if it was far away. Tell him that you would like to have a shorter route as you don't have much time but would like to avoid congested streets as you have already lost your way once in such a street.

Dialogue 3 (Audio 2: 31)

At the doctor's

DOCTOR:	vaanga. ukkaarunga. oɖambukku enna? *What is your problem?*
LEBÈGUE:	enakku reɳɖu naaɭaa vayittupookkaa irukku.
DOCTOR:	vaandi irukkaa?
LEBÈGUE:	ille. aanaa koɖale peraʈʈikiʈʈu varudu.
DOCTOR:	naakke kaaʈʈunga.

(*After examination*)

DOCTOR:	*serious*-aa oɳɳum ille. mundaanaaɭu enna saapʈiinga?
LEBÈGUE:	oru ooʈʈalle kooʐi biriyaaɳi saapʈeen.
DOCTOR:	niinga kaɳɖa oʈʈalleyum saapɖakuuɖaadu. *non-vegetarian* saapɖaama irukkiradu nalladu.
LEBÈGUE:	sari, ɖaakʈar.
DOCTOR:	eppavum kodikka vacca taɳɳiyee kuɖinga. alladu *mineral water* kuɖinga. kaɳɖadeyum saapʈu peragu kaʂʈapaɖradukku jaakkiradeyaa irukkiradu nalladu, illeyaa?
LEBÈGUE:	aamaa, ɖaakʈar.
DOCTOR:	oru maattire eʐudi tarreen. ade denam muuɳu veeɭe saappaaʈʈukku peragu saapɖunga. sariyaa pooyirum.

DOCTOR:	*Come in. Please sit down. What seems to be the problem?*
LEBÈGUE:	*I've had diarrhoea for a couple of days.*
DOCTOR:	*Has there been any vomiting?*
LEBÈGUE:	*No. But there's been a sort of churning in my stomach.*
DOCTOR:	*Let me see your tongue.*

(After examination)

DOCTOR:	*There's nothing serious. What did you eat the day before yesterday?*
LEBEGUE:	*I ate chicken biryani in a restaurant.*
DOCTOR:	*You shouldn't eat in just any restaurant. If you avoid eating non-vegetarian food, it would be better.*
LEBEGUE:	*Fine, doctor.*
DOCTOR:	*Always drink water that has been boiled. Or drink mineral water. It is better to be careful than eating just anything and then having problems, is it not?*
LEBEGUE:	*Yes, doctor.*
DOCTOR:	*I'll give you a prescription for some tablets. Take one three times a day after meals. It will be fine.*

Vocabulary

oḍambu	health, body	**vayiru**	stomach
vayittupookku	diarrhoea	**vaandi**	vomiting
koḍalu	intestine	**peraṭṭu (-n-)**	churn

koḍale peraṭṭikiṭṭu vaa (-nd-)	feel nauseous
mundaa naaḷu	day before yesterday
kaṇḍa	any (indiscriminately) (*lit.* that you see)
kodi (-cc-)	boil (intr)
kodikka vay (-cc-)	boil (tr), make boil
maattire	tablet

Language points

Talking about being ill

A common way of saying one has some symptom of not being well is to use **enakku** followed by the word for the symptom, and this in turn followed by **irukku** – as if to say 'To me there is . . .' This construction was discussed in Unit 2 as a way of expressing possession. Thus, **enakku vayittupookku irukku** means 'I have diarrhoea.' However, Lebègue uses not just **irukku**, but adds **-aa** to the noun indicating the symptom. The difference between the two is that **iru** states the simple fact of having something, whereas **-aa iru** 'be in a state of' indicates that the state is in an intensive condition and is lasting over a period of time. Without **-aa** (**vayit-tupookku irukku**) it will be a simple statement of having something. Somewhat similar in meaning is the use of **-kiṭṭuvaa** with the verbal participle of verbs to indicate a physical condition. This also means having that physical condition is intense and lasting: **enakku tale suttikiṭṭu varudu** 'I feel giddy'; **enakku kaṇṇe kaṭṭikiṭṭu vandudu** 'I felt dizzy, felt off balance'.

Notice how the doctor asks the initial question of the patient: **oḍambukku enna** – (*lit.* What (is) to (your) body?). He or she then, as is quite common if it seems likely that the patient understands English, repeats the question in English.

Making something happen

To express the notion that one causes something to happen, an infinitive plus **vay(yi)** – which in other contexts can mean 'put' – may be used. Thus, **taṇṇi kodikkidu** means 'the water is boiling', while **naan taṇṇiye kodikka vakkireen** means 'I am causing the water to boil'/'I am boiling the water'.

More on comparing things

In Unit 12 we saw that **viḍa** 'than' can be used when two things are being compared. As an alternative to **viḍa**, the dative case marker **-kku** may be used. Indeed, it can be used even more widely, with adjectives and verbs that are not gradable for comparison. This is comparable to stating the preference of one over the other in English: **Maalaavukku Liilaa evḷavoo paravaayille** 'Leela is much better than (preferable to) Mala'; **sinimaa paakkiradukku kirikeṭ paakkalaam** '(We'd) better watch the cricket rather than the film.'

Exercise 7

There are pairs of objects/actions in the pictures overleaf. You prefer one over the other in the pair. Make a sentence to indicate your preference, using any verb and **-ukku**.

Example: **sooru saapḍradukku cappaatti saapḍalaam.**

1

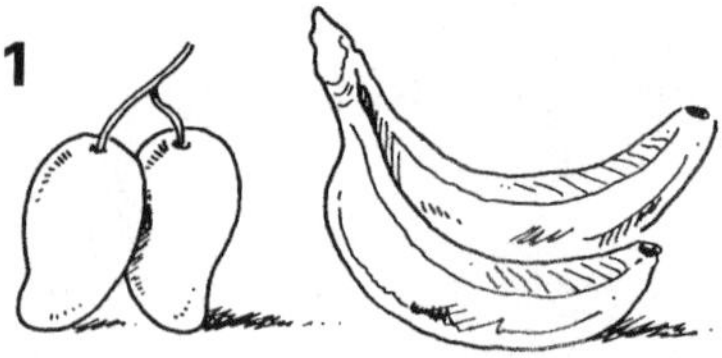

2

3

4

5

Exercise 8 (Audio 2: 32)

You frequently get a headache. You get it before going to a class. It increases in the class. You took some over-the-counter tablets, but they did not help. Explain this to the doctor and ask for a remedy.

Exercise 9 (Audio 2: 33)

Take the prescription from the doctor; ask his/her assistant for the pharmacist's. Go to the pharmacist's. Ask for the medicine and make the payment. You don't understand the dosage written on the prescription; ask the pharmacist to explain it to you. Imagine this transaction and do it in Tamil.

Exercise 10

Try to work out the meaning of these signs in the doctor's waiting room:

1 புகை பிடிக்காதீர்

2 குழந்தைக்கு போலியோ ஊசி போடுங்கள்

3 எய்ட்ஸை தடுப்போம்

4 ஒன்றே போதும்

14 enna sirikkire?

What are you laughing at?

In this unit you will learn to:

- understand Tamil humour
- learn a little about dialect pronunciation
- indicate large quantities of amounts of things
- indicate position in time and space

Dialogue 1 (Audio 2: 34)

What's the joke?

RAJA: enna sirikkire?
RANI: inda tuṇukkugaḷe paḍinga. sirippaa varudu.

கல்யாணம்

குமரன்: என் கல்யாணம் எங்க அப்பாவுக்கு முன்னாலெ நடந்தது.
சிவா: அதெப்படி?
குமரன்: அவரு கல்யாண மேடைக்கு முன்னாலெ உட்கார்ந்தாரு.

சினிமா

பார்வதி: நீ எந்த சினிமா கடெசிலெ பாத்தே?
லட்சுமி: நான் எந்த சினிமாவும் மொதல்லெருந்து பாப்பேன்.

RAJA: *What are you laughing at?*
RANI: *Read these titbits. They make you laugh.*

Marriage

KUMARAN: *I was married before my father.*

SIVAA:	*How was that?*
KUMARAN:	*He sat down before the marriage platform.*

Film

PAARVADI:	*What film did you see in the end?*
LAKSHMI:	*I see every film from the beginning.*

Vocabulary

siri (-cc-)	laugh
tuṇukku	joke, tit-bit
மேடை **meeḍe**	platform, stage
கடெசி **kaḍesi**	end
மொதல் **modal**	beginning

Language points

Writing down spoken Tamil

Though it is possible to say that written and spoken Tamil are in many respects clearly distinct, and though it is the case that for most types of writing the conventions of written, that is to say formal, Tamil must be observed, there are cases where colloquial Tamil forms will be found written down in the script. Examples are the conversational parts of some novels, some plays, and cartoons or jokes in daily or weekly newspapers or journals. There is no universally accepted way of doing this, and a fair amount of variation will be found. There are some compromises. One of these is that sounds that are not pronounced in conversation may be represented when a word is written down. So in the first of the jokes in Dialogue 1, we find a non-pronounced '**r**' in உட்கார்ந்தாரு (**uṭkaarntaaru**), as well as the sequence **-ṭk-** for **-kk-**. In the transcription that we have been using for colloquial utterances, this word would be written **ukkaandaaru**. Similarly, மேடைக்கு (**meeṭaikku**) is the normal written form of a word which in our representation of the colloquial would be **meeḍekki**. One point that all who write down the colloquial would agree on is that ர் **r** and ற் **ṟ** must always be distinguished in writing down spoken forms, even though they are pronounced in the same way when they occur between vowels; கரி (**kari**) 'charcoal' and கறி (**kaṟi**) 'meat', for instance, are homonyms.

Exercise 1

Transcribe the part of dialogue that is printed in Tamil script.

Time and space words

Postpositions and adverbs of time refer to space also. Thus **munnaale**, which follows a noun in the dative case and can carry the meaning of 'before' in a temporal sense, can also mean 'ahead of', 'in front of' in a spatial sense; **kaḍesile** can both mean 'finally'/'at the end' in a temporal sequence and also refer to something that came 'last'/'at the end' in a physical sequence. An appreciation of such points of grammar is, of course, necessary in the understanding of certain types of pun, such as those present in the two jokes above.

Adverbs of quantity

A noun + **-aa** (written -ஆக), when the noun is not a noun of abstract quality of the sort that leads to the formation of an adverb of quality, means 'plenty of same thing', 'exclusion of other things': **sirippaa** 'a lot of laughter'.

Exercise 2

Where I see one of a thing you see many of them. Change my statement to what you see. And translate both sentences.

Example: **inge oru maram irukku.**
There is a tree here.

inge maramaa irukku.
There are plenty of trees here.
(i.e. This place is full of trees.)

1 aasiriyar oru pustagam vaangunaaru.
2 avaḷukku oru parisu keḍeccudu.
3 avan oru paẓam saapṭaan.
4 ammaa oru nalla kade solluvaanga.
5 tambi poy solraan.

Exercise 3

Say your sentences without adding **-aa** to the noun but instead using the quantifiers **romba** and **nereya** 'many'.

Example: **inge maramaa irukku**
inge romba maram irukku
inge nereya maram irukku

Exercise 4

The following sentences refer to time. Give their meaning. Give also their meaning when they refer to space.

Example: **naan Kumaarukku munnaale vandeen.**
I came ahead of/before Kumar.
I came ahead of/in front of Kumar.

1 avaḷukku pinnaale yaaru vandaanga?
2 nii munnaale poo.
3 nii pattu maṇikku munnaale vaa.
(Change the time expression **pattu maṇikku** to the space expression **viiṭṭukku** in (3) and (4).)
4 nii pattu maṇikkuḷḷe vaa.
5 ava kaḍesile ukkaandaa.
6 ava vaguppukku modalle varuvaa.
(Change **vaguppukku** to **vaguppule**.)

Exercise 5 (Audio 2: 35)

Read the joke below, transcribe it, and say in Tamil what makes it humorous:

பேரன்: பாட்டி, வெயிலுலெ என்ன காயுது?

பாட்டி: சாப்பிட கேப்பெ.

பேரன்: கேக்க மாட்டேன், பாட்டி. செல்லு. நான் இப்பதான் சாப்டேன்.

பாட்டி: இல்லைடா, இது சாப்பிட்ற கேப்பெ.

Note: take this tip for your answer. கேப்பை (கேழ்வரகு) 'millet' and கேட்பாய் 'you will ask' are pronounced alike in speech, namely as **keeppe**.

-டா (**-ḍaa**), which can be added to any word in the utterance, is a term used when the addressee is of inferior status or of equal status with intimate relationship. -டி (**-ḍi**) is the feminine equivalent of this. Similarly, **-nga**(ḷ), which is an honorific form, can be added (generally to the last word in the sentence) and is used for both sexes when expressing respect or politeness.

Dialogue 2 (Audio 2: 36)

kallum kaḷḷum – or, How can that be?

Two men in a village near Salem have a conversation and do not immediately understand each other.

VELLACHAMY: koḷattule kuḷiccuṭṭu varriingaḷaa?
PALANICHAMY: aamaa. 'valile' panemarattulerundu 'kallu' erakkikiṭṭurundaanga. niṉṉu reṉḍu nongu tiṉṉuṭṭu varreen.
VELLACHAMY: kallaa? adu epḍi panemarattu meele pooccu?
PALANICHAMY: kallu ille; kuḍikkira 'kallu'.

VELLACHAMY: oo, kaḷḷaa? vaẓile paattingaḷaa? onga vaayile tamiẓ paḍaada paaḍu paḍudu.

VELLACHAMY: *Are you coming from bathing in the tank?*
PALANICHAMY: *Yes. On the way they were taking 'kallu' from a palmyra tree. I stopped and ate a couple of nongu.*
VELLACHAMY: *'kallu'? How did a stone get on the tree?*
PALANICHAMY: *Not a stone; 'kallu' for drinking.*
VELLACHAMY: *Oh, you mean 'kaḷḷu'? You saw it on the way? In your mouth Tamil really goes through the mill!*

Vocabulary

koḷam	(irrigation) tank or lake
panemaram	palmyra tree
nongu	kernel of the tender palmyra fruit before it ripens
kallu	stone
kaḷḷu	toddy
paḍaada paaḍu paḍu (paṭṭ-)	suffer excessively

Language points

Written Tamil, as shown in the sections on Tamil script and as mentioned earlier in this unit, distinguishes between 'r' (ர்) and 'ṟ' (ற்), but both are pronounced alike in speech in the most widely used colloquial variety of the language. On the other hand, in this variety people aim to maintain in speech the difference made in the Tamil script between **l**, **ḷ** and **ẓ**. However, in many dialects **ẓ** is pronounced like **ḷ** and in others like **y**; and in some dialects **ḷ** is pronounced as **l**. In Dialogue 2, words pronounced in a non-standard fashion are indicated by quotes. Thus you will find **kallu** for standard **kaḷḷu**, and **valile** for standard **vaẓile**. Similarly, you may hear **vaaẓeppaẓam** 'banana' pronounced both as **vaaḷeppaḷam** and as **vaayeppayam**.

Exercise 6

You have seen earlier that the ending **-aaga** can be added to dative suffix **-kku** to produce **-kkaaga**, and that this can indicate purpose or the person on behalf of whom an action was performed. In the sentences below, replace the dative (**-kku**) with the purposive (**-kkaaga**) and note the difference in sense.

Example: **Kumaar enakku oru pustagam vaangunaan.**
Kumar bought a book for me.

Kumaar enakkaaga oru pustagam vaangunaan.
Kumar bought a book for my sake.

1 Kumaar ammaavukku paṇam anuppunaan.
2 Kumaar yaarukku ide kuḍuttaan?
3 Kumaar veelekki (for work) vandaan.

Exercise 7

Fill in the blanks with the noun in parentheses followed by **-kkaaga** and give the meaning of the sentences.

Example:
—— onakku naan paṇam kuḍukkireen (onga appaa)
onga appaavukkaaga naan onakku paṇam kuḍukkireen.
I am giving you money for the sake of your father.

1 —— nii een ide seyre? (Maalaa)
2 —— nii vaa. (naan)
3 —— nii vaa. (naan solradu)
4 —— nii engenge poogapoore? (veele)
5 —— nii inge kaatturukke (wait)? (yaaru)

Exercise 8

Fill in the blanks with the noun in parentheses and give the meaning of the sentences.

Example:

ongaḷukku enna —— ? (teeve)	**ongaḷukku enna teeve?**
What is your need?	What do you need?

1 ongaḷukku enna —— ? (aase)
2 ongaḷukku enna —— ? (kaṣṭam)
3 ongaḷukku enna —— ? (koobam)
4 ongaḷukku enna —— ? (tayakkam (hesitation))
5 ongaḷukku enna —— ? (piraccane (problem))

Exercise 9

Answer the questions in Exercise 8 in the negative with **oṇṇum ille** 'not any'. Give the alternative form of this negative also (with **oru . . . -um** replacing **oṇṇum**).

Example: **enakku teeve oṇṇum ille.**
enakku oru teeveyum ille.

Dialogue 3 (Audio 2: 37)

A young what?

Chezhiyan has a conversation with his good friend Singh, a Hindi speaker, who lives in Coimbatore but is still not familiar with all the subtleties of Tamil.

CHEZHIYAN:	en magaḷukku naaykkuṭṭi veeṇumaam, veḷeyaaḍa.
SINGH:	enga viiṭṭule 'maaṭṭukkuṭṭi'daan irukku.
CHEZHIYAN:	ha, ha, ha. 'maaṭṭukkuṭṭi'yaa? kaṇṇukkuṭṭi-nnu sollunga.
SINGH:	viiṭṭule Hindiyee peesuramaa, Tamiẓ peesuradule tappu paṇreen. aaṭṭukkuṭṭi-nnu sollalaam, illeyaa?
CHEZHIYAN:	sollalaam. eliyooḍa kuṭṭikki enna solluviinga?
SINGH:	elikkuṭṭi.
CHEZHIYAN:	ha, ha, ha. ille, elikkunji. kooẓikkunji maadiri.
SINGH:	romba kaṣṭam, poonga.

Vocabulary

naayi	dog
kuṭṭi	young one (generally of animals), young, small
aaḍu	sheep, goat
maaḍu	cow, ox
kaṇṇukkuṭṭi	calf (of a cow) (**kaṉṟu** itself is used to mean 'calf' in written Tamil.)
Hindi, Indi	Hindi
eli	mouse, rat
kunji	young one (generally of birds)
kooẓi	hen

Language points

The particular word for the young of a species is generally predictable by the biological category of the adult. But there are exceptions. **piḷḷe** 'child' is used for the young one of humans, but you also have **tennambiḷḷe** 'sapling of coconut tree'; **kunji** is for the young one that is hatched out of an egg (birds and fish but not snakes), but you also have **elikkunji** 'young mouse'.

Sometimes the interrogative marker **-aa** is used to make a tag question (the equivalent of **illeyaa**), as in **indi peesuramaa** 'We speak Hindi, don't we?'

Note the use of **poo** (in the polite form **poonga**) at the end of a complete sentence to suggest that the speaker is fed up and is dismissive of what went before.

Exercise 10

Summarise the content of Dialogue 3, and explain why there are problems in translating it into English.

Exercise 11

Give the right word for the young of the animals and birds listed.

Example: **puune** cat
puunekkuṭṭi

1 yaane (elephant)
2 puli (tiger)
3 kiḻi (parrot)
4 paambu (snake)
5 eli
6 kaẓude (donkey)
7 kaakkaa

Exercise 12

The generic word for making noise is **kattu**. There are specific words for the noise some animals make and they may be used when you want to be specific. Read the following sentences and give their meaning from the animals and birds mentioned there. If there is no corresponding specific verb in English, use the generic verb.

Example: **naayi kolekkidu.** The dog barks.

1 kaẓude kanekkidu.
2 puli urumudu.
3 singam (lion) karccikkidu.
4 kooẓi (referring to the male) kuuvudu.
5 kaakkaa kareyidu.
6 yaane piḻirudu.
7 nari (fox) uuḻeyiḍudu.

15 naan tamiʐnaaʈʈule reɳɖu naaɭdaan irukka muɖiyum

I can be in Tamil Nadu for just a couple of days

In this unit you will learn to:

- make touristic enquires
- use negatives in relative clauses
- make nouns from verbs
- construct temporal clauses
- express conditions
- explain the reason for something
- report what has been said
- use onomatopoeic expressions

Dialogue 1 (Audio 2: 38)

A place no one has been to

Tom goes to a tourist office to ask how he can best spend a couple of days.

TOM: naan Tamiʐnaaʈʈule reɳɖu naaɭdaan irukka muɖiyum. reɳɖu naaɭule ennenna paakkalaam?

TOURISM OFFICIAL: inda pustagattule Tamiʐnaaʈʈule paakka veeɳɖiya eɖangaɭe patti vevaramaa solliyirukku. idule illaada eɖamee ille.

TOM: veɭinaaʈʈukkaaranga saadaaraɳamaa poogaada eɖattukku pooga naan aaseppaɖureen.

TOURISM OFFICIAL: apḍiyaa? cooz̨ar kaalattu sirpangaḷe pugazaadavanga ille. adu piramaadamaa irukkira oru eḍam Taaraasuram. Kumbakooṇattukku pakkattule irukku. ange poonga.

TOM: *I can be in Tamil Nadu for only two days. What can one see within two days?*

TOURISM OFFICIAL: *In this book are given details of places in Tamil Nadu that ought to be seen. There is no place that is not in it.*

TOM: *I want to go to places that foreigners do not usually go to.*

TOURISM OFFICIAL: *Is that so? There are none who do not praise the sculptures of the Chola period. A splendid place of that sort is Tarasuram. It's near Kumbakonam. (You should) go there.*

Vocabulary

veḷinaaṭṭukkaaranga(ḷ) foreigners

Coozarkaalam the period of Cholas (rulers of Tamil Nadu in the medieval period – approximately 850–1200)

sirpam	sculpture
Taaraasuram	name of a place (in Thanjavur district)
Kumbakooṇam	name of a place

Language points

Negative relative participle

In Unit 9 you learnt to make relative clauses using the relative participle. When using such constructions in which something is not so, it is necessary to use a negative relative participle, that is to say a form in which the negative is incorporated into the verb. This negative participle is formed by adding **-aada** to the verbal stem (i.e. the infinitive form without the suffix **-a**). There is no distinction of tense in the negative:

teriyaada uuru
unknown town, town which someone did not know

paḍikkaada pustagam
unread book, book which someone did not read

Exercise 1

Practise talking about things which were not done by turning the following positive expressions into negative ones. Translate the resulting sentences into English.

Example: **idu naan paḍicca pustagam.**
idu naan paḍikkaada pustagam.
This is a book which I have not read.

1 naan tuungura neeram konjam.
2 enakku piḍicca paaṭṭu inda sinimaavule eduvum ille.
3 naan solra veeleye en tambi seyyamaaṭṭaan.
4 paḍikkira neerattule naan paaṭṭu keeppeen.
5 idu ellaarum seyyakkuuḍiya veele. (Note that the negative of **kuuḍu** (be possible) is **muḍi** (be able.)

Negative participial noun

Just as nouns can be formed from a positive relative participle, so a noun can be formed from the negative. Like its positive counterpart, the negative participial noun is formed by adding a gender and number marker to the participle:

teriyaadavanga
unknown people, people whom someone did not know

paḍikkaadavanga
uneducated people, people who did not study (in school)

If you look back at Unit 9, you will be reminded that **-van** is added for a male human (polite: **-varu**), **-va** for a female human (polite: **-vanga**), **-vanga** for more than one human, and **-du** for non-human.

Exercise 2

The following sentences describe specific kinds of persons and things. Make them general using the participial noun. Translate the sentences you have made.

Example: **viiṭṭuppaaḍam seyyaada payyanga veḷiye poonga.**
viiṭṭuppaaḍam seyyaadavanga veḷiye poonga.
Those who did not do the homework, please leave.

1 neettu vaguppukku varaada payyanga yaaru?
2 eṉṉekkum oru vaartte peesaada poṇṇu iṉṉekki meeḍele peesunaa.
3 avaḷukku piḍikkaada aaḷe kalyaaṇam paṇṇikiḍa sonnaanga.
4 avarukku piḷḷe illaada viṣayam enakku teriyaadu.

Passives

Though the grammar of written Tamil does distinguish between active and passive forms of verbs, passive verbs are hardly ever used in conversation. However, there is one construction for which a convenient translation in English is with a passive. This construction occurs when the neuter singular of **iru** 'be' is added to the verbal participle and there is no expressed subject in the sentence: e.g. **idule enna eẕudiyirukku?** 'What is written in it?'

Exercise 3

While I talk about positive actions, you make them negative. Give the translations of your sentences.

Example: **avan ade sonnadu tappu ille.**
avan ade sollaadadu tappu ille.
His not saying it is not wrong.
(i.e. It is not wrong that he did not say it.)

1 ava paḍikkiradu yaarukkum piḍikkale.
2 nii ide vaangradukku oru kaaraṉam irukkaṉum.
3 ippa maẕe peyradu nalladu.
4 raajaa paṉatte tiruppi keeṭṭadudaan aaccariyam.
5 uurukku poonadunaale enakku paṉam naṣṭam.

Dialogue 2 (Audio 2: 39)

Temple

Tom tells Mahesh about his visit to see the temple at Tarasuram.

MAHESH: Taaraasuram pooniingaḷee; epḍi irundudu?
TOM: adu oru periya kade. surukkamaa solreen.
naan Taaraasuram poonappa oree maẕe. baslerundu erangagunadum maẕe piḍiccukiḍuccu. maẕe niṉṉa peragu pooradukkaaga bas sṭaapleyee niṉṉeen. maẕe nikkira varekkum poẕude pookka pattirikke paḍikka aarambicceen. pattirikke paḍiccukiṭṭurukkumboodu pakkattule niṉṉukiṭṭurundavaru ennooḍa peesa aarambiccaaru. avarukku Taaraasuram kooyile patti nereya terinjurundudu. maẕe niṉṉa oḍane avarum enkuuḍa vandaaru. iruṭṭuradukkuḷḷe kooyile nallaa paattoom. uure viṭṭu keḷamburadukku munnaale innoru sivan kooyileyum avaru odaviyaale paakka muḍinjudu.

MAHESH: *You went to Tarasaram, didn't you? How was it?*
TOM: *It's a long story. I'll tell it to you briefly.*
When I went to Tarasaram, it really rained! When I got down from the bus it started to rain heavily. I stood at the bus stop ready to leave after the rain stopped.

To pass the time till the rain stopped, I began to read the newspaper. While I was reading the newspaper, a man who was standing next to me began to talk to me. He knew a lot about the Tarasaram temple. As soon as the rain stopped, he too came along with me. We had a good look round the temple until it became dark. Before leaving the town and setting off, I was able with his help to see another Shiva temple.

Vocabulary

surukkamaa	briefly
maẕe piḍi (-cc-)	start to rain heavily
iruṭṭu (-n-)	get dark
Sivan	the god Shiva

Language points

Time clauses

Time clauses or temporal clauses are clauses expressing such ideas as: 'when', 'after', 'before', 'as soon as', 'until', 'as long as'. In English, such words and phrases come at the beginning of the clause. To make temporal clauses in Tamil, the equivalent indicators of time relationships are added to a relative participle at the end of a clause. These indicators include **appa** 'when', **samayam** 'at the time of', **peragu** 'after', **munnaale** 'before', **varekkum** 'until', **oḍane** 'immediately after', 'as soon as'. Of these, **peragu** and **oḍane** are added to the past relative participle; **munnaale** to the future relative participle (which becomes identical with the infinitive form in speech) and **varekkum** to the past and present relative participle.

peragu 'after' and **munnaale** 'before' may also be added to a nominalised verb in the dative case in past and present tenses respectively. **uḷḷe** 'inside of', 'before (another action)' is added only to this form in the present tense. A nominalised verb in past tense with **-um** added means 'immediately after', like **oḍane** after a past relative participle. Remember that a nominalised verb in this context is a verb form in which the neuter suffix **-adu** is added to either a present or a past stem. A number of these occur in Dialogue 2. The various possibilities are set out below using the verb **paḍi**:

paḍiccappa/paḍicca samayam	when (some one) was reading
paḍikkirappa/paḍikkira samayam	when (some one) is reading
paḍicca peragu	after (some one) read
paḍiiccadukku peragu	after (some one) read
paḍicca oḍane	as soon as (some one) read
paḍiccadum	as soon as (some one) read
paḍikka munnaale	before (some one) reads
paḍikkiradukku munnaale	before (some one) reads or finishes reading
paḍikkiradukkuḷḷe	before (some one) reads or finishes reading
paḍicca varekkum	as far as (some one) has read, i.e. to the extent (some one) has read
paḍikkira varekkum	until (some one) reads or finishes reading

Exercise 4

I am not good at remembering time. When I say that something happened earlier, you correct me and say that it happened later. Correct the following sentences of mine and also translate both sentences.

Example:

I: **maẓe vara munnaale Kumaar viiṭṭukku vandaan.**
Kumar came to the house before the rain came.

You: **maẓe vanda peragu Kumaar viiṭṭukku vandaan.**
Kumar came to the house after the rain came.

1 appaa solla munnaale Kumaar paḍikka aarambiccaan.
2 Maalaa keekka munnaale Raajaa paṇam kuḍuttaan.
3 bas nikka munnaale taattaa erangunaaru.
4 kaapi aara munnaale ammaa kuḍippaanga.
5 taattaa saapḍa munnaale konja neeram tuunguvaaru.

Exercise 5

Redo my sentences in Exercise 4 using **uḷḷe** instead of **munnaale**, and yours using **oḍane** instead of **peragu**.

Example:

maẓe varradukkuḷḷe Kumaar viiṭṭukku vandaan.
Kumar came to the house before it rained (started to rain).

maẓe vanda oḍane Kumaar viiṭṭukku vandaan.
Kumar came to the house as soon as it rained (started to rain).

Exercise 6

Combine each of these pairs of simple sentences into a single complex sentence starting with a temporal clause. Translate your sentences.

Example:

naan kooyilukku pooneen. appa adu puuṭṭiyirundudu.
naan kooyilukku poonappa adu puuṭṭiyirundudu.
When I went to the temple it was locked.

1 naan kaaleejule paḍicceen. appa ittane bas ille.
2 naan kaaramaa saapṭeen. appa kaṇṇule taṇṇi vandudu.
3 naan Kumaarṭṭe paṇam keeṭṭeen. appa avan kuḍukkale.
4 naan kaaleejukku pooveen. appa vaẓile onne paakkireen.
5 naan naaḷekki Kumaare paappeen. appa avan enakku pustagam kuḍuppaan.

Exercise 7

Once again, combine two simple sentences into one complex one, and translate them.

Example:

naan viiṭṭule irundeen. aduvarekkum Kumaar paḍikkale.
naan viiṭṭule irunda varekkum Kumaar paḍikkale.
Kumar did not read until I was at home.

1 naan kaaleejule irundeen. adu varekkum Kumaar varale.
2 naan kaaleejule paḍicceen. adu varekkum appaa paṇam kuḍuttaaru.

3 enakku anda viṣayam teriyaadu. adu varekkum naan kavaleppaḍale.
4 naan saapḍuveen. adu varekkum ava saappiḍa maaṭṭaa.
5 naan varreen. adu varekkum nii viiṭṭuleyee iru.

Dialogue 3 (Audio 2: 40)

Wildlife sanctuary

Robert: naan Tamiẓnaaṭṭukku poonaa ennenna paakkalaam?
Ramesh: kooyil paakkiradu ellaarum seyradu. niinga pudusaa edaavadu seyyaṉum-naa sollunga.
Robert: aamaa. naan pudusaa edaavadu seyyaṉum-nu nenekkireen.
Ramesh: niinga apḍi nenekkiradunaale solreen. niinga saraṇaalayattukku poogalaam.
Robert: saraṇaalayam-naa enna?
Ramesh: saraṇaalayam-naa kaaṭṭule miruganga paadukaappaa irukkira oru pagudi. niinga puli-nnaa bayappaḍa maaṭṭiingaḷee?
Robert: bayappaḍa maaṭṭeen. enda kaaṭṭukku poonaalum saraṇaalayam irukkumaa?

RAMESH: ille. Tamiẓnaaṭṭule Mudumalele irukku. adu enga irukku-nnaa Uuṭṭilerundu Maysuurukku poora vaẓile irukku. ange kaaṭṭukkuḷḷe yaanemeele poogalaam.
ROBERT: naan angeyee pooreen. yaane tiḍiirnu kaaṭṭukkuḷḷe ooḍa aarambiccuradee?
RAMESH: anda yaanega paẓaguna yaanega. aduga maḍamaḍannu kaaṭṭukkuḷḷe naḍakkirade paattaa payamaa irundaalum oru aabattum varaadu. tayriyamaa poogalaam.

ROBERT: *If I go to Tamil Nadu, what are all the things I can see?*
RAMESH: *Looking at temples is something everyone does. Say if you want to see something new.*
ROBERT: *Yes. I'm thinking of seeing something new.*
RAMESH: *It's because you're thinking like that that I mention it. You can go to a 'saranalayam'.*
ROBERT: *What's a 'saranalayam'?*
RAMESH: *A 'saranalayam' is an area in the forest for the conservation of wild animals. You won't be afraid of tigers, will you?*
ROBERT: *I won't be afraid. Will there be a wildlife sanctuary, whatever forest one goes to?*
RAMESH: *No. In Tamil Nadu there's Mudamalai. As for where it is, it's on the way from Ooty to Mysore. There you can go into the forest on an elephant.*
ROBERT: *That's where I'll go. Will an elephant suddenly start to run in the forest?*
RAMESH: *Those elephants are trained elephants. Even if you see them running fast in the forest and you feel scared, there's no danger. You can go there confidently.*

Vocabulary

saraṇaalayam	wildlife sanctuary		
paadukaappu	preservation, conservation		
mirugam	animal	**pagudi**	part, area
puli	tiger	**yaane**	elephant
Mudumale, Uuṭṭi, Maysuur	Mudumalai, Ooty, Mysore (place names in the western range of hills in South India)		
tiḍiir	onomatopoeic word for suddenness		
paẓagu	be trained, be skilled		
maḍamaḍa	onomatopoeic word for speed		
tayriyam	courage, boldness		

Language points

Cause

To express the cause of something, **-naale** is added to a nominalised form of a verb (that is to say, one ending in **-adu**). It means 'because', 'since':

avan vandadunaale	because he came
avan varradunaale	because he is coming
avan varaadadunaale	because he did/does not come

When the predicate is not a tensed verb, **-ngradunaale** is added to the predicate itself (see the section on 'Quoting' in Unit 12):

avan varaṉum-ngradunaale	because he must come
adu tappu-ngradunaale	because it is a mistake

The causal form **-ngradunaale** can also be added to a tensed verb to give alternatives to the examples given above:

avan vandaan-ngradunaale	because he came
avan varale-ngradunaale	because he did not come

Mention

When a word is 'mentioned' in a sentence (as opposed to its being used in a sentence), the form introduced earlier as a way of expressing a conditional, namely **-(n)naa**, is added to that word (**-nnaa** occurring with words that end in a vowel and **-naa** with words ending in a consonant). This construction is also used when one is defining a word or highlighting it. 'Mentioning' can also occur without **-(n)naa**.

puli-nnaa oru mirugam.	The tiger is an animal.
puli oru mirugam.	The tiger is an animal.
doose-nnaa enakku piḍikkum.	I like dosa.
doose enakku piḍikkum.	I like dosa.
puli-nnaa enakku payam.	I am afraid of tigers.
puliṭṭe enakku payam.	I am afraid of tigers.

Exercise 8

Explain the meaning of the words asked for in the following questions by naming the class to which it belongs or by giving a synonym. Translate your answer.

Example: **Tamiẓ-naa enna?**
Tamiẓ-naa oru moẓi.
Tamil is a language.

1 puli-nnaa enna?
2 iḍli-nnaa enna?
3 maamaa-nnaa yaaru?

Onomatopoeic expressions

Tamil has a good number of onomatopoeic words, and these often occur in conversation. They may be a direct imitation of a sound, or they may be intended to express a type of movement, or even a mood. Most of them are in duplicated form. They are followed by **-(n)nu** (a major use of which is discussed below under 'quotative').

maḍamaḍannu	briskly
tiḍiirnu	suddenly

When these expressions are modifiers of nouns like **sattam** 'sound', **-ngra**, rather than **-(n)nu**, is added to them:

jaljal-ngra sattam	the sound of jingling
ṭak-ngra sattam	the noise of 'tak'

Exercise 9

Make nouns from the following onomatopoeic words and guess their meaning.

Example: **kalakala** (jingle)
kalakalappu (boisterous happiness)

1 paḍapaḍa (flutter)
2 veduvedu (be warm (as of water))
3 kadakada (be warm (as of place, clothes))
4 kurukuru (be irritated)
5 viruviru (be fast (tempo))

Reported speech

As mentioned briefly in Unit 12, when a statement made by another person is directly quoted or indirectly reported the quoted or reported sentence takes the 'quotative' **-(n)nu** at the end.

Directly quoted sentence

'naan naaḷekki varreen'-nu Kumaar sonnaan.
Kumar said 'I will come tomorrow.'

'nii naaḷekki varriyaa'-nnu Kumaar Umaave keeṭṭaan.
Kumar asked Uma 'Are you coming tomorrow?'

'nii naaḷekki varaṇum'-nu Kumaar enakku uttaravu pooṭṭaan.
Kumar ordered me 'You must come tomorrow.'

Reported sentence

(Note that, in contrast with English, the tense does not change.)

taan naaḷekki varreen-nu Kumaar sonnaan.
Kumar said that he would come tomorrow.

ava naaḷekki varraaḷaa-nnu Kumaar Umaave keeṭṭaan.
Kumar asked Uma whether she was coming tomorrow.

naan naaḷekki varaṇum-nu Kumaar sonnaan.
Kumar said that I must come tomorrow.

Even when no actual statement, question, or order is being quoted or reported, **-nnu** may be added to indicate what somebody is thinking or supposing, for instance. The construction itself is not distinguishable from reported speech:

Kumaar taan keṭṭikkaaran-nu nenekkiraan.
Kumar thinks he is clever.

naan naaḷekki uurukku poogalaam-nu irukkeen.
I am thinking of going to my home town tomorrow.

idu periya veeleyaa irukkee-nnu paakkiriyaa?
Do you think it is a big task?

rusiyaa irukku-nnu Maalaa anju doose saapṭaa.
Mala ate five dosas as they were tasty/that she found tasty.

pandu keḍekkale-nnu naayi tirumbi vandudu.
The dog returned as he could not get the ball.

When a positive statement is reported (and not directly quoted), there is an alternative construction. The tensed verb of the reported sentence is nominalised (that is to say that **-adu** is added to the past or present stem) and **-aa**(**ga**) is added to it.

taan naaḷekki varrad*aa* Kumaar sonnaan.
Kumar said that he would come tomorrow.

A further possibility with directly quoted statements, questions, or commands is for the quotative/marker **-nnu** to be conjugated; that is to say that personal endings may be added to it. In such cases it functions as a (past tense) verb meaning 'say', 'ask', 'request':

'naaḷekki varreen'-naan Kumaar.
Kumar said '(I) am coming tomorrow.'

Umaave 'naaḷekki varriyaa'-nnaan Kumaar.
Kumar asked Uma 'Are (you) coming tomorrow?'

enne 'naaḷekki vaa'-nnaan Kumaar.
Kumar told me '(You) come tomorrow.'

Exercise 10

The following sentences are said to have been spoken by Raja to you. Confirm it. Translate your confirming sentences.

Example:

'naaḷekki maẓe peyyum.'
naaḷekki maẓe peyyum-nu Raajaa engiṭṭe sonnaan.
Raja told me 'It will rain tomorrow.'

1 'naaḷekki maẓe peyyumaa?'
2 'maẓeyile naneyaade.'
3 'maẓe evḷavu neeramaa peyyudu.'
4 'maẓeyile naneyakkuuḍaadunnu ammaa solluvaanga.'
5 'naaḷekki maẓe peyyumnu reeḍiyoovule sonnaanga-nnu appaa sonnaar.'

Exercise 11

The following are the actual words spoken by Raja. Report them, changing the reference of the persons to fit the new context. Translate the reported sentences.

Example: **'nii keṭṭikkaaran.'**
naan keṭṭikkaaran-nu raajaa sonnaan.
Raja said that I was clever.

1 'naan keṭṭikkaaran.'
2 'naanum niiyum keṭṭikkaaranga.'
3 'niiyum Maalaavum enge pooriinga?'
4 'nii enge poore-nnu en tambi keekkiraan.'
5 'nii enge poore-nnu on tambi keekkiraan-nu en tangacci solraa.'

Exercise 12

Say the following quotative sentences using the alternative construction with **-aa**(**ga**). Translate those sentences.

Example: **doose rusiyaa irukku-nnu *Barbara* sonnaanga.**
doose rusiyaa irukkiradaa *Barbara* sonnaanga.
Barbara said that dosa is tasty.

1 veele nereya irundudu-nnu *John* sonnaaru.
2 roojaa puutturukku-nnu tooṭṭakkaaran solraan.
3 Maalaa sinimaavule naḍikkapooraa-nnu ellaarum solraanga.
4 Maalaa kaaleejukku varraa-nnu yaarum sollale.
5 veele nereya irundudu-nnu *John* sonnaar-nu *Barbara* sonnaanga.

Exercise 13

It is possible to imagine that an event, that did not happen, would have happened if another event had happened. This is commonly referred to as an unfulfilled condition. This is expressed in Tamil by adding the conditional marker to the past perfect of a verb; i.e. the one formed by adding **iru** to the verbal participle. In the following pairs of sentences, the first sentence is in the negative. Imagine that if the first event had happened, the situation reported in the second sentence would have been different. Link the sentences to indicate the imagined situation in each case. Translate your sentence of imagined happening.

Example:

Kumaar enne viiṭṭukku kuuppiḍale; naan poogale.
Kumaar enne viiṭṭukku kuuppiṭṭurundaa, naan pooyiruppeen.
If Kumar had invited me to his house, I would have gone.

1 Kumaar nallaa paḍikkale; nalla maark vaangale.
2 appaa Madurekki poogale; kooyilukku poogale.
3 nii enkiṭṭe mannippu keekkale; naan aasiriyarṭṭe sonneen.
4 nii pattu maṇikki varale; naan tuungiṭṭeen.
5 taattaa kaḍekki pooga muḍiyale; patrikke vaangale.

Exercise 14 (Audio 2: 41)

Read silently the following description given by Robert about his visit to the wildlife sanctuary and translate it:

mudumalekkuḷḷe bas noẓenjappa ṭamaarnu oru sattam keeṭṭudu. bas ninṇa odane ellaarum maḍamaḍannu erangi ooḍunaanga. en manasu tiktiknu aḍiccudu. naanum pinnaaleyee ooḍunaa ange yaanegaḷukku oru pandayam naḍattikkiṭṭurundaanga. ade aarambikkattaan veeṭṭu pooṭṭurukkaanga. ooṭṭappandayattule oru kuṭṭi yaane kuḍukuḍunnu ooḍi modalle vandudu. pandu piḍikkira veḷeyaaṭṭule oru yaane pande ṭakṭaknu piḍiccudu. kayiru iẓukkira veḷeyaaṭṭule oru yaane edirppakkam irunda nuuru peere paṭnu oru nimiṣattule iẓutturuccu. ellaa nigaẓcciyum romba kalakalappaa irundudu.

16 Tamiẓḷe oru siranda nuulu

A famous book in Tamil

In this unit you will learn to:

- discuss the meaning of words
- give an account of events you have seen

Dialogue 1 (Audio 2: 43)

Tell me about Tirukkuṟaḷ

Smith has heard that Tiruvaḷḷuvar's Tirukkuṟaḷ *is the most famous book in Tamil. He asks Madhivanan to tell him something about it.*

SMITH: Tirukkuraḷ Tamiẓḷe oru siranda nuul-nu keeḷvippaṭṭirukkeen. ade patti konjam solriingaḷaa?

MADHIVANAN: ade patti solrade viḍa adeyee paḍikkalaam. Tirukkuraḷooḍa sirappe terinjikiḍuradukku adudaan nalla vaẓi-nnu solluveen.

SMITH: enakkum ade paḍikka aasedaan. paẓeya ilakkiyatte paḍiccaa puriyamaaṭṭeengudu. Tirukkuraḷe naanee paḍikka muḍiyumaa?

MADHIVANAN: inda kaalattule eẓuduna oru oreye kayyile vaccukiṭṭiinga-nnaa paḍikkalaam. ippavee paḍiccu paakkiriingaḷaa? ongaḷukku engeyum poogaveeṇḍiyadu illeyee?

SMITH: ille.

MADHIVANAN: inda kuraḷ enna solludu-nnu paappoom.

தீயினால் சுட்ட புண் உள்ளாறும் ஆறாதே
நாவினால் சுட்ட வடு

konjam vittiyaasam irundaalum idule irukkira ellaa vaartteyum ongaḷukku teriyum-nu nenekkireen.

SMITH: apḍittaan teriyidu.

MADHIVANAN: ideyee peesura maadiri solreen. nallaa puriyudaa-nnu sollunga.

tiiyinaale suṭṭa puṇṇu uḷḷe aarum; aaraadu
naakkunaale suṭṭa vaḍu.

SMITH: 'naa'-nnaa naakkaa?

MADHIVANAN: aamaa.

SMITH: vaḍu-nnaa enna?

MADHIVANAN: vaḍu-nnaa taẓumbu, ingliṣle 'scar'-nu solluviinga.

SMITH: ippa ellaam puriyidu.

SMITH: *I've heard that* Tirukkural *is a famous book in Tamil. Will you tell me a bit about it?*

MADHIVANAN: *Better than telling about it we can read it. I would say that for getting to know the significance of* Tirukkural, *that is the best way.*

SMITH: *I too want to read it. If I read old literature, I don't understand it. So can I read* Tirukkural?

MADHIVANAN: *If you get hold of a commentary written in modern times, you can read it. Do you want to try reading it now? You don't need to go anywhere, do you?*

SMITH: *No.*

MADHIVANAN: *Let's see what this* kural *says.*

தீயினால் சுட்ட புண் உள்ளாறும் ஆறாதே
நாவினால் சுட்ட வடு

Although there's a bit of difference, I think you know all the words in it.

SMITH: *So it seems.*

MADHIVANAN: *I'll say it in spoken style. Say if you understand it well.*

tiiyinaale suṭṭa puṇṇu uḷḷe aarum; aaraadu
naakkunaale suṭṭa vaḍu.

SMITH: *Does 'naa' mean 'tongue'?*

MADHIVANAN: *Yes.*

SMITH: *What's 'vaḍu'?*

MADHIVANAN: *'vaḍu' means 'taẓumbu'. In English you say 'scar'.*

SMITH: *Now I understand it all.*

Vocabulary

siranda	famous	**nuul**	book
ore	commentary	**aaru (-in-)**	heal
vaartte	word	**tii**	fire
suḍu (-ṭṭ-)	burn	**puṇṇu**	wound
naakku	tongue		

Tirukkuṟaḷ

Tirukkuṟaḷ (திருக்குறள்) is the best known work in the early ethical literature of Tamil. Probably written in the early centuries after Christ, it is considered in the modern period the greatest symbol and representation of Tamil high culture. It consists of 1330 couplets, divided into 133 chapters of ten couplets each.

Exercise 1

On the basis of Madhivanan's explanation, provide a translation of the **kuṟaḷ** (no. 129) that Smith discusses with him.

Exercise 2 (Audio 2: 44)

With the help of the version in modern colloquial Tamil that is provided, see if you can translate this *kuṟaḷ* (no. 108) too:

நன்றி மறப்பது நன்றன்று; நன்றல்ல(து)
அன்றே மறப்பது நன்று

(oruttar senja) nallade marakkiradu nalladu ille; nalladu illaadade aṇṇekkee marakkiradu nalladu.

(**illaadadu** not being, something which is not)

Exercise 3

Study the following sentence in the second paragraph of the dialogue: **ade patti solrade viḍa adeyee paḍikkalaam**. This compares two actions by using the verbal noun **solradu** (in the 'object' case) followed by **viḍa** 'than'/ 'rather than'/ 'better than'. Look again at the section on 'verbal nouns' in Unit 9, and then write sentences of a similar pattern to give the following meanings:

1 Better than walking to the temple, you may go by auto.
2 Rather than watch TV, we can go to the cinema.
3 Rather than drink coffee you should drink juice.

Dialogue 2 (Audio 2: 45)

Tiruvaḷḷuvar festival

Smith tells Madhivanan about his visit to Cape Comorin, where he saw the inauguration of a colossal statue of Tiruvalluvar.

SMITH: niinga Tirukkuraḷe patti sonna peragu oru naaḷ Kanniyaakumarikku pooneen. tarceyalaa aṇṇekki Tiruvaḷḷuvarukku oru periya viẓaa naḍandudu.

MADHIVANAN: Tiruvaḷḷuvar silai tirappu viẓaave pattidaanee solriinga. adepatti pattirikkeleyum TV-leyum nereya veḷambarapaḍuttiyirundaangaḷee.

SMITH:	epḍiyoo naan ade paakkale. naan poona aṉṉekki Kanniyaakumarile oree kuuṭṭam. Tamiẓnaaḍee ange vandamaadiri irundudu. veḷḷinaaṭṭulerundukuuḍa ariñargaḷ vandurundaanga.
MADHIVANAN:	meeḍele peesunadu ellaam purinjudaa?
SMITH:	ellaarum ilakkiya tamiẓle peesunaanga. puriyiradu kaṣṭamaa irundudu.
MADHIVANAN:	mattapaḍi viẓaa epḍi irundudu?
SMITH:	kalai nigaẓccigaḷ irundudu. inda tiruvaḷḷuvar sele avḷavu oyaramaana sele tamiẓnaaṭṭule veere engeyum ille-nnu nenekkireen.
MADHIVANAN:	uṉmedaan. kooḍikaṉakkaa paṉam selavaẓiccu inda seleye ameccirukkaanga.
SMITH:	*New York*-le *Statue of Liberty* maadiri idu Tamiẓ paṉpaaṭṭin aḍippaḍeye uyartti kaaṭṭudu-nnu sollalaam.

Vocabulary

Kanniyaakumari	Kanya Kumari/Cape Comorin, a place at the southernmost tip of India
tarceyalaa	by chance, accidentally
viẓaa	festival, celebration, function
silai/sele	statue
tiṟappu/terappu	opening, inauguration
veḷambaram	advertisement, publicity
veḷambarapaḍuttu (-n-)	advertise, publicise
ariñargaḷ	scholars
mattapaḍi	otherwise
kalainigaẓcci/kale-	cultural programme
oyaram	height
kooḍi	crore, ten million
kooḍikaṉakkaa	in crores, in tens of millions
ame (-cc-)	make, set up
paṉpaaḍu	culture
aḍippaḍai/aḍippaḍe	core, basic element

Exercise 4

Answer in Tamil the following questions based on Dialogue 2.

1 Where did the Tiruvaḷḷuvar festival take place?
2 Why didn't Smith know about the festival?
3 Who spoke at the function apart from people from Tamil Nadu?
4 Why did Smith not understand all the speeches from the platform?
5 What does the statue symbolise?

Calendars in Tamil

Calendars are published annually showing both universal and traditional sets of dates. Wedding invitations may also give both dates. Most newspapers and periodicals are dated in terms of the universal era. On the other hand, some writers and publishers who take particular pride in their Tamil cultural heritage and its distinctiveness use the Tamil system. The traditional system includes cycles of sixty years, each named. The use of the traditional Tamil system can be seen in the Tamil part of the wedding invitation that follows. Before this we give the names of the twelve Tamil months in their written and colloquial forms:

சித்திரை	**sittire**
வைகாசி	**vaygaasi**
ஆனி	**aani**
ஆடி	**aaḍi**
ஆவணி	**aavaṇi**
புரட்டாசி	**puraṭṭaasi**
ஐப்பசி	**ayppasi**
கார்த்திகை	**kaarttige**
மார்கழி	**maargaẓi**
தை	**tay**
மாசி	**maasi**
பங்குனி	**panguni**

An invitation to a wedding

Mrs Kalyani Murugan

Dr N.T. Murugan

solicit your esteemed presence with family and friends

on the occasion of the marriage of their son

Selvan: N.T. Gopalan

with

Selvi: K. Tenmozhi

on Thursday the 3rd February 2000 between

8.30 a.m. and 10.00 a.m.

at Raja Mandram, Thanjavur

திருமண அழைப்பு

அன்புடையீர்,

வணக்கம். நிகழும் பிரமாதி ஆண்டு தை மாதம்
27-ஆம் நாள்
காலை 8-30 மணி முதல் 10-00 மணிக்குள்

செல்வன் : நா. தி. கோபாலன் செல்வி : க. தேன்மொழி

ஆகியோரின் திருமணம் தஞ்சாவூர் இராசா மன்றத்தில்
நடைபெற உள்ளது.
தாங்கள் குடும்பத்துடன் வந்து மணமக்களை வாழ்த்த
வேண்டுகிறோம்.

தங்களன்புள்ள,
டாக்டர் நா. தி. முருகன்
திருமதி கல்யாணி முருகன்

Vocabulary

அழைப்பு	invitation
அன்புடையீர்	a common beginning to a letter: 'Dear friend'
நிகழும்	current
ஆண்டு	year
நாள்	day
பிரமாதி	the name of a year in the sixty-year cycle of the Tamil calendar
தை	the name of the tenth Tamil month
திருமணம்	marriage
மன்றம்	hall, auditorium
மணமக்கள்	bride and bridegroom
வாழ்த்து	bless
வேண்டு	request

It is culturally expected that the wedding invitation is given personally to relatives and friends. They are orally invited as well. The oral invitation (as given by the groom's parents) will be of the form: **enga payyan goopaalanukku tay maasam irubatti eeẓaam teedi kalyaaṇam vaccirukkoom. Tanjaavuurle Raajaa manrattule pattu maṇikkuḷḷe muguurttam. niinga kuḍumbattooḍa varaṇum**.

Exercise 5

Read aloud the wedding invitation in Tamil. Get its meaning with the help of the English version. Which words in the colloquial version of the wedding invitation correspond to the following: ஆண்டு, மாதம், நாள், திருமணம், நடைபெறு?

Exercise 6

Read the names of the Tamil months in Tamil. The first day of சித்திரை **sittire** roughly corresponds to 15 April. Give the corresponding months and dates in the English calendar.

Mixture of formal and informal styles in speech

Note that when talking informally about topics of formal content, words from the formal style are often used and are partially pronounced in the formal style: e.g. **ariñargaɭ**, **silai**, **tirappu**, **ilakkiyam**, **kalai nigaɻcci**. The same word may be pronounced as in colloquial speech depending on the context in the conversation: e.g. **sele**. The phrases may have the grammatical features of formal Tamil, e.g. the genitive **-in̲** in **paɳpaaʈʈin̲ aɖippaɖai**. In the vocabulary for Dialogue 2, the first represents the formal style and the second the colloquial. The sound represented by **ñ** is similar to that represented by the same symbol in Spanish.

Counting in large numbers

In numbering systems in Indian languages figures higher than thousands are spoken of in terms of lakhs (100 thousand) and crores (100 lakhs). The Tamil terms are **laʈcam** (or **laccam**) and **kooɖi**.

Exercise 7 (Audio 2: 46)

If the third day of a month is **muuɳaam teedi**, tell us that:

1 Lakshmi went to Kanya Kumari by car on the 4th of Sittirai.
2 Father went to Chengam by van on the 5th of Aani.
3 John went to Chennai by ship (kappal) on the 6th of Tai.
4 Melli went to Madurai by train on the 7th of Panguni.
5 Raja and Mohan went to London by plane (vimaanam) on 8th June.
6 You went to college by cycle (saykiɭ) on the 9th of last month.
7 You and Kumar will go to Tiruvannamalai (Tiruvaɳɳaamale) by bus on the 10th of next month.

Exercise 8 (Audio 2: 47)

Tell your Tamil friend in Tamil about a festival in your own country that you enjoyed.

Exercise 9 (Audio 2: 48)

Say in five sentences why you want to go to Tamil Nadu.

Appendix 1

The Tamil alphabet

		a	aa	i	ii	u	uu	e	ee	ai	o	oo	au
		அ	ஆ	இ	ஈ	உ	ஊ	எ	ஏ	ஐ	ஒ	ஓ	ஔ
k	க்	க	கா	கி	கீ	கு	கூ	கெ	கே	கை	கொ	கோ	கௌ
ŋ	ங்	ங											
c	ச்	ச	சா	சி	சீ	சு	சூ	செ	சே	சை	சொ	சோ	சௌ
ñ	ஞ்	ஞ	ஞா										
ʈ	ட்	ட	டா	டி	டீ	டு	டூ	டெ	டே	டை	டொ	டோ	
ɳ	ண்	ண	ணா	ணி	ணீ	ணு	ணூ	ணெ	ணே	ணை	ணொ	ணோ	
t	த்	த	தா	தி	தீ	து	தூ	தெ	தே	தை	தொ	தோ	
n	ந்	ந	நா	நி	நீ	நு	நூ	நெ	நே	நை	நொ	நோ	
p	ப்	ப	பா	பி	பீ	பு	பூ	பெ	பே	பை	பொ	போ	பௌ
m	ம்	ம	மா	மி	மீ	மு	மூ	மெ	மே	மை	மொ	மோ	மௌ
y	ய்	ய	யா	யி	யீ	யு	யூ	யெ	யே	யை	யொ	யோ	யௌ
r	ர்	ர	ரா	ரி	ரீ	ரு	ரூ	ரெ	ரே	ரை	ரொ	ரோ	
l	ல்	ல	லா	லி	லீ	லு	லூ	லெ	லே	லை	லொ	லோ	
v	வ்	வ	வா	வி	வீ	வு	வூ	வெ	வே	வை	வொ	வோ	வௌ
ʐ	ழ்	ழ	ழா	ழி	ழீ	ழு	ழூ	ழெ	ழே	ழை	ழொ	ழோ	
ɭ	ள்	ள	ளா	ளி	ளீ	ளு	ளூ	ளெ	ளே	ளை	ளொ	ளோ	
ṟ	ற்	ற	றா	றி	றீ	று	றூ	றெ	றே	றை	றொ	றோ	
ṉ	ன்	ன	னா	னி	னீ	னு	னூ	னெ	னே	னை	னொ	னோ	
j	ஜ்	ஜ	ஜா	ஜி	ஜீ	ஜு	ஜூ	ஜெ	ஜே	ஜை	ஜொ	ஜோ	
ʂ	ஷ்	ஷ	ஷா	ஷி	ஷீ	ஷு	ஷூ		ஷே	ஷை		ஷோ	
s	ஸ்	ஸா	ஸ	ஸி	ஸீ	ஸு	ஸூ	ஸெ	ஸே	ஸை		ஸோ	
h	ஹ்	ஹா	ஹ	ஹி	ஹீ	ஹு	ஹூ		ஹே	ஹை		ஹோ	
kʂ		க்ஷ		க்ஷி	க்ஷீ				க்ஷே				
śrii					ஸ்ரீ								

Note: There are gaps in the above table to indicate that the syllable in question does not occur in any Tamil word.

Appendix 2

The Tamil writing system

To give a clearer indication of letter shapes, the basic vowels and consonants follow in larger size. Where letters begin with a loop, the writing of the letter begins at this point. Where letters begin with a straight line, the writer starts at the top left hand point. In the writing of a single letter, the pen is usually not lifted from the paper. This means that the pen may go over some short segments twice. Except in the case of a vowel sign that precedes the consonant letter, vowel signs are added when the consonant shape is complete.

அ	ஆ	இ	ஈ	உ	ஊ
a	aa	i	ii	u	uu
எ	ஏ	ஐ	ஒ	ஓ	ஔ
e	ee	ai	o	oo	au
க	ங	ச	ஞ	ட	ண
ka	ŋa	ca	ña	ṭa	ṇa
த	ந	ப	ம	ய	ர
ta	na	pa	ma	ya	ra
ல	வ	ழ	ள	ற	ன
la	va	ẓa	ḷa	ṟa	ṉa
ஜ	ஷ	ஸ	ஹ	க்ஷ	
ja	ṣ	sa	ha	kṣa	

Grammatical summary

This grammatical sketch is limited to bringing together in one place for ease of reference the different forms under which nouns, pronouns, and verbs can appear. Details of how these various forms are used in the formation of words and sentences can be found by looking up the range of topics given in the grammatical index at the end of the book.

1 Nouns

A noun can (1) indicate the difference between singular and plural, and (2) show the function of a noun in a sentence by the use of a range of case endings. These comments apply equally to pronouns, though the difference between singular and plural is a little more complicated for some pronouns.

Case endings

In order to talk about case endings or suffixes, we need to label them. What matters, however, is the meanings, not the labels. Apart from this paragraph, abbreviated forms will be used for these. For Tamil, the commonly used labels are:

1 Nom(inative): the subject of a sentence, the basic form of a noun with no added suffix.
2 Acc(usative): the object of a sentence; **-e**. Remember that the accusative is always used if the noun in question refers to a human being and is generally used if the noun refers to an animal. For inanimate objects it is not used if the noun has a general sense, but it is used if the reference is to something specific (in instances where English would use the definite article 'the'): **puune paalu kuḍikkum** 'Cats drink milk'; but **puune paale kuḍiccudu** 'The cat drank the milk.'

3 Dat(ive): 'to', **-kku** or **-kki** (the latter for nouns ending in **i**, **ii** or **e**).
4 Gen(itive): 'of', indicates possession: **-ooḍa**. Optional.
5 Instr(umental): 'by', 'with', indicates the instrument with which, or the person by whom, an action was performed: **-aale**.
6 Soc(iative): 'along with'; indicates the person or thing in association with which something happened; **-ooḍa**.
7 Loc(ative): 'at', 'on', 'in', indicates location: **-le** for things, **-(gi)ṭṭe** for persons (usually).
8 Abl(ative): 'from', **-lerundu** for things, **-(gi)ṭṭerundu** for persons. The optional **-gi-** in the locative and ablative is more commonly dropped in normal speech with third person pronouns and with nouns than with first and second person and reflexive pronouns.

These case forms are illustrated below for two nouns, **payyan** 'boy' and **taḍi** 'rod', 'staff'. Note how **y** is used to link the latter to a following vowel:

Nom	**payyan**	**taḍi**
Acc	**payyane**	**taḍiye**
Dat	**payyanukku**	**taḍikki**
Gen	**payyan(ooḍa)**	**taḍi(yooḍa)**
Instr	**payyanaale**	**taḍiyaale**
Soc	**payyanooḍa**	**taḍiyooḍa**
Loc	**payyangiṭṭe**	**taḍile**
Abl	**payyangiṭṭerundu**	**taḍilerundu**

For cases other than nominative, some nouns have what we have called a 'non-subject' form. The largest set consists of nouns ending in **-am**, which is replaced by **-att-**: **maram** 'tree', but **marattukku** 'to the tree'. Another set consists of nouns ending in **-ḍu**, if this is preceded by a long vowel or by more than one syllable. In these, the non-subject form has **-ṭṭ-**, not **-ḍ-**: **viiḍu** 'house', but **viiṭṭukku** 'to the house'. Finally, a few nouns for which the subject or nominative form ends in **-ru**, the non-subject stem has **-tt-**: **aaru** 'river', but **aattukku** 'to the river'; **keṇaru** 'well', but **keṇattukku** 'to the well'.

Plural of nouns

To indicate more than one of something, **-ga(ḷ)** is added to the singular form. This plural suffix comes before the case ending. If this ending begins with a vowel, the bracketed **ḷ** is pronounced:

Singular		*Plural*	*Dative plural*
aaḷu	man	**aaḷuga**	**aaḷugaḷukku**
poṇṇu	girl	**poṇṇuga**	**poṇṇugaḷukku**
puune	cat	**puunega**	**puunegaḷukku**
maram	tree	**maranga**	**marangaḷukku**

For nouns referring to humans, the plural suffix is always used. When the reference is to non-humans, it is optional, and it is unusual for it to occur when a numeral precedes the noun: **pattu aaḍu** 'ten sheep'; **aaru tennamaram** 'six coconut trees'. One exception to the rule about nouns denoting humans is **peeru** 'person', but this is always preceded by a numeral (or some other quantifier such as **pala** 'several'): **muuṇu peeru vandaanga** 'Three people came.' Note (with regard to **maranga** in the table) the change of **m** to **n** before **-ga** in the case of nouns ending in **-am**.

2 Pronouns

Case endings

The same set of case endings is used for pronouns as for nouns, but as first and second person pronouns have different non-subject forms, the full set of pronoun forms is given below. For third person pronouns, remember that for those listed with initial **a-**, there is an otherwise identical set beginning with **i-**. The difference between the two relates to closeness to or remoteness from the speaker. One uses **a-** forms to refer to that person or thing, and **i-** forms to refer to this person or thing. The **a-** forms hold in addition a 'neutral' position, when one does not aim to be specific as between 'this' and 'that' – as when one uses a pronoun to refer to a person or thing mentioned earlier by name or by the use of a noun. The pronouns are: **naan** 'I', **naama(ḷ)** 'we (inclusive of speaker)', **naanga(ḷ)** 'we (exclusive of speaker)', **nii** 'you (singular)', **niinga(ḷ)** 'you (plural and polite singular)', **avan** 'he', **avaru** 'he (polite)', **ava(ḷ)** 'she', **avanga(ḷ)** 'they (human)', 'she (polite)', **adu** 'it', **aduga(ḷ)** 'they (non-human)', **taan** 'self', **taanga(ḷ)** 'selves'.

Nom	**naan**	**naama**	**naanga**
Acc	**enne**	**namme**	**engaḷe**
Dat	**enakku**	**namakku**	**engaḷukku**
Gen	**en(nooḍa)**	**nam(mooḍa)**	**engaḷ(ooḍa)**

Instr	**ennaale**	**nammaale**	**engaɭaale**
Soc	**ennooɖa**	**nammooɖa**	**engaɭooɖa**
Loc	**engiʈʈe**	**nammagiʈʈe**	**engagiʈʈe**
Abl	**engiʈʈerundu**	**nammagiʈʈerundu**	**engagiʈʈerundu**

Nom	**nii**	**niinga**
Acc	**onne**	**ongaɭe**
Dat	**onakku**	**ongaɭukku**
Gen	**onnooɖa**	**ongaɭooɖa**
Instr	**onnaale**	**ongaɭaale**
Soc	**onnooɖa**	**ongaɭooɖa**
Loc	**ongiʈʈe**	**ongagiʈʈe**
Abl	**ongiʈʈerundu**	**ongagiʈʈerundu**

Nom	**avan**	**avaru**	**ava**
Acc	**avane**	**avare**	**avaɭe**
Dat	**avanukku**	**avarukku**	**avaɭukku**
Gen	**avan(ooɖa)**	**avar(ooɖa)**	**ava(ɭooɖa)**
Instr	**avanaale**	**avaraale**	**avaɭaale**
Soc	**avanooɖa**	**avarooɖa**	**avaɭooɖa**
Loc	**avangiʈʈe**	**avarʈʈe**	**avagiʈʈe**
Abl	**avangiʈʈerundu**	**avarʈʈerundu**	**avagiʈʈerundu**

Nom	**avanga**	**adu**	**aduga**
Acc	**avangaɭe**	**ade**	**adugaɭe**
Dat	**avangaɭukku**	**adukku**	**adugaɭukku**
Gen	**avanga(ɭooɖa)**	**adu/adooɖa**	**aduga(ɭooɖa)**
Instr	**avangaɭaale**	**adunaale**	**adugaɭaale**
Soc	**avangaɭooɖa**	**adooɖa**	**adugaɭooɖa**
Loc	**avangagiʈʈe**	**adule/aduʈʈe**	**adugaɭɭe/ adugaʈʈe**
Abl	**avanga-giʈʈerundu**	**adulerundu/ aduʈʈerundu**	**adugaɭɭerundu/ aduʈʈerundu**

Nom	**taan**	**taanga**
Acc	**tanne**	**tangaɭe**
Dat	**tanakku**	**tangaɭukku**
Gen	**tan(nooɖa)**	**tanga(ɭooɖa)**
Instr	**tannaale**	**tangaɭaale**
Soc	**tannooɖa**	**tangaɭooɖa**
Loc	**tangiʈʈe**	**tangagiʈʈe**
Abl	**tangiʈʈerundu**	**tangagiʈʈerundu**

As regards the neuter pronouns **adu** and **aduga**, the suffixed forms of the genitive are used (optionally) if the reference is to something animate. Similarly the second forms for locative and ablative are used only with animates.

Postpositions

As examples given above show, case endings on nouns and pronouns in Tamil often correspond to prepositions (such as 'to', 'at', 'in', 'from') in English. Some of the case forms can be extended by a further suffix or can have a postposition added to them to give another meaning that cannot be expressed by a case form alone (a postposition being something placed after a noun, as compared with a preposition, which comes before a noun). In this section we look at some of the more common of these.

To express the notion of 'on behalf of' or 'for the sake of', **-aaga** is added to the dative to give **-ukkaaga**: **kaḍekki pooyi ammaavukkaaga konjam saaman vanguneen** 'I went to the shop and bought a few things for mother.'

To express the notion of 'inside', **uḷḷe** is added to the dative, and to express the notion of 'outside', **veḷiye** is added: **viiṭṭukkuḷḷe** 'inside the house'; **viiṭṭukku veḷiye** 'outside the house'.

The noun **pakkam** 'side' is used as a postposition to mean 'near'. It can be added to the 'non-subject' stem or to the dative case: **viiṭṭupakkam** or **viiṭṭukku pakkattule** 'near the house', 'in the vicinity of the house'. Words that occur as adverbs are used in this way to indicate various types of location; e.g. **pinnaale** 'behind', **munnaale** 'in front of', and **meele** 'above': **viiṭṭukku pinnaale** 'behind the house', **viiṭṭukku munnaale** 'in front of the house', **viiṭṭukku meele** 'above the house'. For the meaning 'on top of' (i.e. in contact with the object in question), **meele** is used after the nominative of a noun: **meese meele** 'on the table'; after a dative, **meele** means 'above' or 'over': **meesekki meele** 'above the table'. Finally in this set, **kiiẓe** is used after a dative to mean 'under': **meesekki kiiẓe** 'under the table'.

Postpositions may follow other cases. A commonly used one that follows the accusative (object) case is **patti** 'concerning': **avaḷe patti** 'about her'. Another that follows the accusative is **tavira** 'except': **ade tavire** 'other than that'. In comparative constructions, **viḍa** is used after a noun in the accusative as the equivalent of English 'than': **ade viḍa perisu** 'bigger than that'. An alternative to the instrumental case is the accusative followed by **vacci**: **kattiye vacci veṭṭu** 'cut with a knife'. Note also the addition of **kuuḍa** to the sociative case: **avanooḍa kuuḍa** 'along with him'.

3 Verbs

The main verb in a sentence typically consists of three parts: (1) the root, which indicates the basic meaning of the verb, (2) a suffix to indicate tense, and (3) a personal ending. What we call the root can occur on its own as an imperative form, used to instruct someone to do something. It is the root that is used as the heading for an entry in a dictionary – and is therefore the form under which verbs are listed in the glossaries found towards the end of this book.

Tenses

Three tenses are distinguished – past, present, and future. These relate in meaning to past, present, and future time. As the grammar points in the units in which the tense forms are introduced explain, however, the matching between tenses is not exact. For example, the present tense can be used to refer to an action that will take place in the future. English sentences such as 'Jack arrives tomorrow evening at seven', can be compared to this. The future tense can indicate future time, but it can also be used to refer to an action which is habitual.

On the basis of present and future tense markers, verbs are classified into two main groups. These are commonly labelled 'strong' and 'weak'. Strong verbs take **-kkir-** to mark the present tense and **-pp-** to mark the future. Weak verbs take **-r-** to mark the present tense and **-v-** to mark the future. From this it follows that, if one knows the present tense of a verb, one knows the future, and vice versa. The past tense is somewhat more complicated, since the range of endings is larger, and some of these occur with both strong and weak verbs. For each verb it is therefore necessary to learn both the present and past markers (and these are given alongside each verb in the glossaries). With this knowledge it is possible to predict all other verb forms. Past tense markers that occur with strong verbs are: **-tt-**, **-cc-**, **-ṭṭ-** and **-nd-**. Past tense markers that occur with weak verbs are: **-d-**, **-ḍ-**, **-ṭṭ-**, **-nd-**, **-nj-**, **-ṇṇ-** and **-n-**.

Examples of each of these are given in the table that follows. The hyphens at the end of the different tenses are to indicate that the personal ending is still to be added (see next section). The most frequently occurring past tense suffixes are **-tt-** and **-cc-** for strong verbs, and **-n-** and **-nj-** for weak verbs.

The vowel **i** in the present tense marker **-kkir-** tends to be dropped, and what you hear will most commonly sound like **-kr-**.

Verb	*Meaning*	*Past*	*Present*	*Future*
kuḍu	give	**kuḍutt-**	**kuḍukkir-**	**kuḍupp-**
paḍi	read	**paḍicc-**	**paḍikkir-**	**paḍipp-**
keeḷu	hear	**keeṭṭ-**	**keekkir-**	**keepp-**
naḍa	walk	**naḍand-**	**naḍakkir-**	**naḍapp-**
aẓu(vu)	weep	**aẓud-**	**aẓu(vu)r-**	**aẓuv-**
kaaṇ	see	**kaṇḍ-**	**kaangr-**	**kaamb-**
pooḍu	put	**pooṭṭ-**	**pooḍr-**	**pooḍuv-**
viẓu	fall	**viẓund-**	**viẓur-**	**viẓuv-**
seyyi	do	**senj-**	**seyr-**	**seyv-**
uruḷu	roll	**uruṇḍ-**	**uruḷur-**	**uruḷuv-**
kollu	kill	**koṇṇ-**	**kolr-**	**kolluv-**
ooḍu	run	**ooḍun-**	**ooḍr-**	**ooḍuv-**

Rules can be formulated to account for the loss in past tense forms of such consonants as **ḷ**, **l**, and **r** that appear in the base form, but it is simpler to learn the forms for each verb separately. In 'strong' verbs, these consonants are dropped in each tense form. Examples are **keeḷu** (in the table) and **paaru** 'see' (**paatt-**, **paakkir-**, **paapp-**). In many languages, common verbs are slightly irregular. Two such verbs in Tamil follow:

vaa	come	**vand-**	**varr-**	**varuv-**
iru	be	**irund-**	**irukk-**	**irupp-**

From a knowledge of these four parts of a verb – root, and past, present, and future stems – it is possible to predict all other forms, such as the infinitive, verbal participle, relative participle and verbal noun, as well as such complex forms as those that indicate that an action is continuous (progressive) or completed (completive). This can be understood by looking up such terms in the grammatical index. A full account of the verbal (or past) participle and the most frequently occurring complex verb forms that are based on it can be found in Unit 8.

Personal endings

With each pronoun is associated a different personal verb ending. This ending occurs on verb forms, past, present, or future, which are the main verbs of sentences. Except for **maaʈʈ-**, it does not occur on negative verbs. Nor does it occur with verbs with such meanings as 'may', 'can', 'must', 'should' (sometimes called modal verbs). There are two instances of a single verb ending sufficing for two pronouns. First person plural pronouns 'we', both inclusive of the person spoken to (**naama**) and exclusive (**naanga**), go with the ending **-oom**. For third person neuter nouns or pronouns (i.e. those that do not refer to humans), there is no distinction between singular and plural as far as the verb ending is concerned. The endings are illustrated below with the three tenses of the verbs **ooɖu** 'run' and **naɖa** 'walk'. The reasons for giving two verbs are explained above in the paragraph on tense.

Pronoun	*Past*	*Present*	*Future*
naan	**ooɖuneen**	**ooɖureen**	**ooɖuveen**
naama(ɭ)	**ooɖunoom**	**ooɖuroom**	**ooɖuvoom**
naanga(ɭ)	**ooɖunoom**	**ooɖuroom**	**ooɖuvoom**
nii	**ooɖune**	**ooɖure**	**ooɖuve**
niinga(ɭ)	**ooɖuniinga(ɭ)**	**ooɖuriinga(ɭ)**	**ooɖuviinga(ɭ)**
avan	**ooɖunaan**	**ooɖuraan**	**ooɖuvaan**
avaru	**ooɖunaaru**	**ooɖuraaru**	**ooɖuvaaru**
ava(ɭ)	**ooɖunaa(ɭ)**	**ooɖuraa(ɭ)**	**ooɖuvaa(ɭ)**
avanga(ɭ)	**ooɖunaanga(ɭ)**	**ooɖuraanga(ɭ)**	**ooɖuvaanga(ɭ)**
adu	**ooɖuccu**	**ooɖudu**	**ooɖum**
aduga(ɭ)	**ooɖuccu**	**ooɖudu**	**ooɖum**

Pronoun	*Past*	*Present*	*Future*
naan	**naɖandeen**	**naɖakkireen**	**naɖappeen**
naama(ɭ)	**naɖandoom**	**naɖakkiroom**	**naɖappoom**
naanga(ɭ)	**naɖandoom**	**naɖakkiroom**	**naɖappoom**
nii	**naɖande**	**naɖakkire**	**naɖappe**
niinga(ɭ)	**naɖandiinga(ɭ)**	**naɖakkiriinga(ɭ)**	**naɖappiinga(ɭ)**
avan	**naɖandaan**	**naɖakkiraan**	**naɖappaan**
avaru	**naɖandaaru**	**naɖakkiraaru**	**naɖappaaru**
ava(ɭ)	**naɖandaa(ɭ)**	**naɖakkiraa(ɭ)**	**naɖappaa(ɭ)**
avanga(ɭ)	**naɖandaanga(ɭ)**	**naɖakkiraanga(ɭ)**	**naɖappaanga(ɭ)**
adu	**naɖandudu**	**naɖakkudu**	**naɖakkum**
aduga(ɭ)	**naɖandudu**	**naɖakkudu**	**naɖakkum**

Though the forms are in general quite regular, a few points need to be noted. Firstly, the bracketed (ḷ) at the end of some pronouns and verb forms is pronounced only when a suffix beginning with a vowel (e.g. the question suffix **-aa**) follows: **ava** 'she', **avaḷaa** 'she?'; **naḍakkiraanga** 'They are walking', **naḍakkiraangaḷaa?** 'Are they walking?'

Two endings change when such a suffix is added. First person plural **-oom** becomes **-am-**, and second person singular **-e** becomes **i-**: **naḍappoom** 'We shall walk', **naḍappamaa?** 'Shall we walk?'; **naḍappe** 'You will walk', **naḍappiyaa?** 'Will you walk?'

Particular attention needs to be paid to the third person neuter forms. In present tense forms, the ending for this is **-udu**. The **r** of the present markers appearing before this disappears. This means that for strong verbs **-kkir-** becomes **-kk-**, whilst in weak verbs there is no actual segment to indicate the present. In future tense forms, the third person neuter is indicated by the ending **-um**. In strong verbs, this is preceded by **-kk-** (and not **-pp-**). In weak verbs, **-v-** disappears and **-um** is added directly to the root of the verb. In past tense forms, there are two endings for neuter: **-udu** and **-uccu**. For one set of verbs, those that have **-n-** as indicator of the past tense, **-uccu** alone is used. With these verbs, the **-n-** is dropped (see **ooḍu** in the table above). With other markers of the past tense, either ending (without the loss of the past marker) is possible; e.g. **vandudu** or **vanduccu** 'it came'.

Key to exercises

Note: Where answers to questions involve personal names, it is often the case that a correct answer does not necessarily require that the name you use should be the one given below.

Unit 1

Exercise 1

1 nii Goovindan. **2** avan Arasu. **3** niinga Nittilaa. **4** peeraasiriyar Lakşmi. **5** peeraasiriyarooḍa maaṉavan Raaman.

Exercise 2

1 onga peeru Goovindan. **2** en maaṉavan peeru Arasu. **3** onga maaṉavan peeru Raaman.

Exercise 3

1 avan Goovindanaa? **2** avaru Arasaa? **3** ava Nittilaavaa? **4** onga peeru Lakşmiyaa? **5** onga maaṉavan peeru Raamanaa?

Exercise 4

1 niinga poonga. **2** niinga irunga. **3** niinga kuḍunga.

Exercise 5

1 inda ooṭṭalu, anda ooṭṭalu. **2** inda viiḍu, anda viiḍu. **3** inda ruum, anda ruum. **4** inda maaṉavan, anda maaṉavan. **5** inda peeraasiriyar, anda peeraasiriyar.

Exercise 6

1 nii biiccukku pooviyaa? **2** ava biiccukku poovaaḷaa? **3** avanga biiccukku poovaangaḷaa? **4** Murugan biiccukku poovaanaa? **5** Kalyaaṇi biiccukku poovaaḷaa? **6** peeraasiriyar biiccukku poovaaraa? **7** onga maaṇavan biiccukku poovaanaa?

Exercise 7

(a) 1 nii ooṭṭalukku pooviyaa? **2** ava ooṭṭalukku poovaaḷaa? **3** avanga ooṭṭalukku poovaangaḷaa? **4** Murugan ooṭṭalukku poovaanaa? **5** Kalyaaṇi ooṭṭalukku poovaaḷaa? **6** peeraasiriyar ooṭṭalukku poovaaraa? **7** onga maaṇavan ooṭṭalukku poovaanaa?
(b) 1 nii Cennekki pooviyaa? **2** ava Cennekki poovaaḷaa? **3** avanga Cennekki poovaangaḷaa? **4** Murugan Cennekki poovaanaa? **5** Kalyaaṇi Cennekki poovaaḷaa? **6** peeraasiriyar Cennekki poovaaraa? **7** onga maaṇavan Cennekki poovaanaa?

Exercise 8

1 Goovindan karumbu caaru kuḍippaanaa? **2** Lakṣmi ṭii kuḍippaaḷaa? **3** niinga paalu kuḍippiingaḷaa? **4** avanga mooru kuḍippaangaḷaa?

Exercise 9

1 b; **2** d; **3** a; **4** c

Unit 2

Exercise 1

1 naama sinimaavukku pooroom. **2** naanga sinimaavukku pooroom. **3** nii viiṭṭukku poore. **4** niinga viiṭṭukku pooriinga. **5** avan ooṭṭalukku pooraan **6** ava ooṭṭalukku pooraa. **7** avaru biiccukku pooraaru **8** avanga biiccukku pooraanga **9** Murugan Cennekki pooraan. **10** Mr Smith Laṇḍanukku pooraaru. **11** peeraasiriyar kaaleejukku pooraaru. **12** adu Nungambaakkattukku poogudu. **13** ṭæksi Nungambaakkattukku poogudu.

Exercise 2

1 naama sinimaavukku poovoom. **2** naanga sinimaavukku poovoom. **3** nii viiʈʈukku poove. **4** niinga viiʈʈukku pooviinga. **5** avan ooʈʈalukku poovaan **6** ava ooʈʈalukku poovaa. **7** avaru biiccukku poovaaru **8** avanga biiccukku poovaanga **9** Murugan Cennekki poovaan. **10** Mr Smith Laɳɖanukku poovaaru. **11** peeraasiriyar kaaleejukku poovaaru. **12** adu Nungambaakkattukku poogum. **13** ʈæksi Nungambaakkattukku poogum.

Exercise 3

1 f; **2** e; **3** b; **4** a; **5** c; **6** d

Exercise 4

1 avan viiʈʈukku pooraan. **2** avan ruumukku pooraan. **3** avan Meɖraasukku pooraan. **4** avan Laɳɖanukku pooraan. **5** avan Amerikkaavukku pooraan.

Exercise 5

1 ooʈʈalu pinnaale irukku; ooʈʈalu munnaale irukku. **2** viiɖu pinnaale irukku; viiɖu munnaale irukku. **3** ruum pinnaale irukku; ruum munnaale irukku. **4** maaɳavan pinnaale irukkaan; maaɳavan munnaale irukkaan. **5** peeraasiriyar pinnaale irukkaaru; peeraasiriyar munnaale irukkaaru. **6** Murugan pinnaale irukkaan; Murugan munnaale irukkaan. **7** Mr Smith pinnaale irukkaaru; Mr Smith munnaale irukkaaru.

Exercise 6

1 onakku tambi irukkaanaa? **2** onakku aɳɳan irukkaaraa? **3** onakku tangacci irukkaaɭaa? **4** onakku akkaa irukkaangaɭaa? **5** ongiʈʈe peenaa irukkaa?

Exercise 7

Listen to the tape for the pronunciation.

Exercise 8

1 ettane ooʈʈalu irukku? naalu ooʈʈalu irukku. **2** ettane viiɖu irukku? aaru viiɖu irukku. **3** ettane ʈæksi irukku? anju ʈæksi irukku. **4** ettane naaɭu irukku? eeẓu naaɭu irukku. **5** ettane maaɳavanga irukkaanga? muuɳu maaɳavanga irukkaanga.

Exercise 9

1 f; **2** c; **3** g; **4** d; **5** a; **6** e; **7** b

Unit 3

Exercise 1

1 avanukku enna veeɳum? avanukku iɖli veeɳum. **2** avaɭukku enna veeɳum? avaɭukku puuri veeɳum. **3** Muruganukku enna veeɳum? Muruganukku uppumaa veeɳum. **4** Robert-ukku enna veeɳum? Robert-ukku vaɖe veeɳum.

Exercise 2

1 avanukku iɖli veeɳɖaam. **2** avaɭukku puuri veeɳɖaam. **3** Muruganukku uppumaa veeɳɖaam. **4** *Robert*-ukku vaɖe veeɳɖaam.

Exercise 3

1 avanukku paalu veeɳumaa? kaapi veeɳumaa? avanukku paalu veeɳum. **2** avaɭukku juus veeɳumaa? paalu veeɳumaa? avaɭukku juus veeɳum. **3** Muruganukku caʈni veeɳumaa? saambaar veeɳumaa? avanukku caʈni veeɳum. **4** Robert-ukku vengaaya saambaar veeɳumaa? kattarikkaa saambaar veeɳumaa? avanukku vengaaya saambaar veeɳum.

Exercise 4

1 avanukku kaapi veeɳɖaam. **2** avaɭukku paalu veeɳɖaam. **3** avanukku saambaar veeɳɖaam. **4** avanukku kattarikkaa saambaar veeɳɖaam.

Exercise 5

1 idu enna? idu veṇḍekkaa. **2** idu enna? idu meḷagaa. **3** idu enna? idu maangaa. **4** idu enna? idu takkaaḷi. **5** idu enna? idu biins. **6** idu enna? idu vengaayam. **7** idu enna? idu uruḷekkeẓangu.

Exercise 6

1 idu veṇḍekkaayaa? aamaa, idu veṇḍekkaa. **2** idu meḷagaayaa? aamaa, idu meḷagaa. **3** idu maangaayaa? aamaa, idu maangaa. **4** idu takkaaḷiyaa? aamaa, idu takkaaḷi. **5** idu biinsaa? aamaa, idu biins. **6** idu vengaayamaa? aamaa, idu vengaayam. **7** idu uruḷekkeẓangaa? aamaa, idu uruḷekkeẓangu.

Exercise 7

1 pattu ruubaa sṭaampu anju kuḍunga. **2** anju ruubaa sṭaampu pattu kuḍunga. **3** padinanju ruubaa sṭaampu muuṇu kuḍunga. **4** muuṇu ruubaa sṭaampu padinanju kuḍunga. **5** naalu eer leṭṭar kuḍunga. **6** anju inlaaṇḍ kuḍunga.

Exercise 8

1 idu Cennekki poogudu; evḷavu aagum? **2** idu Madurekki poogudu; evḷavu aagum? **3** idu Paarisukku poogudu; evḷavu aagum? **4** idu Amerikkaavukku poogudu; evḷavu aagum?

Exercise 9

1 doose, iḍli, sooru, vade (cooked items). **2** uppu, maavu, arisi, puḷi, cakkare (ingredients for cooking).

Exercise 10

1 d; **2** a; **3** g; **4** b; **5** i; **6** e; **7** c; **8** j; **9** f; **10** h

Unit 4

Exercise 1

1 haloo, naan *Jones* peesureen. Lakṣmi irukkaangaḷaa? **2** haloo, naan *Jones* peesureen. Murugeesan irukkaaraa? **3** haloo, naan *Jones* peesureen. Raaman irukkaanaa? **4** haloo, naan *Jones* peesureen. Mulle irukkaaḷaa?

Exercise 2

1 maṇi enna? maṇi anju. **2** maṇi enna? maṇi aaru. **3** maṇi enna? maṇi eeẓu. **4** maṇi enna? maṇi eṭṭu. **5** maṇi enna? maṇi ombadu. **6** maṇi enna? maṇi pattu.

Exercise 3

(a) maṇi enna? maṇi anju. (b) maṇi enna? maṇi anjee kaal. (c) maṇi enna? maṇi anjare. (d) maṇi enna? maṇi anjee mukkaa. (e) maṇi enna? maṇi aaru. (f) maṇi enna? maṇi aaree kaal. (g) maṇi enna? maṇi aarare. (h) maṇi enna? maṇi aaree mukkaa. (j) maṇi enna? maṇi eeẓu.

Exercise 4

maṇi anju pattu; maṇi aaru pattu; maṇi eeẓu pattu; maṇi eṭṭu pattu; maṇi ombadu pattu; maṇi pattu pattu.

Exercise 5

1 oṇṇu. **2** reṇḍu. **3** muuṇu. **4** naalu. **5** anju. **6** aaru. **7** eeẓu. **8** eṭṭu. **9** ombadu. **10** pattu.

Exercise 6

1 oṇṇaam vaguppu. **2** reṇḍaam vaguppu. **3** muuṇaam vaguppu. **4** naalaam vaguppu. **5** anjaam vaguppu. **6** aaraam vaguppu. **7** eeẓaam vaguppu. **8** eṭṭaam vaguppu. **9** ombadaam vaguppu. **10** pattaam vaguppu.

Exercise 7

1 oṇṇaavadu viiḍu. **2** reṇḍaavadu viiḍu. **3** muuṇaavadu viiḍu. **4** naalaavadu viiḍu. **5** anjaavadu viiḍu. **6** aaraavadu viiḍu. **7** eeẓaavadu viiḍu. **8** eṭṭaavadu viiḍu. **9** ombadaavadu viiḍu. **10** pattaavadu viiḍu.

Exercise 8

1 oṇṇaavadu teru. **2** reṇḍaavadu teru. **3** muuṇaavadu teru. **4** naalaavadu teru. **5** anjaavadu teru. **6** aaraavadu teru. **7** eeẓaavadu teru. **8** eṭṭaavadu teru. **9** ombadaavadu teru. **10** pattaavadu teru.

Exercise 9

1 paakkaade. **2** peesaadinga. **3** nikkaade. **4** ukkaaraadinga. **5** saapḍaade. **6** kuḍikkaadinga.

Exercise 10

1 Murugan, niinga kaaleejule peesa muḍiyumaa? muḍiyum.
2 Murugan, niinga kaḍekki pooga muḍiyumaa? muḍiyaadu.
3 Murugan, niinga peeraasiriyare paakka muḍiyumaa? muḍiyum.
4 Murugan, niinga enakku odavi seyya muḍiyumaa? muḍiyaadu.

Exercise 11

1 Muruganaale kaaleejule peesa muḍiyum. **2** Muruganaale kaḍekki pooga muḍiyaadu. **3** Muruganaale peeraasiriyare paakka muḍiyum. **4** Muruganaale enakku odavi seyya muḍiyaadu.

Exercise 12

1 Raajaa viiṭṭule irukkaan. **2** peenaa payyile irukku. **3** pustagam meesele irukku. **4** payyi sovarle tongudu. **5** nii basle vaa. **6** peenaave kayyile piḍi. **7** kayye taṇṇile kaẓuvu.

Exercise 13

1 Raajaa viiʈʈule ille. **2** peenaa payyile ille. **3** pustagam meesele ille. **4** payyi sovarile tongale. **5** nii basle varaade. **6** peenaave kayyile piɖikkaade. **7** kayye taɳɳile kaɻuvaade.

Exercise 14

1 Raajaa ombadu maɳikki kaaleejle peesaɳum. **2** Raajaa ombadu maɳikki peeraasiriyare paakkaɳum. **3** Raajaa ombadu maɳikki viiʈʈule irukkaɳum. **4** Raajaa ombadu maɳikki tambikki pustagam kuɖukkaɳum.

Exercise 15

1 Kumaar kaɖekki pooganumaa? aamaa, pooganum. **2** Raajaa kaaleejle peesaɳumaa? aamaa, peesaɳum. **3** Maalaa peeraasiriyare paakkaɳumaa? aamaa, paakkaɳum. **4** Murugan viiʈʈule irukkaɳumaa? aamaa, irukkaɳum.

Exercise 16

1 reɳɖu maɳikki porappaɖum. **2** muuɳee kaal maɳikki porappaɖum. **3** naalre maɳikki porappaɖum. **4** pattee mukkaa maɳikki porappaɖum.

Exercise 17

1 avan enge pooraan? **2** avan edule varraan? avan epɖi varraan? **3** avan ettane maɳikki peesapooraan? avan eppa peesapooraan? **4** ava ettane pustagam vaangapooraa? **5** ava evɭavu ruubaa kuɖuppaa? **6** ava yaare paappaa?

Exercise 18

1 அது. **2** ஆம். **3** இந்த. **4** ஈ **5**. உப்பு. **6** ஊசி. **7** என். **8** ஏன்.
9 ஐந்து **10** ஒரு. **11** ஓட்டல். **12** ஔஷதம்.

Unit 5

Exercise 1

1 (a) meduvaa peesunga; (b) meduvaa peesaꞃum. **2** (a) avanukku sollunga; (b) avanukku sollaꞃum. **3** (a) pinnaale ukkaarunga; (b) pinnaale ukkaaraꞃum.

Exercise 2

1 ille. **2** maaʈʈeen. **3** maaʈʈeen. **4** maaʈʈeen. **5** veeɳɖaam. **6** ille. **7** ille. **8** muɖiyaadu.

Exercise 3

paalu, ʈii, karumbu caaru, kaapi.

Exercise 4

1 Smith taamadamaa vandaan. **2** avan basle vandaan. **3** avan kaapi kuɖiccaan. **4** avaru oru kuuʈʈattukku poogaꞃum.

Exercise 5

1 ille, paɖikkale. **2** ille, peesa maaʈʈaan. **3** ille, vara maaʈʈaan. **4** ille, varale. **5** ille, irukka maaʈʈaan. **6** ille, viiʈʈule ille.

Exercise 6

1 paɖikkalaam. **2** peesalaam. **3** varalaam. **4** varalaam. **5** irukkalaam. **6** irukkalaam.

Exercise 7

1 Raajaa paɖikkiraanaa? Paaʂaa paɖikkiraanaa? reɳɖupeerum paɖikkale. **2** Raajaa peesuvaanaa? Paaʂaa peesuvaanaa? reɳɖupeerum peesa maaʈʈaanga. **3** Raajaa varuvaanaa? Paaʂaa varuvaanaa? reɳɖupeerum vara maaʈʈaanga. **4** Raajaa varraanaa? Paaʂaa varraanaa? reɳɖupeerum varale. **5** Raajaa viiʈʈule iruppaanaa? Paaʂaa viiʈʈule iruppaanaa? reɳɖupeerum irukka maaʈʈaanga. **6** Raajaa viiʈʈule irukkaanaa? Paaʂaa viiʈʈule irukkaanaa? reɳɖupeerum viiʈʈule ille.

Exercise 8

1 Raajaa paɖikkiradu enakku teriyaadu. **2** Raajaa peesuradu enakku teriyaadu. **3** Raajaa varradu enakku teriyaadu. **4** Raajaa varradu enakku teriyaadu. **5** Raajaa viiʈʈule irukkiradu enakku teriyaadu. **6** Raajaa viiʈʈule irukkiradu enakku teriyaadu.

Exercise 9

1 kaɳɖakʈargaɭ ellaarum. **2** kaaleej ellaam. **3** koʐaayellaam. **4** taragargaɭ ellaarum.

Exercise 10

1 bas denam varaadu. **2** Smith kaalele doose saapɖa maaʈʈaan. **3** Maalaa nallaa paaɖa maaʈʈaa. **4** Jaanukku Tamiʐ teriyaadu. **5** ellaarukkum iɖli pidikkaadu.

Exercise 11

1 ஆமா / அம்மா **2** இலை / இல்லை **3** புளி / புள்ளி **4** மகள் / மக்கள் **5** கனம் / கன்னம் **6** பாடு / பாட்டு **7** குதி / குத்தி.

Unit 6

Exercise 1

1 kaalele ombadare maɳikki keɭamburoom. **2** kaalele padinoru maɳikki keɭamburoom. **3** madyaanam reɳɖee mukkaa keɭamburoom. **4** madyaanam muuɳee kaal maɳikki keɭamburoom.

Exercise 2

1 Aɳi puɭiyoodareyum tayirccoorum uurugayum koɳɖuvaruvaa. **2** Melli puuri keʐangum medu vaɖeyum koɳɖuvaruvaa. **3** *Sarah* oɳɳum koɳɖuvara maaʈʈaa; paʐam vaanguradukku paɳam kuɖuppaa.

Exercise 3

1 Liilaa. **2** Lakṣmi. **3** muuṉu. **4** oru aaṉu, reṉḍu poṉṉu. **5** Mulle. **6** Mulle, Kalyaaṉi, Kumaari. **7** reṉḍu peeru. **8** Kriṣṉan. **9** paaṭṭi. **10** atte. **11** maamaa. **12** maamaa.

Exercise 4

1 b; **2** c; **3** d; **4** b; **5** d; **6** b; **7** a; **8** b

Exercise 5

1 naḍa (walk) – ooḍu (run). **2** poo (go) – vaa (come). **3** eeru (climb up, get on) – erangu (climb down, get off).

Exercise 6

1 murukku saapḍuvoom; adu valuvaa irukkum. **2** karumbu caaru kuḍippoom; adu inippaa irukkum. **3** iḍli saapḍuvoom; adu meduvaa irukkum. **4** paayasam saapḍuvoom; adu inippaa irukkum. **5** medu vaḍe saapḍuvoom; adu kaaramaavum meduvaavum irukkum. **6** rasam saapḍuvoom; adu kaaramaavum puḷippaavum irukkum. **7** tayirccooru saapḍuvoom; adu puḷippaa irukkum. **8** paẓam saapḍuvoom; adu inippaa irukkum. **9** puḷiyoodare saapḍuvoom; adu puḷippaa irukkum. **10** cappaatti kuruma saapḍuvoom; adu kaaramaa irukkum.

Exercise 7

GANAPATHY: piḷḷega mirugakkaacci saalekki pooga aasepaḍaraanga. naaḷekki kuḍumbattule ellaarum poovoom.

ARUMUGAM: naangaḷum varroom. ellaarum pooroom.

GANAPATHY: vaṉḍaluurukku neere bas irukku. basleyee poovoom.

(*In the zoo*)

KUMAAR: appaa, aaḍu, maaḍu, kudire ellaam een inge irukku. idugaḷe viiṭṭuleyee paakkalaamee?

GANAPATHY: paakkalaam. mirugakkaacci saalele ellaa mirugangaḷum irukkaṉum, illeyaa?

MALA:	maamaa, idu oru aaḍaa?
GANAPATHY:	ille, idu maanu. onga appaavukku maane patti romba teriyum. avare keeḷu.
MALA:	appaa, kaaṭṭule singam maane saapḍumee, inge enna saapḍum?
ARUMUGAM:	inge singam, pulikki aaṭṭukkari, maaṭṭukkari pooḍuvaanga.
MALA:	aaḍu, maaḍu paavam. enakku singam, puli piḍikkale.

Exercise 8

1 yaane, kudire, maaḍu, maan, puli, singam, karaḍi, aaḍu, naayi, korangu, puune. **2** puli, singam, karaḍi, naayi, puune. **3** yaanekkuṭṭi, kudirekkuṭṭi, kaṉṉukkuṭṭi, maankuṭṭi, pulikkuṭṭi, singakkuṭṭi, karaḍikkuṭṭi, aaṭṭukkuṭṭi, naaykkuṭṭi, korangukkuṭṭi, puunekkuṭṭi.

Exercise 9

Your choice of activities may, of course, be different from those given in the answers.

1 tingakkeẓame naan kaaleejukku pooveen. On Mondays I go to college. **2** sevvaakkeẓame naan viiṭṭule paḍippeen. On Tuesdays I study at home. **3** budankeẓame naan en paaṭṭiyooḍa viiṭṭukku pooveen. On Wednesdays I go to grandma's house. **4** viyaaẓakkeẓame naan viiṭṭukku saamaan vaanguveen. On Thursdays I buy things for the house. **5** veḷḷikkeẓame naan kooyilukku pooveen. On Fridays I go to the temple. **6** sanikkeẓame naan ṭi vi paappeen. On Saturdays I watch TV. **7** nyaayittukkeẓame naan ooyvu eḍuppeen. On Sundays I take a rest.

Exercise 10

1 kaalele, madyaanam, saayangaalam, raatri. **2** varuṣam, maasam, vaaram, naaḷu. **3** anju naaḷekki munnaale; oru naaḷekki munnaale; pattu naaḷekki peragu; oṉṉare naaḷekki peragu. **4** neettu kaalele, yesterday morning; naaḷekki raatri, tomorrow night; mundaanaaḷu madyaanam, on the afternoon of the day before yesterday; naaḷekkaẓiccu saayngaalam, in the evening of the day after tomorrow; iɳɳekki kaalele, this morning **5** kaalele pattu maɳikki, at ten in the morning; raatri padinoru maɳikki, at eleven at night; madyaanam oru maɳikki, at one in the afternoon; saayangaalam anju maɳikki, at five in the evening; kaalele aaru maɳikki, at six in the morning

Exercise 11

a: iɳɳekki raatri sinimaavukku poogalaamaa?
b: iɳɳekki konjam veele irukku; naaɭekki poogalaamaa?
a: nyaayittukkeʐame poovoom. aɳɳekki oru veeleyum ille.
b: enda paɖattukku pooroom?
a: nii sollu.
b: onakku tamiʐ paɖam piɖikkumaa? hindi paɖam piɖikkumaa?
a: naan tamiʐ paɖamdaan paappeen.
b: *Sun Theatre*-le oru nalla tamiʐ paɖam ooɖudu.
a: adukkee poovoom.

Exercise 12

Washington, Japan, Spain, Beijing, Assam, Moscow.

Exercise 13

1 பஸ். **2** ஜூன். **3** ஷூஸ்.

Unit 7

Exercise 1

1 Raajaa enne Cennekki pooga connaaru. **2** Raajaa enne Amerikkavukku pooga connaaru. **3** Raajaa enne peeraasiriyarooɖa pustagatte paɖikka connaaru. **4** Raajaa enne Madurele eranga connaaru.

Exercise 2

1 naan Raajaave Cennekki pooga conneen. **2** naan Raajaave Amerikkavukku pooga conneen. **3** naan Raajaave peeraasiriyarooɖa pustagatte paɖikka conneen. **4** naan Raajaave Madurele eranga conneen.

Exercise 3

1 ille, Maalaa neettu kaaleejle paaḍunaa. No, Mala sang in the college yesterday. **2** ille, Saaraa appa solla tayangunaanga. No, Sarah hesitated to say then. **3** ille, Jaan inge baslerundu erangunaan. No, John got down from the bus here. **4** ille, Murugan neettu uurukku poonaan. No, Murugan went to his home town yesterday. **5** ille, paaṭṭi neettu kade sonnaanga. No, Grandmother told stories yesterday. **6** ille, Raajaa neettu viiṭṭukku vandaan. No, Raja came home yesterday. **7** ille, Maalaa inda viiṭṭule irundaanga. No, Mala was in this house. **8** ille, Saaraa inge ukkaandaanga. No, Sarah sat here. **9** ille, ellaarum neettu raatri sinimaa paattaanga. No, everyone saw a movie last night. **10** ellaarum raatri enge paḍuttaanga? Where did everyone sleep last night? **11** yaaru yaaru inda paḍattule naḍiccaanga? Who are all those who acted in this picture?

Exercise 4

1 naan neettu ooḍuneen. **2** Raaman naaḷekki naḍappaan. **3** ava Raamane neettu paattaa. **4** niinga neettu sonniinga. **5** Lakṣmi naaḷekki paḍippaa.

Exercise 5

1 Jaanum Saaraavum sinimaavukku poonaanga. **2** Maalaavum Saaraavum Madurele irundaanga. **3** naanum Raajaavum eṭṭu maṇikkee paḍuttoom. **4** niiyum naanum Tamiẓ paḍiccoom. **5** niiyum avaḷum nidaanamaa vandiinga.

Exercise 6

1 Jaan Saaraavooḍa Madurekki vandaan. **2** Jaan Saaraavooḍa Tamiẓ paḍiccaan. **3** naan onnooḍa inda kaaleejle paḍicceen. **4** nii avaḷooḍa enge poone? **5** Maalaa Tamiẓ paaṭṭooḍa Hindi paaṭṭum paaḍunaa.

Exercise 7

1 nii Madurele irundadu enakku teriyaadu. I didn't know you had been in Madurai. **2** Kumaar viiṭṭukku vandadu enakku piḍikkale. I didn't like it that Kumar came to the house. **3** Maalaa paaḍunade yaarum enakku sollale. No one told me Mala sang. **4** nii ade solla tayangunadu saridaan. It was right that you hesitated to say that.

Exercise 8

1 Raajaa peesaama veele senjaan. Raja worked without speaking. **2** Maalaa sollaama viiṭṭukku vandaa. Mala came home without informing (anyone). **3** nii tayangaama peesu. Speak without hesitating. **4** appaa kaalelerundu saapḍaama irukkaaru. Father goes without food from the morning onwards. **5** naan onakkaaga tuungaama irundeen. I went without sleep for you. **6** niinga yaarum varaama naan poogale. Without any of you coming, I wouldn't go. **7** naan veele seyyaama irukkale. I wasn't (there) not working. **8** Kumaar enakku teriyaama sinimaavukku poonaan. Kumar went to the cinema without my knowing.

Exercise 9

1 Kumaar oru periya viiḍu vaangunaan. Kumar bought a big house. **2** oru aẓagaana poṇṇu kaaleejukku vandaa. A beautiful girl came to college. **3** ammaa renḍu meduvaana iḍli kuḍuttaanga. Mother gave two soft idlis. **4** suuḍaana kaapi kuḍu. Give (me) a hot coffee.

Exercise 10

1 koobappaḍu 'be angry, feel anger'. **2** aaseppaḍu 'desire'. **3** teeveppaḍu 'need'. **4** kavaleppaḍu 'feel sorrow, be anxious/ concerned'. **5** erakkappaḍu 'feel pity, sympathise'.

Exercise 11

9, 7, 5, 3, 2, 1, 10, 8, 6, 4

Unit 8

Exercise 1

1 paattu – paaru 'see'; **2** muḍiccu – muḍi 'finish, complete'; **3** seendu – seeru 'join'; **4** senju – seyyi 'do'; **5** pooyi – poo 'go'; **6** aarambiccu – aarambi 'begin, start'; **7** tayaariccu – tayaari 'prepare'; **8** vittu – villu 'sell'; **9** pooṭṭu – pooḍu 'put, set up'.

Exercise 2

1 Kumaar kaḍele doose vaangi viiṭṭule saapṭaan. Kumar bought a doosa in the shop and ate it at home. **2** Kumaar kaaleejukku pooyi peeraasiriyare paattaan. Kumar went to the college and saw the professor. **3** Kumaar viiṭṭukku vandu ennooḍa peesunaan. Kumar came home and spoke to me. **4** Kumaar pattu ruubaa kuḍuttu inda peenaave vaangunaan. Kumar gave ten rupees and bought this pen. **5** Kumaar paaṭṭu paaḍi ellaareyum sandooṣappaḍuttunaan. Kumar sang a song and made everyone happy. **6** Kumaar kaṣṭappaṭṭu paḍiccu paas paṇṇunaan. Kumar studied hard and passed.

Exercise 3

1 naan kaaleejukku pooneen; appa Kumaar veḷiye vandukiṭṭurundaan. I went to the college; Kumar was coming out then. **2** neettu Maalaa paaḍunaa; appa Kumaar veḷiye niṇṇukiṭṭurundaan. Yesterday Mala sang; Kumar was standing outside then. **3** ammaa kaalele doose paṇṇuvaanga; appa nii tuungikiṭṭuruppe. Mother will make dosa in the morning; you'll be sleeping then. **4** innum oru varuṣattule Kumaar kampenile veele paattukiṭṭuruppaaru. Kumar will be working in the company for one more year. **5** Maalaa paaḍraa; nii peesikiṭṭurukke. Mala is singing; you are talking. **6** Kumaar onne paaraaṭṭuraan; nii veḷiye paattukiṭṭurukke. Kumar is eulogising you; you are looking outside. **7** raatri maṇi pattu aagudu; bas innum ooḍikiṭṭurukku. It's ten o'clock at night; the buses are still running.

Exercise 4

1 Raajaa kaaleejukku pooyṭṭaan. **2** appaa pattu maṇikki paḍuttuṭṭaaru. **3** kaḍekkaaran kadave muuḍiṭṭaan. **4** ḍaakṭar palle piḍungiṭṭaaru. **5** paappaa kiiẓe viẓunduṭṭudu/viẓunduruccu. **6** enakku paṇam keḍeccuṭṭudu/keḍeccuruccu.

Exercise 5

1 appaa Laṇḍanukku pooyirukkaaru; aḍutta vaaram tirumbi varuvaaru. Father has gone to London; he'll come back next week. **2** naan nallaa paḍiccurukkeen; nalla maark vaanguveen. I've studied hard; I shall get good marks. **3** naan appaaṭṭe onakku paṇam kuḍukka solliyirukkeen; pooyi vaangikka. I've asked father to give you some money; go and get it. **4** ivan aaru maṇi neeram veele paatturukkaan; kuuḍa paṇam kuḍutturu. He's worked for six hours; give him more money. **5** naan sinna vayasule sigareṭṭu kuḍiccurukkeen; ippa viṭṭuṭṭeen. I smoked when I was young; now I've given up. **6** niinga Laṇḍan pooyirukkiingaḷaa? ille, poonadulle. Have you been to London? No, I never went there.

Exercise 6

1 neettu raatri maẓe penjurukku; tare iiramaa irukku. It must have rained last night; the ground is wet. **2** Maalaa aẓudurukkaa; ava kaṇṇu sevappaa irukku. Mala must have been crying; her eyes are red. **3** Raajaa edoo tappu paṇṇiyirukkaan; reṇḍu naaḷaa enne paakka varale. Raja must have done something wrong; he hasn't been to see me for two days. **4** Kumaar veḷeyaaḍa pooyiruppaan; avan pande kaaṇoom. Kumar must have gone to play; his ball's nowhere to be found. **5** Kumaar nallaa paḍiccuruppaan; alladu veḷeyaaḍa pooyirukkamaaṭṭaan. Kumar must have done his studies, or he wouldn't have gone to play.

Exercise 7

1 Kumaar saapṭukiṭṭurundaan; appa Umaa vandaa. Kumar was eating; Uma came then. **2** Kumaar viiṭṭukku pooyikiṭṭurundaan; vaẓile Umaave paattaan. Kumar was going home; on the way he met Uma. **3** appaa pattu maṇikki tuungikiṭṭuruppaaru; appa naama ṭi vi paakkalaam. Father will be sleeping at ten o'clock; at the time we shall watch TV.

Exercise 8

1 (a) Kumaar kaapi kuḍiccuṭṭu veḷiye vandaan. Kumar drank his coffee and then went out. (b) Kumaar kaapi kuḍiccukiṭṭee veḷiye vandaan. Kumar went while drinking his coffee. **2** (a) maamaa irumiṭṭu peesa aarambiccaaru. Uncle coughed and then began to speak. (b) maamaa irumikiṭṭee peesa aarambiccaaru. Uncle began to speak while coughing. **3** (a) ammaa tuungiṭṭu ṭi vi paakkiraanga. Mother sleeps and then watches TV. (b) ammaa tuungikiṭṭee ṭi vi paakkiraanga. Mother watches TV while sleeping. **4** (a) nii paḍiccuṭṭu veele paaru. Study and then work. (b) nii paḍiccukiṭṭee veele paaru. Work while studying. **5** (a) Madurele irunduṭṭu Jaan Tamiẓ peesa kaṣṭappaḍraaru. After being in Madurai, John has trouble in speaking Tamil. (b) Madurele irundukiṭṭu Jaan Tamiẓ peesa kaṣṭappaḍraaru. While in Madurai, John has trouble in speaking Tamil.

Exercise 9

Moohan sinimaavukku pooyikiṭṭirundaan. vaẓile Raajaave paattaan. avan bassukkaaga kaattukiṭṭirundaan. avanooḍa avan tambi Kumaarum niṉṉukiṭṭurundaan. Kumaare Moohan oru taḍave kaaleejule paatturukkaan. Moohan sinimaavukku reṇḍu ṭikkeṭ vaangiyirundaan. Raajaaveyum sinimaavukku kuupṭaan. Raajaa tambiye basle viiṭṭukku anuppiṭṭu sinimaavukku vara ottukiṭṭaan. reṇḍu bassu nikkaama pooyiruccu. sinimaavukku neeram aagikiṭṭurundudu. Raajaa tambi kayyile pattu ruubaa kuḍuttu basle pooga colliṭṭu Moohanooḍa keḷambunaan. tambi paṇatte vaccukiṭṭu bassukkaaga niṉṉaan. Moohanum Raajaavum veegamaa naḍandaanga. sariyaana neerattukku sinimaavukku pooyiṭṭaanga.

Mohan was going to the cinema. On the way he met Raja. He was waiting for a bus. His younger brother Kumar was standing there with him. Mohan had seen Kumar once in college. Mohan had bought two tickets for the cinema. He invited Raja (to go with him) to the cinema. Raja agreed to send his brother home by bus and go to the cinema. Two buses went by without stopping. It was almost time for the cinema. Raja handed his brother ten rupees, told him to take the bus and set off with Moohan. Taking the money, the younger brother waited for the bus. Mohan and Raja walked quickly. They arrived at the cinema on time.

Exercise 10

1 Elections in Tamil Nadu in the month of March. **2** Terrible railway accident in Assam. **3** India win cricket match.

Unit 9

Exercise 1

1 varra ṭaaksi. A taxi's coming. The taxi that's coming. **2** Raaman neettu paḍicca patrikke. Raman read a newspaper yesterday. The newspaper that Raaman read yesterday. **3** Lakṣmi vanda bas. Lakshmi came by bus. The bus Lakshmi came by. **4** naan Goovindanukku kuḍutta paṇam. I gave Govindan some money. The money I gave Govindan.

Exercise 2

1 paambu (snake) – the others are all birds. **2** maambaẓam (mango) – the others are all vegetables. **3** nari (fox) – the others are all domesticated animals. **4** arisi ((uncooked) rice) – the others are all cooked items. **5** kuṭṭi (the young of an animal) – the others are all verbs.

Exercise 3

1 Kumaar viiṭṭukku vandu pustagam keeṭṭaan. Kumar came home and asked for a book. **2** Sundar pudu saṭṭe pooṭṭukiṭṭu veḷiye keḷambunaan. Sundar put on a new shirt and went out. **3** Raajaa peenaave toleccuṭṭu aẓudaan. Raja cried after losing his pen. **4** naan keeḷvi keeṭṭu avan padil sollale. When I asked a question, he didn't answer. **5** Umaa naaḷekki kaaleejukku vandu ange onne paappaa. Uma will come to college tomorrow and see you there. **6** Murugan kaṇṇe muuḍikiṭṭu epḍi kaare ooṭraan? How can Murugan drive the car with his eyes closed?

Exercise 4

1 neettu paḍicca kade romba nallaa irundudu. The story I read yesterday was very good. **2** neettu vaanguna pustagam romba vele. The book I bought yesterday was very expensive. **3** naan eḍuttukiṭṭa paṇam enga appaa paṇam. The money I took was our father's money. **4** naan paḍikkira kaaleej romba duurattule irukku. The college I study in is a long way off. **5** naan paḍiccukiṭṭurukkira paaḍam kaṣṭamaa irukku. The lesson I am studying is very difficult. **6** naan sonna veeleye senjuṭṭiyaa? Did you do the work I told you? **7** naan solra veeleye siikram seyyi. Do the work I'm telling you (to do) quickly. **8** naan keekkira odaviye nii kaṭṭaayam seyyaṇum. You must certainly do the favour I'm asking of you.

Exercise 5

1 engiṭṭe Laṇḍanle Tamiẓ paḍiccavanga Indiyaavukku vandurukkaanga. The English people who studied Tamil with me in London have come to India. Those who studied Tamil with me in London have come to India. **2** engiṭṭe Tamiẓ paḍiccavaru Amerikkaavule irukkaaru. Jim who studied Tamil with me is in America. The man who studied Tamil with me is in America. **3** bas-sṭaaple nikkiravaḷe engeyoo paatturukkeen. I've seen the girl who is standing at the bus stop somewhere. I've seen the one who is standing at the bus-stop somewhere. **4** enakku piḍiccade inge saapḍa muḍiyale. I can't eat the food I like here. What I like, I can't eat here.

Exercise 6

1 naan kaaleejukku basle poonadu kaṣṭamaa irundudu. My going to college by bus was troublesome. **2** naan kaaleejukku kaarle pooradu nallaa irukku. My going to college by car is good. **3** naan nalla maark vaangunade aasiriyar paaraaṭṭunaaru. The teacher complimented me on getting good marks. **4** naan uurukku pooradukku aasiriyar anumadi kuḍuttuṭṭaaru. The teacher gave me permission to go home. **5** naan onne patti aasiriyarṭṭe sonnadule enna tappu? What was wrong in my telling the teacher about you? **6** naan paṇatte tiruppi keeṭṭadunaale avanukku koobam. He got angry because of my asking for the money back.

Exercise 7

1 tambikki vayiru valikkidaam. The younger brother has stomach ache. It appears the younger brother has stomach ache. **2** Raajaa amerikkaavukku pooraanaam. Raja's going to America. They say Raja's going to America. **3** inda veelekki irubadu ruubaa aagumaam. This work will come to twenty rupees. It seems this work will come to twenty rupees. **4** inda pustagam eranuuru ruubaayaam. This book is two hundred rupees. I gather this book is two hundred rupees. **5** naan senjadu tappaam. What I did was wrong. They say that what I did was wrong. **6** Moohan Ingilaandulerundu vandurukkaanaam. Mohan has come back from England. I hear Mohan has come back from England. **7** nii niccayam parisu vaanguviyaam. You'll certainly get a prize. They say you'll certainly get a prize. **8** puunekki pasikkidaam. The cat's hungry. It seems the cat's hungry. **9** Kumaar appaaṭṭe enne patti enna sonnaanaam? What did Kumar say about me to father? What is Kumar supposed to have said about me to father?

Exercise 8

Raajaa paḍicca vaguppuledaan Raaṇiyum paḍiccaa. maark vaanguradule reṇḍu peerukkum pooṭṭi. Tamiẓ aasiriyarṭṭe nuuttukku arubadu maarkkukku meele vaangurudu romba kaṣṭam. avaru Tamiẓ ilakkiyam nereya paḍiccavaru. ilakkiya varigaḷe apḍiyee kaṭṭurele eẓuduradu avarukku romba piḍikkum. Raajaavum Raaṇiyum kaṣṭappaṭṭu paḍiccaanga. tuungura neeram tavira matta neeram ellaam paḍikka selevaẓiccaanga. adu terinja Tamiẓ aasiriyar avangaḷe romba paaraaṭṭunaaru. vaguppule irukkira ellaareyum avanga paḍikkira maadiri kaṣṭappaṭṭu paḍikka sonnaaru.

Rani too studied in the same class as Raja. The two of them competed to get marks. Getting more than sixty marks out of a hundred from the Tamil teacher was very difficult. He was very well read in Tamil literature. Writing literary quotations in an essay was very much to his liking. Raja and Rani studied hard. They used all the time they had apart from sleeping time for study. The Tamil teacher, who got to know about that, praised them for it. He told all those in the class to study hard in the way they did.

Exercise 9

1 (d); **2** (c); **3** (a); **4** (b)
(a) grain of rice; (b) cash-box/safe; (c) silk cloth; (d) prescription

Unit 10

Exercise 1

1 Stephen kalyaaṉattukku poonaan. **2** avanga kalyaaṉattukku munnaale peesale. **3** anda kaalattule paakkiradukuuḍa ille. **4** payyanum poṇṇum oree maadiri kuḍumba suuẓnelele vaḷandadu.

Exercise 2

1 payyanum poṇṇum kalyaaṉattukku munnaale oruttare oruttar paattukaanga. **2** avanga kalyaaṉattukku munnaale oruttarooḍa oruttar peesikiṭṭaanga. **3** Jaanum Raajaavum oruttarukku oruttar pustagam koḍuttukiṭṭaanga.

Exercise 3

1 (i) (B) I tried to give the cat some milk, but it didn't drink it. (ii) (A) I was about to give the cat some milk, but there wasn't time. **2** (i) (A) I tried to read this novel, but it's not a good one. (ii) (B) I meant to read this novel, but mother didn't let me. **3** (i) (B) I tried to give Mala a piece of advice, but she wouldn't listen. (ii) (A) I was going to give Mala a piece of advice, but she wasn't around. **4** (i) (B) The dog tried to climb on to the wall, but it couldn't. (ii) (A) The dog was going to climb on to the wall, but I dragged it off. **5** (i) (A) Kumar tries to drink some wine, but he can't. (ii) (B) Kumar tries to drink some wine, but he's also scared.

Exercise 4

Raajaa tannooḍa paḍicca Maalaave kalyaaṉam paṇṇikiḍa aaseppaṭṭaan. aanaa avanooḍa appaa adukku ottukiḍale. taan paatturukkira poṇṇe kalyaaṉam paṇṇikiḍa sonnaaru. Raajaa tan ammaaṭṭe tan aaseye sonnaan. avangaḷukku Maalaave piḍikkum. ava appaaṭṭe paṇam romba ille; aanaa avaḷooḍa kuḍumbam romba nalla kuḍumbam. adunaale avangaḷukku avaḷe piḍikkum. maganooḍa aaseye appaaṭṭe solli avaḷe ottukiḍa vaccaanga. Raajaavukku oree sandooṣam.

Raja wanted to marry Mala, who studied with him. But his father didn't agree to it. He told him (Raja) to marry the girl that he himself had selected. Raja told his mother about his wish. She liked Mala. Her father didn't have much money, but her family was a good one (i.e. well thought of). So she liked her. She told his father of her son's wish and got him to agree. Raja was very happy.

Exercise 5 (Audio 2: 17)

enakku kalyaaṉam aagi oru maasam kuuḍa aagale. Laṉḍanle naḍandudu. en manevi *Jackie*-um naanum oree kaaleejule paḍiccoom. reṇḍu peerum modalle kaaleejule olagattulerundu marenjikiṭṭurukkira mirugangaḷe patti naḍanda oru kuuṭṭattule paattoom. adukku peragu sandikkirappa anda maadiri viṣayaangaḷe patti peesunoom. engagiṭṭa pala viṣayaanga poduvaa irundudu. enga reṇḍu peeru kuḍumbamum mattiyadara (*middle class*) kuḍumbam. kalyaaṉam paṇṇikiḍra eṇṇattule oru varuṣam *dating* poonoom. oruttare oruttar nallaa purinjikiṭṭa peragu kalyaaṉam paṇṇikiḍa muḍivu senjoom. appaa ammaaṭṭe solliṭṭu *church*-ule kalyaaṉam paṇṇikiṭṭoom.

Exercise 6 (Audio 2: 18)

kuḍumbattule kaṉavan manevikki eḍele kasappu varradukku ettaneyoo kaaraṉam irukku. paṇam selevaḷikkiradulerundu piḷḷegaḷe vaḷakkiradu vare evḷavoo viṣayattule karuttu veerubaaḍu varalaam. veele paakkira eḍattule varra piraccaneyaale viiṭṭule oruttar meele oruttar ericcal paḍalaam. ipḍipaṭṭa viṣayangaḷaale manastaabam perusaagi vivaagarattule muḍiyalaam. aarambattuleyee kaṉavanum maneviyum oruttarukku oruttar viṭṭukuḍuttu vittiyaasangaḷe eettukiḍradu oṉṉudaan kuḍumbattule sandooṣattukku vaẓi.

Exercise 7

1 P; **2** C; **3** N; **4** R; **5** M; **6** E; **7** S; **8** T; **9** J; **10** A

Unit 11

Exercise 1

CHEZHIAN: naandaan vandu vandu onne paakkaɳumaa? nii enne paakka varakkuuɖaadaa?

ANBAN: on arekki vara evɭavoo muyarcci paɳɳuneen. muɖiyale. oree veele.

CHEZHIAN: apɖi enna veele, naɳbane kuuɖa paakka muɖiyaama?

ANBAN: periya periya taɳikkekkaaranga talame aluvalagattulerundu vandurukkaanga enga aluvalagattukku. avanga keeɭvigaɭukku padil tayaar paɳɳi vaccuʈʈu viiʈʈukku vara raatri pattu, padinooru maɳi aaccu. oru vaaram idee maadiridaan.

CHEZHIAN: onakku on veeleye viʈʈaa veere olagamee keɖeyaadu. sari. *stereo*-e pooɖu. Rahmaanooɖa paaʈʈe keeppoom.

Exercise 2

1 naan paale viʈʈaa veere oɳɳum kuɖikka maaʈʈeen. I won’t drink anything other than milk. **2** Maalaavukku Kamalaave viʈʈaa veere yaareyum piɖikkaadu. Mala doesn’t like anyone other than Kamala. **3** en tambi iɖliye viʈʈaa veere eduvum saapɖamaaʈʈaan. My younger brother won’t eat anything other than idli. **4** enga ammaa Madureye viʈʈaa veere enda uurukkum poonadulle. Apart from Madurai, our mother hasn’t been anywhere. **5** mannippu keekkirade viʈʈaa veere vaʐi ille. There’s no way out other than to apologise.

Exercise 3

1 Raajaa Kumaarʈʈe solli solli paattaan; avan keekkale. Raja tried to tell Kumar time and again; he wouldn’t listen. **2** Raajaa kadave terandu terandu paattaan; muɖiyale. Raja kept trying to open the door; he couldn’t. **3** Raajaa paɳatte tiruppi tiruppi kuɖuttaan; kumaar vaangale. Raja kept offering to give the money back; Kumar wouldn’t take it.

Exercise 4 (Audio 2: 22)

YOU:	neettu Indiyaavukkum Bangḷadeeṣukkum naḍanda *football match*-e paattiingaḷaa?
FRIEND:	*T V*-le paatteen. *half-time*-ukku peragudaan paakka muḍinjudu.
YOU:	adukku peragudaan aaṭṭam romba viruviruppaa irundudu.
FRIEND:	kaḍesi pattu nimiṣattule daane Indiyaa oru *goal* pooṭṭudu. paakka vanda kuuṭṭam naḍandukiḍrade paakkiradum veeḍikkeyaa irundudu.
YOU:	aamaa. adu uurukku uuru vittiyaasapaḍum. Kalkattaavule romba ragaḷe naḍakkum.
FRIEND:	Laṇḍanleyum apḍidaan. *police* vandudaan kuuṭṭatte aḍakkaṇum.
YOU:	jananga *emotional*-aa engeyum ipḍidaan naḍakkiraanga.

Exercise 5

1 naan viiṭṭukku varradukkuḷḷe, avan pooyṭṭaan. He had left before I came home. **2** appaa aapiisukku pooradukkuḷḷe, avarooḍa peesuveen. I shall speak to father before he goes to the office. **3** naan keeḷviye keeṭṭu muḍikkiradukkuḷḷe, ava padil solliṭṭaa. She had answered before I finished asking the question. **4** naan naaye kaṭṭi vakkiradukkuḷḷe, tabaalkaararu uḷḷe vanduṭṭaaru. The postman had come in before I had tied up the dog.

Exercise 6

1 ille, maalaa kaṣṭappaṭṭaa. **2** ille, ammaa paaṭṭu keeṭṭaanga. **3** ille, suuriyan marenjudu. **4** ille, tambi veele senjaan. **5** ille, cakkaram veegamaa uruṇḍudu. **6** ille, puli maane koṇṇudu. **7** ille, maaḍu teruvule ooḍuccu.

Exercise 7

1 aamaa, paatteen. **2** aamaa, paḍicceen. **3** aamaa, naḍandeen. **4** aamaa, senjeen. **5** aamaa, saapṭeen. **6** aamaa, keeṭṭeen. **7** aamaa, aẓudeen. **8** aamaa, kaṇḍeen. **9** aamaa, uruṇḍeen. **10** aamaa, koṇṇeen.

Exercise 8

1 Lakshmi Lodge. **2** Meals ready. **3** Raja Hotel. **4** Pizza Corner.

Unit 12

Exercise 1

1 ennooḍa uuru Cidambaram. **2** ennooḍa uuru Cikkaagoo. **3** ennooḍa uuru Koẕumbu. **4** ennooḍa uuru Laṉḍan. **5** ennooḍa uuru Kocci. **6** ennooḍa uuru Paaris. **7** ennooḍa uuru Kiyooṭṭoo. (*Note*: In all cases, **en** or **enga** may be substituted for **ennooḍa**. Kochi (Cochin) is in Kerala.)

Exercise 2

1 enakku pasikkira maadiri irukku. I'm sort of hungry. **2** veḷiye maẕe peyra maadiri irukku. It looks like it's raining outside. **3** pakkattu viiṭṭule yaaroo paaḍra maadiri irukku. I've a feeling someone's singing in the house next door. **4** raatri maẕe penja maadiri irukku. It appears that it rained during the night. **5** appaa kaarle vanda maadiri irukku. It appears father came by car.

Exercise 3

1 (d) Walk quickly. **2** (c) a fast walk, a fast gait. **3** (b) Sing beautifully. **4** (e) beautiful song. **5** (f) Answer correctly. **6** (a) correct answer.

Exercise 4

டாக்டர் தொழில் மக்களுக்கு சேவை செய்கிற தொழில். அது இப்போது வியாபாரமாக ஆகிக்கொண்டிருக்கிறது. டாக்டர் பணம் பண்ண(க்) கூடாது என்று சொல்லவில்லை. பணத்தை எடுத்துவைத்தால்தான் வைத்தியம் பார்ப்பேன் என்று சொல்ல(க்) கூடாது.

இப்போது புது(ப்) புது வியாதி எல்லாம் வருகிறது. அதை(ப்) பற்றி எவ்வளவோ ஆராய்ச்சி நடக்கிறது. அதை(ப்) படித்து தெரிந்துகொண்டால் புது வியாதிகளை முழுதாக புரிந்துகொள்ள முடியும்; புது சிகிச்சை முறைகளை(ப்) பயன்படுத்த முடியும் என்று நினைக்கிறேன். அதற்கு டாக்டர் நேரம் ஒதுக்க வேண்டும்.

வியாதியை(க்) குணப்படுத்த எந்த மருத்துவ முறையில் நல்ல வழி இருந்தாலும் அதை எடுத்துக்கொள்ள வேண்டும் . . .

Exercise 5

1 naaḷekki kaaleej irundaa Kumaar Umaa viiṭṭukku pooga maaṭṭaan. If there's college tomorrow, Kumar won't go to Uma's

house. **2** Maalaa sinimaavukku vandaa Raajaa sinimaavukku
varuvaan. If Mala comes to the cinema, Raja will come to the
cinema. **3** appaa Madurekki poonaa tavaraama kooyilukku
poovaaru. If father goes to Madurai, he will without fail go to the
temple. **4** Ramees̩ nalla maark vaangan̩um-naa kas̩t̩appat̩t̩u
pad̩ikkan̩um. If Ramesh wants to get good marks, he'll have to
work hard at his studies. **5** naan sonnadu tappu-nnaa enne
manniccuru. Excuse me if what I said was wrong.

Exercise 6

1 naal̩ekki kaaleej ille-naa Kumaar Umaa viit̩t̩ukku poovaan.
If there's no college tomorrow, Kumar will go to Uma's house.
2 Maalaa sinimaavukku varale-nnaa Raajaa sinimaavukku
varuvaan. If Mala doesn't come to the cinema, Raja will come
to the cinema. **3** appaa Madurekki poogale-nnaa appaa
kooyilukku pooga mud̩iyaadu. If father doesn't go to Madurai,
he won't be able to go to the temple. **4** Ramees̩ nalla maark
vaanga veen̩d̩aam-naa enda neeramum vel̩eyaad̩ikkit̩t̩urukkalaam.
If Ramesh doesn't need to get good marks, he'll be able to play
all the time. **5** naan sonnadu sari ille-nnaa enne manniccuru.
Excuse me if what I said was not right.

Exercise 7

1 naal̩ekki kaaleej ille-nnaalum Kumaar Umaa viit̩t̩ukku pooga
maat̩t̩aan. Even if there's no college tomorrow, Kumar won't go
to Uma's house. **2** Maalaa sinimaavukku vandaalum Raajaa
sinimaavukku vara maat̩t̩aan. Even if Mala comes to the cinema,
Raja won't come to the cinema. **3** appaa Madurekki poonaalum
kooyilukku pooga maat̩t̩aaru. Even if father goes to Madurai,
he won't go to the temple. **4** Ramees̩ nalla maark vaangan̩um-
naalum kas̩t̩appat̩t̩u pad̩ikka maat̩t̩aan. Even though Ramesh
wants to get good marks, he won't work hard at his studies.

Unit 13

Exercise 1

1 (a) The cat is smaller than the dog. (ii) The dog is bigger than
the cat. **2** (b) My younger brother is taller than me. (iv) I am
shorter than my younger brother. **3** (c) Our house is closer to the
college than yours. (v) Your house is further away from the

college than ours. **4** (d) English is more difficult than Tamil. (i) Tamil is easier than English. **5** (e) I am cleverer than anyone. (iii) No one is cleverer than me.

Exercise 2

1 (a) Sarah speaks Tamil better than I do. (v) Sarah speaks Tamil better than me. **2** (b) He has studied more than you have studied. (iii) He has studied more than you. **3** (c) Father knows more about Madurai than I know. (i) Father knows more about Madurai than me. **4** (d) It rains more in Kodaikanal than it rains in Madurai. (ii) It rains more in Kodaikanal than in Madurai. **5** (e) Mother tells stories better than you do or I do. (iv) Mother tells stories better than you or me.

Exercise 3

1 (a) inda viiḍu anda viiṭṭe viḍa perusu. This house is bigger than that house. (b) anda viiḍu inda viiṭṭe viḍa sirusu. That house is smaller than this house. **2** (a) maaḍi viiḍu ooṭṭu viiṭṭe viḍa oyaram. The storeyed house is higher than the tiled house. (b) ooṭṭu viiḍu maaḍi viiṭṭe viḍa oyaram korevu. The tiled house is less high than the storeyed house. **3** (a) inda maram anda maratte viḍa perusu. This tree is bigger than that tree. (b) anda maram inda maratte viḍa sirusu. That tree is smaller than this tree. **4** (a) laari basse viḍa baankukku pakkattule nikkidu. The lorry is parked closer to the bank than the bus. (b) bas laariye viḍa baankukku duurattule nikkidu. The bus is parked further from the bank than the lorry. **5** (a) ivan naḍakkirade viḍa avan veegamaa naḍakkiraan. This man is walking faster than that one. (b) avan naḍakkirade viḍa ivan meduvaa naḍakkiraan. That man is walking more slowly than this one. **6** (a) inda maratte viḍa anda marattule ele romba irukku. There are more leaves on that tree than on this tree. (b) anda maratte viḍa inda marattule ele korevaa irukku. There are fewer leaves on this tree than on that tree.

Exercise 4

(Note that (depending, for instance, on an individual's assumed age) in the answers that follow, avan and avaru are mutually substitutable for male persons, and avaḷ and avanga for females.)

1 (a) ava Japaan. (b) ava Japaankaari. (c) ava Japaaniyan. **2** (a) avan Jermani. (b) avan Jermankaaran. (c) avan Jermaniyan. **3** (a) avan Ittaali. (b) avan Ittaalikkaaran. (c) avan Ittaaliyan. **4** (a) avanga Fraansu. (b) avanga Frencukkaaranga. (c) avanga Frencu. **5** (a) ava Amerikkaa. (b) ava Amerikkaakkaari. (c) ava Amerikkan. **6** (a) avaru Fraansu. (b) avaru Frencukkaararu. (c) avaru Frencu. **7** (a) avanga Singapuur. (b) avanga Singapuurkaaranga. (c) avanga Singapuuriyan. **8** (a) avaru Maleeşiyaa. (b) avaru Maleeşiyaakkaararu. (c) avaru Maleeşiyan. **9** (a) avanga Skaaţlaandu. (b) avanga Skaaţlaandukkaaranga. (c) avanga Briţiş.

Exercise 5

HE: (*Approaching you with a smile*) inge pakkattule *post office* irukkaa?
YOU: irukku. ongaļukku Karpagam teru teriyumaa?
HE: teriyaadu. naan inda pakkam idukku munnaale vandadulle.
YOU: sari. inda teruvule neere poonga. oru *municipal school* varum. ange eḍadu pakkam tirumbunga. adu daan Karpagam teru. *Post office* ange daan.

Exercise 6

YOU: naan are maņi neerattule rayile piḍikkaņum. vaẓi tappiţţeen. rayilvee sţeeşan ingerundu evļavu duuram?
HE: oru kiloomiiţţar irukkum. inda eḍattulerundu ange pooga ongaļukku bas ille.
YOU: veegamaa pooga kurukku vaẓi irukkaa?
HE: kurukku vaẓile poogalaam. pattu mimişattule sţeeşanukku pooyiralaam.
YOU: vaẓile kuuţţam illaama irukkumaa? veegamaa naḍakka muḍiyumaa?
HE: ippa madyaanam illeyaa? teruvule kuuţţam irukkaadu. siikkiram poonga.

Exercise 7

1 vaaẓeppaẓam vaanguradukku maambaẓam vaangalaam. It is preferable to buy mangoes than to buy bananas. **2** basle pooradukku aaţţoorikşaavule poogalaam. Going by autorickshaw is preferable to going by bus. We shall go by by autorickshaw instead of by bus. **3** puu pooṭṭa saṭṭekki nuuru ruubaa kuḍukkiradukku kooḍu pooṭṭa saṭṭekki nuutti irubadu ruubaa kuḍukkalaam. Giving 120 rupees for the striped shirt is preferable to giving 100 rupees for the flowered shirt. **4** 'tinandoor̲um'-ukku 'iḷamai uuñjalaaḍugir̲adu' nalla paḍam. 'iḷamai uuñjalaaḍugir̲adu' is a better film than 'tinandoor̲um. **5** kalyaaṇattukku eepril reṇḍaam teedikki maarccu pattombadaam teedi nallaa irukku. March 19th is a better (= more auspicious) day for the wedding than April 2nd.

Exercise 8 (Audio 2: 32)

ḍaakṭar, enakku aḍikkaḍi talevali varudu. mukkiyamaa, vaguppukku pooradukku munnaale varudu. vaguppule irukkirappa talevali adigamaagudu. naanaa kaḍe maattire vaangi saapṭeen. keekkale. adunaale ongagiṭṭe vandeen.

Doctor, I often get a headache. Mainly it comes before I go to a class. When I'm in the class it gets worse. I bought some tablets by myself in the shop and took them. They didn't work. So I came to you.

Exercise 9 (Audio 2: 33)

YOU:	inda marundu enge keḍekkum?
ASSISTANT:	veḷiye valadu pakkam naalaavadu kaḍe marundu kaḍe. ange ellaa marundum keḍekkum.
YOU:	(*To the pharmacist*) ḍaakṭar inda marunde ez̲udi kuḍutturukkaaru. irukkaa?
PHARMACIST:	irukku. . . . indaanga.
YOU:	ḍaakṭar kayyez̲uttu puriyale. oru naaḷekki ettane maattire saapḍaṇum?
PHARMACIST:	kaalele oṇṇu, madyaanam oṇṇu, raatri oṇṇu, saappaaṭṭukku peragu.

Exercise 10

1 No smoking. **2** Inject children against polio. **3** Prevent AIDS. **4** One is enough (i.e. one child per family).

Unit 14

Exercise 1

kalyaaṇam

KUMARAN: en kalyaaṇam enga appaavukku munnaale naḍandadu.
SIVAA: adeppaḍi?
KUMARAN: avaru kalyaaṇa meeḍaikku munnaale uṭkaarndaaru.

sinimaa

PAARVATI: nii enda sinimaa kaḍecile paattee?
LAṬCUMI: naan enda sinimavum modallerundu paappeen.

Exercise 2

1 aasiriyar pustagamaa vaangunaaru. The teacher bought a book. The teacher bought lots of books. **2** avaḷukku parisaa keḍeccudu. She won a prize. She won stacks of prizes. **3** avan paẓamaa saapṭaan. He ate a banana. He ate piles of bananas. **4** ammaa nalla kadeyaa solluvaanga. Mother tells a good story. Mother tells no end of good stories. **5** tambi poyyaa solraan. Younger brother tells lies. Younger brother tells one lie after another.

Exercise 3

1 aasiriyar nereya pustagam vaangunaaru. **2** avaḷukku nereya parisu keḍeccudu. **3** avan nereya paẓam saapṭaan. **4** ammaa nereya nalla kade solluvaanga. **5** tambi nereya poy solraan.

Note: 'romba' can be substituted for 'nereya' in each case.

Exercise 4

1 Who came after/later than her? Who came after/behind her? **2** You go first./You go before (me). You go first./You go in front (of me). **3** Come before ten o'clock. Come in front of the house. **4** Come by ten o'clock. Come inside the house. **5** She sat down last. She sat down at the end (of the row). **6** She'll come to the class first. She'll come first in the class.

Exercise 5

PEERAN: paaʈʈi, veyilule enna kaayudu?
PAAʈʈI: saappiɖa keeppe.
PEERAN: keekka maaʈʈeen, paaʈʈi. sollu. naan ippadaan saapʈeen.
PAAʈʈI: illeɖaa, idu saapiɖra keeppe.

'keepekki' reɳɖu arttam. oɳɳu 'you will ask'; innoɳɳu 'millet'. paaʈʈi sonnadu 'millet'; peeran purinjukiʈʈadu 'you will ask'. ipɖi tappaa purinjukiʈʈadu sirippaa irukku.

Exercise 6

1 kumaar ammaavukkaaga paɳam anuppunaan. Kumar sent the money for mother's sake. **2** kumaar yaarukkaaga ide kuɖuttaan? For whose sake did Kumar give this? **3** kumaar veelekkaaga vandaan. Kumar came for the sake of the job.

Exercise 7

1 maalaavukkaaga nii een ide seyre? Why are you doing this for Mala's sake? **2** enakkaaga nii vaa. Come for my sake. **3** naan solradukkaaga nii vaa. Come for the reason that I told you to. **4** veelekkaaga nii engenge poogapoore? Where are all the places you are going to in search of work? **5** yaarukkaaga nii inge kaatturukke. Who are you waiting here for?

Exercise 8

1 ongaɭukku enna aase? What is your desire? What do you want? **2** ongaɭukku enna kaʂʈam? What's your trouble? What's troubling you? **3** ongaɭukku enna koobam? What are you angry about? Why are you angry? **4** ongaɭukku enna tayakkam? What's your hesitation? Why are you hesitating? **5** ongaɭukku enna piraccane? What's your problem?

Exercise 9

1 enakku aase oɳɳum ille; enakku oru aaseyum ille. I don't want anything. **2** enakku kaʂʈam oɳɳum ille; enakku oru kaʂʈamum ille. Nothing's troubling me. **3** enakku koobam oɳɳum ille; enakku oru koobamum ille. I'm not angry. **4** enakku tayakkam oɳɳum ille; enakku oru tayakkamum ille. I'm not hesitating. **5** enakku piraccane oṇṇum ille; enakku oru piraccaneyum ille. I don't have a problem.

Exercise 10

On hearing Chezhiyan, who is a Tamil speaker, use the word 'naaykkuṭṭi' for 'puppy', Singh works on the assumption that 'kuṭṭi' is used in a similar way for the young of all animals. He therefore produces a compound word, 'maaṭṭukkuṭṭi' for 'calf', that does not exist in Tamil – to the great amusement of Chezhiyan. Producing an English translation is difficult because it is almost impossible to produce similar erroneous forms in English.

Exercise 11

1 yaanekkuṭṭi. **2** pulikkuṭṭi. **3** kiḷikkunji. **4** paambukkuṭṭi. **5** elikkunji. **6** kaẓudekkuṭṭi. **7** kaakkaakkunji.

Exercise 12

1 The donkey brays. **2** The tiger growls. **3** The monkey chatters. **4** The cock crows. **5** The crow caws. **6** The elephant trumpets. **7** The fox barks.

Unit 15

Exercise 1

1 naan tuungaada neeram konjam. The time when I don't sleep is little. **2** enakku piḍikkaada paaṭṭu inda sinimaavule eduvum ille. There's no song in this film that I don't like. **3** naan sollaada veeleye en tambi seyyamaaṭṭaan. My younger brother will not do work that I have not told (him to do). **4** paḍikkaada neerattule naan paaṭṭu keeppeen. At times when I am not studying, I listen to songs. **5** idu ellaarum seyya muḍiyaada veele. This is work that no one can do.

Exercise 2

1 neettu vaguppukku varaadavanga yaaru? Who are the ones who did not come to the class yesterday? **2** eṇṇekkum oru vaartte peesaadava iṇṇekki meedele peesunaa. One who never says a word spoke on the platform today. **3** avaḷukku piḍikkaadavane kalyaaṇam paṇṇikiḍa sonnaanga. They told her to marry someone she does not like. **4** avarukku piḷḷe illaadadu enakku teriyaadu. I did not know about his not having children.

Exercise 3

1 ava paḍikkaadadu yaarukkum piḍikkale. No one liked her not studying. **2** nii ide vaangaadadukku oru kaaraṇam irukkaṇum. There must be a reason for your not buying this. **3** ippa maẓe peyyaadadu nalladu. It's good that it's not raining now. **4** raajaa paṇatte tiruppi keekkaadadudaan aaccariyam. It's surprising that Raja doesn't ask for the money back. **5** uurukku poogaadadunaale enakku paṇam naṣṭam. Because of not going home, I lost money.

Exercise 4

1 appaa sonna peragu Kumaar paḍikka aarambiccaan. Kumar began to study before father told (him to). Kumar began to study after father told (him to). **2** Maalaa keeṭṭa peragu Raajaa paṇam kuḍuttaan. Raja gave the money before Mala asked (for it). Raja gave the money after Mala asked (for it). **3** bas niṇṇa peragu taattaa erangunaaru. Grandfather got off before the bus stopped. Grandfather got off after the bus stopped. **4** kaapi aaruna peragu ammaa kuḍippaanga. Mother drinks coffee before it has cooled. Mother drinks coffee after it has cooled. **5** taattaa saapṭa peragu konja neeram tuunguvaaru. Grandfather sleeps for a short while before eating. Grandfather sleeps for a short while after eating.

Exercise 5

1 (a) appaa solradukkuḷḷe kumaar paḍikka aarambiccaan. (b) appaa sonna oḍane kumaar paḍikka aarambiccaan. **2** (a) maalaa keekkiradukkuḷḷe raajaa paṇam kuḍuttaan. (b) maalaa keeṭṭa oḍane raajaa paṇam kuḍuttaan. **3** (a) bas nikkiradukkuḷḷe taattaa erangunaaru. (b) bas niṇṇa oḍane taattaa erangunaaru.

4 (a) kaapi aarradukkuḷḷe ammaa kuḍippaanga. (b) kaapi aaruna oḍane ammaa kuḍippaanga. **5** (a) taattaa saapḍradukkuḷḷe konja neeram tuunguvaaru. (b) taattaa saapṭa oḍane konja neeram tuunguvaaru.

Exercise 6

1 naan kaaleejule paḍiccappa ittane bas ille. When I was studying at college, there weren't this many buses. **2** naan kaaramaa saappiṭṭappa kaṇṇule taṇṇi vandudu. When I ate something hot, my eyes watered. **3** naan kumaarṭṭe paṇam keeṭṭappa avan kuḍukkale. When I asked Kumar for money, he didn't give it. **4** naan kaaleejukku poorappa vaẓile onne paakkireen. I'll see you on the way when I go to college. **5** naan naaḷekki kumaare paakkirappa avan enakku pustagam kuḍuppaan. Kumar will give me a book when I see him tomorrow.

Exercise 7

1 naan kaaleejule irunda varekkum Kumaar varale. As long as I was in college, Kumar didn't come. **2** naan kaaleejule paḍicca varekkum appaa paṇam kuḍuttaaru. Until I studied in college, Father gave me money. **3** enakku anda viṣayam teriyra varekkum naan kavaleppaḍale. Until I got to know about this matter, I did not worry. **4** naan saapḍra varekkum ava saapḍa maaṭṭaa. He won't eat till I eat. **5** naan varra varekkum nii viiṭṭuleyee iru. Stay in the house until I come.

Exercise 8

1 pulinnaa oru mirugam. **2** iḍlinnaa oru saappaaḍu. **3** maamaannaa ammaavooḍa aṇṇan alladu tambi.

Exercise 9

1 paḍapaḍappu 'fluttering'. **2** veduveduppu 'the state of being lukewarm'. **3** kadakadappu 'warmth'. **4** kurukuruppu 'irritation'. **5** viruviruppu 'excitement', 'tempo'.

Exercise 10

1 naaḷekki maẓe peyyumaa-nnu Raajaa enne keeṭṭaan. Raja asked me, 'Will it rain tomorrow?' **2** maẓeyile naneyaade-nnu Raajaa engiṭṭe sonnaan. Raja said to me, 'Don't get wet in the rain.' **3** maẓe evḷavu neeramaa peyyudunnu Raajaa engiṭṭe keeṭṭaan. Raja asked me, 'How long has it been raining?' **4** maẓeyile naneyakkuuḍaadu-nnu ammaa solluvaanga-nnu Raajaa engiṭṭe sonnaan. Raja said to me, 'Mother always says, "Don't get wet in the rain".' **5** naaḷekki maẓe peyyum-nu reeḍiyoovule sonnaanga-nnu appaa sonnaar-nu Raajaa engiṭṭe sonnaan. Raja said to me, 'Father said, "They said on the radio, it will rain tomorrow".'

Exercise 11

1 taan keṭṭikkaaran-nu raajaa sonnaan. Raja said that he was clever. **2** taanum naanum keṭṭikkaaranga-nnu raajaa sonnaan. Raja said that he and I were clever. **3** naanum Maalaavum enge pooroom-nnu Raajaa keeṭṭaan. Raja asked where Mala and I were going. **4** naan enge pooreen-nu tan tambi keekkiraan-nu Raajaa sonnaan. Raja said that his younger brother was asking where I was going. **5** naan enge pooreen-nu en tambi keekkiraan-nu tan tangacci solraa-nnu Raajaa sonnaan. Raja said that his sister said that my brother was asking where I was going.

Exercise 12

1 veele nereya irundadaa Jaan sonnaaru. John said that he had a lot of work. **2** roojaa puutturukkiradaa tooṭṭakkaaran solraan. The gardener says that the rose had blossomed. **3** Maalaa sinimaavule naḍikkapooradaa ellaarum solraanga. Everyone says that Mala was going to act in films. **4** Maalaa kaaleejukku varradaa yaarum sollale. No one said that Mala was coming to college. **5** veele nereya irundadaa Jaan sonnadaa Baarbaraa sonnaanga. Barbara said that John said he had a lot of work.

Exercise 13

1 Kumaar nallaa paḍiccurundaa nalla maark vaangiyiruppaan. If Kumar had studied well, he would have got good marks. **2** appaa Madurekki pooyirundaa kooyilukku pooyiruppaaru.

If father had gone to Madurai, he would have gone to the temple. **3** nii engiṭṭe mannippu keeṭṭurundaa naan aasiriyarṭṭe solliyirukka maaṭṭeen. If you had apologised to me, I would not have spoken to the teacher. **4** nii pattu maṇikki vandurundaa naan tuungiyirukka maaṭṭeen. If you had come at ten o'clock, I shouldn't have gone to sleep. **5** taattaa kaḍekki pooga muḍinjirundaa patrikke vaangiyiruppaaru. If grandfather had been able to go to the shop, he would have bought a newspaper.

Exercise 14

When the bus got into Mudumalai, there was a loud bang. As soon as the bus stopped, everybody got down in a rush and ran. My heart palpitated. When I too ran behind them, (I found) they were staging a contest for elephants. To start it off they had let off firecrackers. In the race an elephant calf running with short quick steps came first. In the grabbing the ball game, an elephant grabbed the balls one by one in a flash. In the tug-of-war game, an elephant unbelievably quickly pulled the hundred people on the other side over the line in a minute. All the events were very lively.

Unit 16

Exercise 1

A wound caused by burning will heal, but a scar caused by a sharp tongue will not heal.

Exercise 2

Forgetting a good thing (that someone has done) is not good; something which is not good – it is good to forget it on that very day.

Exercise 3

1 kooyilukku naḍakkirade viḍa niinga aaṭṭoole poogalaam.
2 ṭi vi paakkirade viḍa naama sinimaavukku poogalaam.
3 kaapi kuḍikkirade viḍa niinga juus kuḍikkalaam.

Exercise 4

1 adu kanniyaakumarile naḍandudu. **2** pattirikke paḍikkaadadunaale Smith-ukku viẓaave patti teriyale. **3** veḷinaaṭṭulerundu vanda ariñargaḷum peesunaanga. **4** ange peesunavanga ilakkiya tamiẓle peesunaanga. **5** sele Tamiẓ paṇpaaṭṭin aḍippaḍeye kaaṭṭudu.

Exercise 5

1 ஆண்டு – varuṣam. **2** மாதம் – maasam. **3** நாள் – teedi. **4** திருமணம் – kalyaaṇam. **5** நடைபெறு – naḍa.

Exercise 6

சித்திரை	mid-April to mid-May
வைகாசி	mid-May to mid-June
ஆனி	mid-June to mid-July
ஆடி	mid-July to mid-August
ஆவணி	mid-August to mid-September
புரட்டாசி	mid-September to mid-October
ஐப்பசி	mid-October to mid-November
கார்த்திகை	mid-November to mid-December
மார்கழி	mid-December to mid-January
தை	mid-January to mid-February
மாசி	mid-February to mid-March
பங்குனி	mid-March to mid-April

Exercise 7

1 Lakṣmi sittire maasam naalaam teedi Kanniyaakumarikki kaarle poonaa. **2** appaa aani anjaam teedi Cengattukku vænle poonaaru. **3** John tay aaraam teedi Cennekki kappalle poonaan. **4** Melli panguni eeẓaam teedi Madurekki ṭreynle poonaa. **5** Raajaavum Moohanum juun eṭṭaam teedi Laṇḍanukku vimaanattile poonaanga. **6** naan poona maasam ombadaam teedi kaaleejukku saykkiḷḷe pooneen. **7** naanum Kumaarum aḍutta maasam pattaam teedi Tiruvaṇṇaamalekki basle poovoom.

Exercise 8

enga naaṯṯule kristumas oru periya paŋḏige. appa pani penjirukkum. kristumas maram maṯṯum pacceyaa irukkum. adule sondakaarangaḻukkum naŋbarkaḻukkum kuḏukkira parisugaḻe kaṯṯivaccuruppoom. kristumas taattaa anda parisugaḻe koŋḏuvandu vaccadaa nambikke. adunaale kristumas-naa piḻḻegaḻukku oru kuṣi.

Exercise 9

Tamiẓnaaṯṯu kooyilgaḻe patti naan sinna vayasule paḏiccurukkeen. ade paakka enakku romba naaḻaa aase. kooyille irukkira sirpatte paakkiradu maṯṯum ille. saadaaraŋa janangaḻooḏa vaaẓkkele kooyilukku enna eḏam-nu paakkavum aase. enga naaṯṯule jananga carccukku pooradu romba korenju pooccu. adooḏe, kooyille paaṯṯu kacceeri irukkum-nu keeḻvipaṯṯurukkeen. ade keekkavum aase.

Tamil–English glossary

A note on the Tamil–English glossary

Though there is an accepted alphabetical order for Tamil, the order followed here – on the grounds of simplicity – is that of the roman alphabet as used for English. Some modification is needed to account for the special letters used for 'retroflex' consonants. Each of these follows the English letter that it most resembles. This gives the following order: **a**, **æ**, **b**, **c**, **d**, **ḍ**, **e**, **f**, **g**, **h**, **i**, **j**, **k**, **l**, **ḷ**, **m**, **n**, **ṇ**, **o**, **p**, **r**, **s**, **ṣ**, **t**, **ṭ**, **u**, **v**, **y**, **z**, **ẓ**.

For verbs the present and past tense suffixes are given in parentheses, since on the basis of these it is possible to predict all other verb forms. Where this information may seem insufficient, the full past or present stem is given. Verbs that can take only a neuter or inanimate subject present a slight problem here, in that present tense forms lack the **-r-** that is found with other subjects. So for 'strong' verbs, present tense here is indicated by **-kk-** (rather than **-kkir-**). In the case of 'weak' verbs, it is the lack of any overt sign of tense that indicates present tense for neuter subjects. This absence of a tense marker is shown below by a 'zero' (-Ø-) or, in the case of stems ending in **-i** or **-e**, by the linking consonant **-y-**.

Where a noun or pronoun has a different stem for 'non-subject' forms, this is indicated. There is one exception to this: all nouns ending in **-am** can be assumed to have a 'non-subject' stem ending in **-att-**, and this is therefore not separately indicated.

The numbers indicate the unit in which the word is introduced. Where there is no number the word in question appears in an exercise devised expressly for the tape that accompanies the book.

Abbreviations: adj(ective), fem(inine), masc(uline), intr(ansitive), tr(ansitive), subj(ect).

A

aa(gu) (-r-, -n-)	become, be 3
aaccariyam	surprise 15
aaccee	is it not (equivalent to the tag question form **illeyaa**) 7
aaccu	happened 5
aadaravu	support 10
aaḍi	the name of the fourth month in the Tamil calendar 16
aaḍu (aaṭṭ-)	goat, sheep 7
aaḍu (-r-, -n-)	play (a game) 11
aafiis/aapiis	office 11
aafiisar	officer 8
aaḷu	man, person 15
aamaa	yes 1
aanaa	but 10
aani	the name of the third month in the Tamil calendar 16
aaṇ	man (**aaṇgaḷ** 'men') 10
aaraaycci	research 12
aarambam (-kkir, -cc-)	beginning, start 6
aarambi (-kkir, -cc-)	begin, start 8
aaru	six 2
aaru (-Ø-, -n-)	cool off 15, heal (intr) 16
aase	desire (noun) 11
aaseppaḍu (-r-, -ṭṭ-)	desire (verb) 11
aasiriyar	teacher 9
aaṭci	government 9
aaṭṭam	game 11
aaṭṭoo/ aaṭṭoorikṣaa	autorickshaw 2
aaṭṭook-kaaranga(ḷ)	autorickshaw drivers 2
aaṭṭukkari	mutton 6
aavaṇi	the name of the fifth month in the Tamil calendar 16
aayiram	thousand 2
adee maadiri	likewise, in the same manner 7
adigam	much 5
adigamaagu (-ø-, -n-)	get worse 13
adu	that, it 1
aduga(ḷ)	they (neuter) 1
adunaale	because of that, so, therefore 5
aḍa	expression of surprise 8
aḍakku (-r-, -n-)	control, subdue 11
aḍa paavamee	what a pity 5
aḍi (-kkir-, -cc-)	hit, beat 2
aḍikkaḍi	often 13
aḍippaḍai/ aḍippaḍe	core, basis 16
aḍutta	next 9
akkaa(ḷ)	elder sister 2
alaral	scream 7
alaru (-r-, -n-)	scream 7
ale (-yr-, -nj-)	run around, wander 8
alladu	or 3
aluvalagam	office 11
aḷavu	measurement 9
aḷavu saṭṭe	model shirt (for measurement) 9
ambadu	fifty 2
ame (-kkir-, -cc-)	make, set up 16

Amerikkaa USA 7
ammaa mother 5
anal heat, fire
anda that, those (adj) 1
ange there 1
aniyaayam unfairness, injustice 9
anju five 2
anumadi approval, permission 8
anuppu (-r-, -n-) send 7
aṇṇan elder brother 2
aṇṇekki on that day, then 1
apḍi like that, so 4
appa then 1
appaa father 6
appaa ammaa parents 10
appḷikeeṣan application 7
aranuuru six hundred 2
arasaangam government 8
are half 4
are room 11
ariñargaḷ scholars 16
arisi rice (uncooked) 3
arivippu announcement
arivu knowledge 9
arttam meaning, sense 13
aruvadu sixty 2
attane that many 1
atte aunt 6
ava(ḷ) she 1
avan he 1
avanga(ḷ) they, she (polite) 1
avaru he (polite) 1
avasiyam necessity, essential 10
avḷavu that much, so much 7
aynuuru five hundred 2
ayppasi the name of the seventh month in the Tamil calendar 16
aẓagaana beautiful 5
aẓagu beauty 5
aẓu (-r-, -d-) cry, weep 7

B

baanku/bænk bank 11
balan benefit 4
Bangḷadeeṣ Bangladesh 11
bas/bassu bus 4
bayam/payam fear 7
bayangaram/ payangaram something terrible 7
biic/biiccu beach 1
bi ii B(achelor of) E(ngineering) 7
biins beans 3
billu bill, invoice 3
biriyaaṇi biryani 13
boorḍu board 4
Britiṣ British 13
budankeẓame Wednesday 6

C

caaru juice 1
cakkaram wheel 11
cakkare sugar 3
cappaatti chapati 6
carc/carccu church 10
caṭni chutney 3
cekku cheque 7

Cenne	Chennai (the capital city of Tamil Nadu) 1
Cidambaram	Chidambaram (name of a town) 3
ciiṭṭukkaṭṭu	pack of playing cards 6
cinna/sinna	small 5
cinnammaa	mother's younger sister 6
cirpam	sculpture 15
cittappaa	father's younger brother 6
citti	mother's younger sister 6
collu (colr-, conn-)/sollu	say 2
cooru/sooru	rice 6
Cooḻarkaalam	the period of Chola dynasty 15

D

denam	daily 6
doose	dosa (a pancake made of fermented rice and black gram flour) 3
duuram	distance 9
ḍaaktar	doctor 8
ḍaalar	US dollar 7
ḍras	garment, dress, clothing 8

E

edirpakkam	opposite side 15
edu	what (pronoun), which thing 3
eduraa	against 10
eḍadu	left (side) 4
eḍam	place, seat 4
eḍele	between, among 10
edirpaaru (-kkir-, -tt-)	expect, wait for
eḍu (-kkir-, -tt-)	take, pick up 1
ee si	AC (air conditioned) 2
eemaattu (-r-, -n-)	cheat 2
een	why 4
eer leṭṭar	air letter 3
eeru (-r-, -n-)	climb, get on (a vehicle) 6
eettukiḍu (-r-, -ṭṭ-)	accept 10
eettumadi	export 8
eeḻu	seven 2
eli	rat, mouse 9
ellaam	all 5
ellaarum	all (humans) 2
embadu	eighty 2
en	my 1
enda	which (adj) 3
enga(ḷ)	our 1
enge	where 3
engeyoo	somewhere 5
enna	what 2
eṇṇe	oil 3
eṇṇekki	on what day, when 4
eṇṇuuru	eight hundred 2
epḍi	how 3
eppa	when 3
eppavum	always 5
erakkam	pity, sympathy 7
erakkumadi	import (noun) 8
erakkumadi seyyi (seyr-, senj-)	import (verb) 8

erangu (-r-, -n-)	climb down, get off (a vehicle) 6
eranuuru	two hundred 2
ere (-kkir-, -cc-)	draw (water from a well) 5
ericcal	annoyance 10
ettane	how many 2
eṭṭu	eight 2
eva(ḷ)	which (female) person 2
evan	which (male) person 2
evanga(ḷ)	which persons 2
evaru	which (male) person (polite) 2
evḷavu	how much 3
eyḍs	AIDS 13
eẓanuuru	seven hundred 2
eẓudi kuḍu (-kkir-, -tt-)	prescribe 13
eẓudu (-r-, -n-)	write 5
eẓuttu	writing, letter 12
eẓuvadu	seventy 2

F

faaram/paaram	form 4
fayil	file 8
Fraansu	France 13
Frencukkaaran	Frenchman 13

G

graam	gram 3

H

haloo	hello 13
Hindi/Indi	Hindi 14
hooṭṭal/ooṭṭal	hotel, restaurant 1

I

idoo	look here, here it is 2
idu	it, this 1
iduga(ḷ)	they (neuter) 1
iḍli	steamed cake made from ground rice and black gram 3
ii	fly 4
iiram	dampness, wetness 8
ilakkiyam	literature 5
Ilange	Sri Lanka 11
illaadadu	not being, something which is not 16
illaama	without 7
ille	no, not 2
inda	this, these (adj) 1
Indi/Hindi	Hindi 14
Indiya	Indian (adj) 10
Indiyaa	India 8
inge	here 1
Ingilaandu	England 8
Ingliṣ	English 1
ini (-kk-, -cc-)	be sweet 1
inippu	sweetness 6
inji	ginger 5
inlaaṇḍ	inland letter form 3
innoru	another 2
innum/innom	still, yet 5
iṇṇekki	today 1
ipḍi	like this, in this manner 2

ipḍipaṭṭa	this sort of 10
ippa	now 1
iru (-kk-, -nd-)	be, have, wait 2
iruṭṭu (-Ø-, -in-)	get dark 15
iruvadu	twenty 2
Ittaali	Italy 13
iva(ḷ)	she 1
ivan	he 1
ivanga(ḷ)	they 1
ivaru	he (polite) 1
ivḷavu	this much 1
iẕu (-kkir-, -tt-)	pull 15

J

jallikkaṭṭu	bullfight, bull-running
jananga(ḷ)	people 2
Japaan	Japan 13
Jermani	Germany 13
juram	fever 6
juulay	July 6
juun	June 6
juus	juice 3

K

kaa (-kkir-, -tt-)	wait 8
kaa(y) (-Ø-, -nd-)	become heated up, become dry 14
kaadalan	lover (masc) 13
kaadali	lover (fem) 13
kaaḍu (kaaṭṭ-)	forest, jungle 7
kaakkaa	crow 14
kaal	quarter 4
kaaleej	college 4
kaalu	leg 5
kaaṇoom	not to be found, missing 5
kaaṇu (kaangr-, kaṇḍ-)	see (restricted to a few object nouns like **kanavu**) 7
kaapi	coffee 3
kaaram	hotness, pungency 6
kaaraṇam	reason 15
kaaru	car 2
kaarttige	the name of the eighth month in the Tamil calendar 16
kaattiru (-kk-, -nd-)	wait 2
kaattu	wind, breeze
kacceeri	concert, recital 16
kadavu	door 8
kade	story 7
kaḍalkare	beach, sea shore 6
kaḍe	shop 4
kaḍekkaaran	shopkeeper 7
kaḍesi	end 14
kaḍesile	finally 14
kaḍidam	letter (mail) 12
kalainigaẕcci/ kale-	cultural programme 16
kalandukiḍu (-r-, -ṭṭ-)	take part 12
Kalkattaa	Calcutta 11
kalyaaṇam	marriage, wedding, married life 10
kalyaaṇam paṇṇu (-r-, -n-)	marry 10
kaḷeppaa	tired 5
kaḷeppu	tiredness 5
kaḷḷu	toddy 14
kampeni	company, firm 8
kana	a lot of, many 12

kanam	heaviness 5
kanavu	dream 7
kanavu kaaṇu (kaangr-, kaṇḍ-)	have a dream 7
kanivaana	kind
kanivu	kindness, tenderness
kannam	cheek 5
Kanniyaakumari	Kanya Kumari/ Cape Comorin 16
kaṇakku	calculation, account 3
kaṇavan	husband 10
kaṇḍa	any (indiscriminately) (*lit.* that you see) 13
kaṇḍakṭar	bus conductor 5
kaṇṇu	eye 7
kaṇṇukkuṭṭi	calf 14
kappal	ship 16
karaḍi	bear 6
karaṇṭ	electricity, power 8
kari	meat 7
karumbu	sugar cane 1
karuttu	opinion 10
kasa (-kk-, -nd-)	be bitter, have a bitter taste 9
kasappu	bitterness 10
kaṣṭam	difficulty, suffering 7
kaṣṭappaḍu (-r-, -ṭṭ-)	suffer 7
kattarikkaa(y)	brinjal, aubergine, egg plant 3
kaṭṭaayam	certainty, certainly 9
kaṭṭu (-r-, -n-)	fasten, tie, pay 8
kaṭṭuppaaḍu	control 8
kaṭṭure	essay 9
kavale	sorrow, concern 7
kavaru	envelope, cover 3
kayiru (kayitt-)	rope 15
kayyeẓuttu	handwriting, signature 13
kayyi	hand 4
kaẓi (-kkir-, -cc-)	subtract 8
kaẓude	donkey 14
kaẓuvu (-r-, -n-)	wash 4
keḍe (-kk-, -cc-)	get, be available (with dative subj) 1
keeḷu (keekkir-, keeṭṭ-)	ask, ask for 6; hear, listen 7; work, be effective (e.g. a medicine) 13
keeḷvi	question 9
keeḷvipaḍu (-r-, -ṭṭ-)	hear about, hear tell 16
keeppe	millet 14
keḷambu (-r-, -n-)	start, set out, leave 6
keṇaru (keṇatt-)	well 5
keṭṭikkaaran	clever person (masc) 6
keṭṭikkaari	clever person (fem) 6
keṭṭupoo (-r-, -n-)	be ruined 10
keẓame	day of the week 6
keẓangu	potato curry, root vegetable 6
kiiẓe	down, below 8
kiloo	kilogram 3
kiloomiiṭṭar	kilometre 2
kiḷi	parrot 14
kiraamam	village 7

kiṭṭattaṭṭa	about, approximately 10
kiẓi (-y-, -nj-)	tear (intr, and hence with neuter subj only) 9
klinik	clinic (where one consults a doctor) 13
kodi (-kk-, -cc-)	boil (intr) 13
kodikka vay (vakkir-, vacc-)	boil (tr), make boil 13
koḍale peraṭṭ-ikiṭṭu vaa (varr-, vand-)	feel nauseous 13
koḍalu	intestine 13
koḍam	pot 7
koḍumepaḍuttu (-r-, -n-)	ill-treat, make suffer 10
kollu (kolr-, koṇṇ-)	kill 7
koḷam	irrigation tank or lake 14
konjam	a little, some, somewhat 1
kombu	horn (of a cow)
koṇapaḍuttu (-r-, -n-)	cure, treat 12
koṇḍuvaa (-varr-, -vand-)	bring 6
koobam	anger 7
koodume	wheat 3
kooḍi	crore, ten million 16
kooḍikaṇakkaa	in crores, in tens of millions 16
kooḍu	line, stripe 13
kooṭṭu	coat, jacket 9
kooyil	temple 11
kooẓi	hen, fowl 14
korangu	monkey 6
kore/korevu	shortage, lack 14
kore (-Ø-, -nj-)	diminish, lessen 16
kosu	mosquito 7
koẓaa(y)	tap, faucet 5
koẓande	child 13
Koẓumbu	Colombo 11
krikeṭ	cricket 13
kristumas	Christmas 16
kristumas taattaa	Father Christmas 16
kudi (-kkir-, -cc-)	jump 5
kudire	horse 6
kuḍi (-kkir-, -cc-)	drink 1
kuḍu (-kkir-, -tt-)	give 2
kuḍumbam	family 10
Kumbakooṇam	name of a town 15
kuni (-r-, -nj-)	bend down 7
kunju	young one (generally of birds) 14
kurukku teru	cross street 13
kurukku vaẓi	short cut 13
kurumaa	thick spiced sauce with potato and other vegetables or meat 6
kuṣi	jollity, bubbling enthusiasm 16
kuṭṭe	short(ness) 13
kuṭṭi	child, young of an animal 15
kuuḍa	even 5
kuuḍa-perandavanga(ḷ)	siblings 6
kuuḍaadu	must not 11
kuuḍu (-r-, -n-)	gather, come together, meet 7

kuuḍum can, be possible 11
kuupḍu (-r-, -ṭ-) call, invite 6
kuuṭṭam crowd, meeting 5
kuuṭṭikiṭṭuvaa (-varr-, -vand-) bring along 6

L

laaḍj lodge, modest hotel 13
laari lorry, truck 13
Laṇḍan London 3
laṭcam lakh, 100,000 16
leesaa slightly 12
leesu light (in weight), easy 13
liṭṭar litre 2

M

maadiri manner; like, as, as if 9
maaḍi viiḍu storeyed house 13
maaḍu (maaṭṭ-) ox, bull, any bovine creature 6
maale/maalai afternoon 6
maamaa uncle 6
maambaẓam mango 3
maamuul bribe 2
maangaa(y) mango (unripe) 3
maanu deer 6
maaṇavan student (male) 1
maaṇavi student (female) 1
maargaẓi the name of the ninth month in the Tamil calendar 16
Maariyamman goddess of rain 7
maark mark 9
maaru (-r-, -n-) change (intr) 10
maasam month 5
maasi the name of the eleventh month in the Tamil calendar 16
maattire tablet 13
maattu (-r-, -n-) change (tr) 10
maaṭṭ- will not 5
maaṭṭukkari beef 6
maavu flour 3
maayamaa without a trace 7
Madure Madurai, a major city in Tamil Nadu 3
madyaanam afternoon (from noon till about 4 p.m.) 6
maḍamaḍa onomatopoeic word for speed 15
maga(ḷ) daughter 5
magan son 5
magiẓcci happiness 1
makkaḷ people 12
Malayaaḷam Malayalam 12
Malayaaḷi Malayalee 12
Maleṣiyaa Malaysia 13
manappaanme attitude 10
manastaabam difference of mind, misunderstanding 10
manasu mind, heart 15
mandiri minister 8
manevi wife 10
manni (-kkir-, -cc-) excuse, forgive, pardon 5

mannippu	forgiveness, pardon 1
manram	hall, auditorium 16
maṇi	hour, time 4
mara (-kkir-, -nd-)	forget 5
maram	tree, wood 2
mare (-r-, -nj-)	disappear 7
marundu	medicine, pharma-ceuticals 8
marundu kaḍe	pharmacy 13
maruttuvam	medical practice, medical treatment 12
masaalaa	spice, curry made of potatoes and ground spices 3
masaalaa vaḍe	savoury snack made of yellow split pea flour and deep fried 6
matta	other 2
mattapaḍi	otherwise 16
mattavanga(ḷ)	others 7
mattiyadara	middle class 10
maṭṭum	only 2
Maysuur	Mysore 15
maẓe	rain 8
maẓe kaalam	rainy season, monsoon 8
maẓe piḍi (-kk-, -cc-)	start to rain heavily 15
medu	soft 6
medu vaḍe	savoury snack made of black gram flour and deep fried 6
meduvaa	softly, gently, slowly 6
meduvaana	soft 6
Meḍraas	Madras (now Chennai) 1
meeḍe	platform, dais, stage 14
meele	on, above 10
meese	table 4
Meriinaa	Marina 1
meḷagaa(y)	chilli 3
miiṭṭar	meter; metre 2
mikka	very, extremely 13
mirugakkaacci saale	zoological garden 6
mirugam	animal 6
modal	first 4
modalle	at first 15
mogam	face 7
mooru	buttermilk 1
moosamaana	bad, of poor quality 8
more	system 12
moẓi	language 15
Mudumale	Mudumalai 15
muḍi (-kkir, -cc-)	finish 8
muḍi (-y-, -nj-)	be over 8
muḍivu	decision 10
muḍivu seyyi (-r-, senj-)	decide 10
muḍiyaadu	cannot 4
muḍiyum	can, be able, be possible 4
muguurttam	in a wedding ceremony, the main event of tying the taali 16
mukkiyam	that which is important 13

mukkiyamaa	particularly, mainly, chiefly 13
mundaanaaḷu	day before yesterday 6
munnaale	before, in the front 2
munnuuru	three hundred 2
munpaṇam	advance 5
muppadu	thirty 2
murukku	a snack (shaped like pretzel) 1
muuccu	breath 7
muuḍu (-r-, -n-)	close 13
muuṇu	three 2
muyarci	effort, attempt 12
muyarci paṇṇu (-r-, -n-)	try 11
muẓusaa	completely 8
muẓusum	whole, all 9

N

naakku/naa	tongue 16
naalu	four 2
naaḷekaẓicci	day after tomorrow 6
naaḷekki	tomorrow 5
naaḷu	day (24 hours) 2
naama(ḷ) (nam-)	we (inclusive) 1
naan (en-)	I 1
naanga(ḷ) (enga(ḷ)-)	we (exclusive) 1
naanuuru	four hundred 2
naappadu	forty 2
naaval	novel 10
naayi	dog 6
naaykkuṭṭi	puppy 14
naḍa (-kkir-, -nd-)	walk 1
naḍattivay (-vakkir-, -vacc-)	conduct (something for it to stay on) 10
naḍattu (-r-, -n-)	run, conduct, organise 8
naḍe	walk, gait 12
naḍi (-kkir-, -cc-)	act 7
naḍippu	acting 7
nalla	good 3
nallaa	well, good 4
nalladu	good, good thing; fine 2
nambar	number 4
nanme	goodness, benefit 9
nanri	gratitude, thanks 5
naṇban	friend 16
nari	fox 14
naṣṭam	loss 15
neeram	time 2
neere	straight, directly 4
neettu	yesterday 6
nellu	paddy, rice as a crop 3
nereya	in plenty, in great numbers 7
niccayam	certainty 10
nidaanam	composure, calmness 5
nidaanamaa	leisurely, unhurriedly 5
nigaẓcci	happening, event 15
nii (on-)	you (singular) 1
niinga(ḷ) (onga(ḷ)-)	you (plural and polite) 1
nillu (nikkir-, niṇṇ-)	stop, stand 4
nimiṣam	minute 4

nongu/nungu	kernel of the tender palmyra fruit before it ripens 14
noẓe (-r-, -nj-)	enter, go into 15
Nungam-baakkam	Nungambakkam, an area in Chennai 2
nuul	book 16
nuulu	thread 7
nuuru	hundred 2
nyaayittuk-keẓame	Sunday 6

O

odaḍu	lip 2
odavi	help 5
odukku (-r-, -n-)	set aside, allocate 12
oḍambu	body, health 8
oḍane	immediately, at once; (as a conjunction) as soon as 15
oḍe (-kkir-, -cc-)	break (tr) 10
oḍe (-y-, -nj-)	break (intr) 10
olagam	world 9
oli	sound 4
oḷi (-kkir-, -cc-)	hide, conceal 8
oḷi (-r-, -nj-)	hide (oneself) 8
ombadu	nine 2
on	your (singular) 1
onga(ḷ)	your (plural) 1
oṇṇare	one and a half 4
oṇṇu	one 2
oṇṇum	anything 6
ooḍu (-r-, -n-)	run 6
ooramaa	along, along the edge of 6
ooṭṭal	hotel, restaurant 1
ooṭṭalkaaran	hotel man (clerk, owner, etc.) 2
ooṭṭam	run (noun) 6
ooṭṭappandayam	running race 15
ooṭṭu (-r-, -n-)	drive 9
ooyvu	rest, relaxation 1
oppandam	contract, agreement 8
ore	commentary 16
oree	too much, excessive 5
oru	one (adj) 2
oruttar	one person, someone 16
oruttar + oruttar	each other (The first **oruttar** takes a case marker.) 10
ottukiḍu (-r-, -ṭṭ-)	agree, accept 8
oṭṭu (-r-, -n-)	stick, paste 3
ovvoruttaru	everyone 6
oyaraam	height 16
oyin	wine 10
oẓeppu	hard work 5
oẓi (-kkir-, -cc-)	eradicate 10
oẓi (-y-, -nj-)	be eradicated 10

P

paadi	half 8
paadukaappu	protection, conservation 15
paaḍam	lesson 9
paaḍu (-r-, -n-)	sing 7
paalu	milk 1
paambu	snake 5
Paaṇḍiyan	Pandian, name of a train 4
paappaa	child, baby 8

paaraaṭṭu congratulation, appreciation 5
paaraaṭṭu (-r-, -n-) appreciate, congratulate, praise 5
paaru (paakkir-, paatt-) see, meet; look up; check, try 2
paas paṇṇu (-r-, -n-) pass 8
paattukka (-kiḍur-, kiṭṭ-) take care, look after 8
paaṭṭi grandmother 6
paaṭṭu song 7
pacce green 5
padil answer 9
padimuuṇu thirteen 2
padinaalu fourteen 2
padinaaru sixteen 2
padinanju fifteen 2
padineeẓu seventeen 2
padineṭṭu eighteen 2
padinoṇṇu/-oru eleven 2
paḍaada paaḍu paḍu (-r-, -ṭṭ-) suffer excessively 14
paḍam picture 7
paḍi (-kkir-, -cc-) read, study 7
-paḍi according to, as 8
paḍippi (-kkir-, -cc-) teach 12
paḍippu education 7
paḍu (-kkir-, -tt-) lie down, go to sleep 7
paḍu (-r-, -ṭṭ-) experience, undergo 7
paḍu (-Ø-, paṭṭ-) sound, seem 10
pagalu daytime 6
pagudi part, portion, area 15
pakkam side, towards, in the direction of, nearby 4
pakkattu viiṭṭuk-kaararu next-door neighbour 6
pakkattule nearby 13
pala many, several
pallu tooth 8
pandayam contest, competition 15
pandu ball 8
panemaram palmyra tree 14
panguni the name of the twelfth month in the Tamil calendar 16
pani snow, dew, mist 16
panireṇḍu twelve 2
paṇam money 6
paṇḍige (religious) festival 16
paṇṇu (-r-, -n-) do, make 7
paṇpaaḍu culture 16
paravaayille does not matter, all right 2
paricce examination 6
parisu award, prize 5; gift 16
parundu kite (bird) 16
pasi hunger 9
pasi (-kk-, -cc-) be hungry (dative subj; neuter ending on verb) 9
pasu cow 5
patrikke, pattirigai newspaper 9
patti about, concerning 5
pattombadu nineteen 2
pattu ten 2
paṭṭu silk 9
payam fear 10
payan usefulness 12

payanpaḍuttu (-r-, -n-)	use 12
payyan	boy, son 5
payyi	bag 4
paẓagu (-r-, -n-)	be used to, be accustomed, be trained 10
paẓakkam	custom, practice, familiarity 7
paẓam	fruit 6
paẓeya	old 1
pæṇṭs	pants, trousers 9
peeccu	speech 7
peenaa	pen 2
peeraasiriyar	professor 1
peeran	grandson 6
peeru	name 1
peeru	person (when preceded by a numeral) 5
peesu (-r-, -n-)	talk, speak 5
peetti	granddaughter 6
peṇ	woman (**peṇgaḷ** 'women') 10
peragu	then, afterwards, after 4
peraṭṭu (-r-, -n-)	churn 13
periya	big 5
periyamma	mother's elder sister 6
periyappa	father's elder brother 6
pettavanga	parents 10
peṭrool	petrol, gas 2
pey (-y-, -nj-)	fall (of rain, dew or snow) 8
piḍi (-kk-, -cc-)	like (with dative subj) 5
piḍi (-kkir-, -cc-)	grasp, catch, be tight 4
piḷaaṭfaaram	platform (railway)
pinnaale	behind, in the back 2
piraccane	problem 8
piramaadam	excellent, splendid 11
pirayaaṇam	journey, travel
pirayaaṇi	passenger, traveller
poduvaa	commonly, generally 10
poge	smoke 13
poge piḍi (-kkir-, -cc-)	smoke (tobacco) 13
pongal	a sweet rice dish 3
poṇṇu	girl, daughter, bride 6
poo (-r-, -n-)	go 1
poodaadu	(it's) not enough/ sufficient 2
poodum	(it's) enough, sufficient 2
pooḍu (-r-, -ṭṭ-)	put, make 3
poola	like, as if
poolis-kaaranga(ḷ)	police officers 2
pooliyoo	polio 13
poona	last (e.g. year) 9
pooṭṭi	competition, match 9
porappaḍu (-r-, -ṭṭ-)	set off, leave 4
poru (-kkir-, -tt-)	bear with, put up with 10
porume	patience 8
poruttam	suitability, being a good fit 9
poy/poyyi	lie, untruth 9
pudiya	new 5
pudu	new 9
Puducceeri	Pondichery 3

pudusu	new thing 3
puli	tiger 6
pulikuṭṭi	tiger cub 14
pullu	grass 7
puḷi	tamarind 3
puḷippu	sourness 6
puḷiyoodare	rice cooked with tamarind powder or juice 6
puḷḷi	dot 1
puṇṇu	wound 16
puraavum	all, entire 11
puraṭṭaasi	the name of the sixth month in the Tamil calendar 16
puriyaadu	not understand (with dative subj) 5
puriyum	understand (with dative subj) 5
pustagam	book 1
puttimadi	advice 10
puu	flower 4
puune	cat 6
puunekkuṭṭi	kitten 14
puuri	flat unleavened wheat bread that is deep fried 3
puẓukkam	humidity, sultriness

R

raatri	night 6
ragaḷe	boisterousness, disturbance, fracas 11
rasam	a kind of soup with a basis of tamarind or lime water 6
rayilu	train 13
rayilvee sṭeeṣan	railway station 2
reḍi	ready 11
reṇḍu peerum	both (people) 5
rippeer	repair 2
risarveeṣan	reservation 2
romba	very; very much 1
rusi	taste 15
rusiyaa(na)	tasty 15
ruubaa(y)	rupee (basic unit of Indian currency) 2
ruum	room 2

S

saadaa	ordinary, not special (short for **saadaa-raṇa(m)**) 3
saadaaraṇam	ordinary, common 2
saamaan	thing, provisions 3
saambaar	sauce made of yellow split peas and spices 3
saapḍu (-r-, saapṭ-)	eat 1
saappaaḍu (saapaaṭṭ-)	food, meal 6
saar	sir, a term of address 2
saayangaalam	evening 1

saivam vegetarian, vegetarianism 7
samaaɭi (-kkir-, -cc-) manage, handle 10
samam equality, equity 10
samayal cooking 3
samayam time; (as a conjunction) when 15
same (-kkir-, -cc-) cook 6
sammadam being agreeable, OK 5
samuuga social 10
samuugam society 10
sandi (-kkir-, -cc-) meet 6
sandooʂam happiness 5
sanikkeʐame Saturday 6
saɳɖe quarrel, fight 7
sarakku goods, commodity 8
saraɳaalayam wild life sanctuary 15
sari OK, fine, right 2
sariyaa exactly 6
sariyaana correct, appropriate 6
sattam sound, noise 7
saʈʈe shirt 7
saykiɭ bicycle 16
seendu together, jointly 10
seeru (-r-, -nd-) reach (a place) (intr) 8
seeve service 12
selavaʐi (-kkir-, -cc-) spend (money) 10
selavu expenses 10
sele/silai statue 16
sevappu redness 8
sevvakkeʐame Tuesday 6
seyyi (seyr-, senj-) do 5
sigicce clinical treatment 12
siikram quickly 9
sila some, a few
sillare small change 4
singam lion 6
Singapuur Singapore 13
sinimaa cinema, film 7
sinna/cinna small 5
siranda famous 16
siri (-kkir-, -cc-) laugh 14
sirippu laugh, laughter 14
sirpam sculpture 6
sittire the name of the first month in the Tamil calendar 16
Sivan the god Shiva 15
Skaaʈlaandu Scotland 13
sollu (solr-, sonn-)/collu say 2
sonda own, native (place) 10
sondakkaaran relative (masc) 16
sondakkaari relative (fem) 16
sooru/cooru rice 6
sovaru wall 4
sʈaampu stamp 3
sʈaap stop 4
sʈayl style 9
sudandiram freedom, independence 10
surukkamaa briefly 15
suttam purity; cleanliness 12

suttipaaru (-paakkir-, -paatt-)	sightsee, visit 7
suuḍu	heat, hot 7
suuriyan	sun 11
suuẓnele/ suuẓnilai	background, environment 10

T

taamadam	delay 5
taamadamaa	late 5
taan	(one)self 2
taan/-daan/ -ttaan	(emphatic word) 1
taanga(ḷ)	(them)selves 10
taaraaḷamaa	by all means, freely 6
Taaraasuram	name of a place (in Thanjavur district) 15
taattaa	grandfather 6
tabaal	mail 3
taḍave	time, occasion 8
taḍu (-kkir, -tt-)	prevent 8
takkaaḷi	tomato 3
talappu	caption, title 12
tale	head 5
taleme aluvalagam	head office, headquarters 11
taleme	leadership 11
talevali	headache 13
tambi	younger brother 1
Tamiẓ	Tamil 8
Tamiẓnaaḍu	the state of Tamil Nadu 5
tangacci	younger sister 6
tangu (-r-, -n-)	stay 5
tanippaṭṭa	individual, particular 10
taṇikke	inspection 11
taṇṇi	water 5
tappu (-r-, -n-)	miss, lose, escape 13
tappu (-r-, -n-)	mistake, fault 5
taragar	agent, broker 5
tarceyalaa	by chance, accidentally 16
tare	ground, floor 8
tavira	except 11
tay/tai	the name of the tenth month in the Tamil calendar 16
tayaar	ready 11
tayaari (-kkir, -cc-)	prepare, produce, make, manufacture 8
tayakkam	hesitation 14
tayangu (-r-, -n-)	hesitate 7
tayircooru	rice mixed in yoghurt 6
tayiru	yoghurt 6
tayriyam	courage, boldness 15
tayyakkaararu	tailor 9
tayyi (takkir-, tacc-)	stitch, sew; get stitched/sewn 9
teedi	day, date 4
teengaa(y)	coconut 14
teeve	need 7
tennamaram	coconut tree 14
tennambiḷḷe	coconut sapling 14
tera (-kkir-, -nd-)	open 8
terappu/tiṟappu	opening, inauguration 16
teriyaadu	not know (with dative subj) 5

teriyum (*past* -**nj**-)	know (with dative subj) 5
teru	street 4
tiḍiir	onomatopoeic word for suddenness 15
tiḍiirnu	suddenly 15
tii	fire 16
tingakkeẓame	Monday 6
tirumba	back, again 8
tirumaṇam	marriage 16
tirumbu (-r-, -n-)	return, go back 8; turn (e.g. at a corner) 13
tiruppi	back, in return 8
tiruppu (-r-, -n-)	return, give back 9
Tiruvaṇṇaamale	Tiruvannamalai (name of a town in N. Arcot District) 16
tiruviẓaa	festival 7
tiṭṭam	plan 8
tiṭṭampooḍu (-r-, ṭṭ-)	plan, draw a plan 8
tiṭṭappaḍi	according to plan 8
tiṭṭu (-r-, -n-)	scold 10
toḍandu	continuously 10
tole (-kkir-, -cc-)	lose 9
toḷaayiram	nine hundred 2
toṇṇuuru	ninety 2
tovaram paruppu	split lentil 3
toẓil	profession, vocation 12
tuṇi	cloth, clothes, garments 8
tuṇukku	joke, titbit 14
tuukkam	sleep 7
tuungu (-r-, -n-)	sleep 5
ṭaaksi/ṭæksi	taxi 2
ṭaaksikkaar-anga(ḷ)	taxi people, taxi drivers 2
ṭeylar	tailor 9
ṭifan/ṭipan	tiffin, snack 5
ṭii	tea 3
ṭikkeṭ	ticket 8
ṭi vi	TV 8
ṭreyn	train 4

U

ukkaaru (-r-, -nd-)	sit down 2
uḷḷe	inside, within; (as a conjunction) until, by (the time that) 11
uṇḍu	be (with no tense difference) 7
uppu	salt 9
uppumaa	cooked cream of wheat 3
urime	right, title 9
uruḷekkeẓangu	potato 3
uruḷu (-r-, uruṇḍ-)	roll 7
uuru	village, town, place where people live 3
uurugaa(y)	a pickle 6
uusi	needle 13
uusi pooḍu (-r-, ṭṭ-)	inject 13
Uuṭṭi	Ooty (a town in the Nilgiri Hills) 15

V

vaa (var-, vand-)	come 1
vaaḍage	rent 5

vaandi	vomiting 13
vaangu (-r-, -n-)	buy 3
vaaram	week 2
vaartte	word 16
vaaẓappaẓam	banana, plantain 14
vaaẓkke	life 10
vaḍe	a snack made of lentil or chick-pea paste and fried in oil 3
vaguppu	class 4
valadu	right (side) 13
vali (-kk-, -cc-)	ache, pain (with dative of person) 9
valu	hardness 6
vaḷaru (-r-, -nd-)	grow, develop, grow up 9
vaḷaru (-kkir-, -tt-)	rear, bring up 10
vaḷatti	tall 13
vaṇakkam	greetings 1
varadaccane	dowry 10
varekkum	up to, until 15
varise	line, queue 4
varuṣam	year 6
vasadi	convenience, facility 5
vavvaa(l)	bat (mammal) 4
vayasu	age 16
vaygaasi	the name of the second month in the Tamil calendar 16
vayiru (vayitt-)	stomach 9
vayittupookku	diarrhoea 13
vayttiyam	medical treatment 12
vayyi (vakkir-, vacc-)	put, place; cause 8
vaẓakkamaana	usual 7
vaẓi	pathway, path, way 4
vaẓi tappu (-r-, -n-)	miss the way, lose one's way 13
vaẓukku (-r-, -n-)	slip, be slippery 10
væn	van 6
vedam	manner, way 10
veeḍikke	fun, amusement, entertainment 11
veegam	speed 8
veele	work 5
veele paaru (paakkir-, paatt-)	work, do a job (usually not a manual job) 7
veeḷe	time, occasion 10
veeṇḍaam	not want 3
veeṇḍiyadu	things needed, the necessary 5
veeṇum	want, need 3
veeppamaram	neem tree 9
veere	else, other, different, some other (thing) 3
veeṭṭu	firecracker, gunshot 15
velagu (-r-, -n-)	withdraw, stay out 12
veḷambaram	advertisement, publicity 16
veḷambara-paḍuttu (-r-, -n-)	advertise, publicise 16
veḷayaadu	fun, game 9
veḷeyaaḍu (-r-, -n-)	play 6
veḷeyaaḍu (-ṭṭ-)	game 15
veḷinaaṭṭuk-kaaranga(ḷ)	foreigners 15
veḷiye	out, outside 6

veḷḷikkeẓame	Friday 6
vengaayam	onion 3
veṇḍekkaa(y)	okra, lady's finger 3
veyil	sunshine 2
veyil aḍi (-kk-, -cc-)	be hot 2
vibattu	accident 8
viḍa	than 12
viḍu (-r-, viṭṭ-)	leave, let go 7
viiḍu (viiṭṭ-)	house, home 2
viiram	courage, valour
viiṭṭukkaararu	man of the house, husband, owner of the house 2
viiṭṭukkaari	wife (informal) 2
viiṭṭuppaaḍam	homework 15
villu (vikkir-, vitt-)	sell 2
vimaanam	aeroplane 16
viruppu veruppu	likes and dislikes 10
viruviruppaa	exciting 11
viseeṣam	special event, function 6
viṣayam	news, matter 6
vittiyaasam	difference 12
viṭṭaa(l)	other than, besides 11
viṭṭukuḍu (-kkir-, -tt-)	concede, give up 10
vivaagarattu	divorce 10
viyaaẓakkeẓame	Thursday 6
viyaadi	disease 2
viẓaa	festival, celebration, function 16
viẓu (-r-, -nd-)	fall 7
vyaabaaram	business 8

Y

yaane	elephant 15
yaanekkuṭṭi	elephant calf 14
yaaroo	someone 5
yaaru	who 1
Yaaẓppaaṇam	Jaffna 3
yoosane	suggestion, advice, thought 9
yoosi (-kkir-, -cc-)	think 10

English–Tamil glossary

A

about (concerning)	**patti** 5
above	**meele** 10
abundant	**nereya** 7
AC (air conditioned)	**ee si** 2
accident	**vibattu** 8
accidentally	**tarceyalaa** 16
according to	**-paḍi** 8
account	**kaṇakku** 3
accustomed (be/become)	**paẓagu (-r-, -n-)** 10
ache	**vali (-kk-, -cc-)** (with dative of person) 9
act	**naḍi (-kkir-, -cc-)** 7
acting	**naḍippu** 7
advance (of money)	**munpaṇam** 5
advertise	**veḷambara-paḍuttu (-r-, -n-)** 16
advertisement	**veḷambaram** 16
advice	**yoosane** 9; **puttimadi** 10
aeroplane	**vimaanam** 16
after(wards)	**peragu** 4
afternoon	**madyaanam** 6; **maale** (more formal) 6
afterwards	**pinnaale** 2
again	**tirumba** 8
against	**eduraa** 10
age	**vayasu** 16
agent	**taragar** 5
agree	**ottukiḍu (-r-, -ṭṭ-)** 8
agreement	**oppandam** 8
ahead	**munnaale** 2
AIDS	**eyḍs** 13
air letter	**eer meyil** 3
all	**ellaam** 5
all (humans)	**ellaarum** 2
allocate	**odukku (-r-, -n-)** 12
along (the edge of)	**ooramaa** 6
always	**eppavum** 5
America	**Amerikkaa** 7
among	**eḍele** 10
anger	**koobam** 7
animal	**mirugam** 6
announcement	**arivippu**
annoyance	**ericcal** 10
another	**innoru** 2
answer	**padil** 9
answer	**padil sollu (solr-, sonn-)** 12
anything	**oṇṇum** 6
application	**appḷikeeṣan** 7
appropriate	**sariyaana** 6
approval	**anumadi** 8; **sammadam** 5

approximately	**kiṭṭattaṭṭa** 10
area	**pagudi** 15
as	**maadiri** 9
ask, ask for	**keeḷu (keekkir-, keeṭṭ-)** 6
attitude	**manappaanme** 10
aubergine	**kattarikkaa(y)** 3
aunt (mother's sister)	**atte** 6
aunt (father's elder sister)	**periyammaa** 6
aunt (mother's younger sister)	**cinnammaa, citti** 6
autorickshaw	**aaṭṭoo, aaṭṭoorik-ṣaa** 2
autorickshaw driver	**aaṭṭookkaaran** 2
award	**parisu** 5

B

baby	**paappaa** 8
background	**suuẓnele/suuẓnilai** 10
bad	**moosamaana** 8
bag	**payyi** 4
ball	**pandu** 8
banana	**vaaẓappaẓam** 14
Bangladesh	**Bangḷadeeṣ** 11
bank	**baanku/bænk** 11
basic element	**aḍippaḍe/ aḍippaḍai** 16
bat (mammal)	**vavvaa(l)** 4
be	**iru (-kk-, -nd-)** 2; **uṇḍu** (with no tense difference) 7
be, become	**aa(gu) (-r-, -n-)** 3
beach	**biic/biiccu** 1; **kaḍalkare** 6
beans	**biins** 3
bear (animal)	**karaḍi** 6
beat	**aḍi (-kkir-, -cc-)** 2
beautiful	**aẓagaana** 5
beauty	**aẓagu** 5
beef	**maaṭṭukkari** 10
before	**munnaale** 2
begin	**aarambi (-kkir-, -cc-)** 8
beginning	**aarambam** 6
behind	**pinnaale** 2
below	**kiiẓe** 8
bend down	**kuni (-r-, -nj-)** 7
benefit	**nanme** 9
besides	**viṭṭaa(l)** 11
between	**eḍele** 10
bicycle	**saykiḷ** 16
big	**periya** 5
bill	**billu** 3
bitter (be, in taste)	**kasa (-kkir-, -nd-)** 9
bitterness	**kasappu** 10
board	**boorḍu** 4
body	**oḍambu** 8
boil (intr)	**kodi (-kkir-, -cc-)** 13
boil (tr)	**kodikka vay (vakkir-, vacc-)** 13
boldness	**tayriyam** 15
book	**pustagam** 1; **nuul** (more formal) 16
both (people)	**renḍu peerum** 5
bovine creature	**maaḍu (maaṭṭ-)** 6
boy	**payyan** 5
break (intr)-	**oḍe (-yr-, -nj-)** 10
break (tr)	**oḍe (-kkir-, -cc-)** 10
breath	**muuccu** 7
bribe	**maamuul** 2
bride	**poṇṇu** 10
briefly	**surukkamaa** 15
bring	**konḍuvaa (-varr-, -vand-)** 6

bring along	**kuuṭṭikiṭṭuvaa (-varr-, -vand-)** 6
bring up	**vaḷaru (-kkir-, -tt-)** 10
brinjal	**kattarikkaa(y)** 3
British	**Britiṣ** 13
broker	**taragar** 5
brother (elder)	**aṇṇan** 2
brother (younger)	**tambi** 1
bull	**maaḍu**
bull-running	**jallikkaṭṭu**
bus	**bas** 4
business	**vyaabaaram** 8
but	**aanaa** 10
buttermilk	**mooru** 1
buy	**vaangu (-r-, -n-)** 3
by (the time that)	**uḷḷe** 11

C

calculation	**kaṇakku** 3
Calcutta	**Kalkattaa** 11
calf	**kaṇṇukkuṭṭi** 14
call	**kuupḍu (-r-, -ṭ-)** 6
calmness	**nidaanam** 5
can	**muḍiyum** 4
cannot	**muḍiyaadu** 4
Cape Comorin	**Kanniyaakumari** 16
caption	**talappu** 12
car	**kaaru** 2
cat	**puune** 6
catch hold of	**piḍi (-kkir-, -cc-)** 4
cause	**vayyi (vakkir-, vacc-)** 8
celebration	**viẓaa** 16
certainty	**kaṭṭaayam** 9; **niccayam** 10
change (intr)	**maaru (-r-, -n-)** 10
change (tr)	**maattu (-r-, -n-)** 10
change (coins)	**sillare** 4
chapati	**cappaatti** 6
cheat	**eemaattu (-r-, -n-)** 2
check	**paaru (paakkir-, paatt-)** 2
cheek	**kannam** 5
Chennai	**Cenne** 1
cheque	**cekku** 7
Chidambaram	**Cidambaram** 3
child	**paappaa** 8; **koẓande** 13; **kuṭṭi** 15
chilli	**meḷagaa(y)** 3
Chola era	**Coozarkaalam** 15
Christmas	**kristumas** 16
church	**carc**, **carccu** 10
churn	**peraṭṭu (-r-, -n-)** 13
chutney	**caṭni** 3
cinema	**sinimaa** 7
class	**vaguppu** 4
cleanliness	**suttam** 12
clever person (fem)	**keṭṭikkaari** 6
clever person (masc)	**keṭṭikkaaran** 6
climb	**eeru (-r-, -n-)** 6
climb down	**erangu (-r-, -n-)** 6
clinic	**klinik** 13
clinical treatment	**sigicce** 12
close	**muuḍu (-r-, -n-)** 13
cloth, clothes	**tuṇi** 8
clothing	**ḍras** 8
coconut	**teengaa(y)** 14
coconut sapling	**tennambiḷḷe** 14
coconut tree	**tennamaram** 14
coffee	**kaapi** 3
college	**kaaleej** 4
come	**vaa (varr-, vand-)** 1

come together	**kuuḍu (-r-, -n-)** 7
commentary	**ore** 16
commodity	**sarakku** 8
common	**saadaaraṇam** 2
commonly	**poduvaa** 10
company	**kampeni** 8
competition	**pooṭṭi** 9; **pandayam** 15
completely	**muẓusaa** 8
composure	**nidaanam** 5
conceal	**oḷi (-kkir-, -cc-)** 8
concede	**viṭṭukuḍu (-kkir-, -tt-)** 10
concern	**kavale** 7
concerning	**patti** 5
concert	**kacceeri** 16
conduct	**naḍattu (-r-, -n-)** 8
conductor (on a bus)	**kaṇḍakṭar** 5
congratulate	**paaraaṭṭu (-r-, -n-)** 5
congratulation	**paaraaṭṭu** 5
conservation	**paadukaappu** 15
contest	**pandayam** 15
continuously	**toḍandu** 10
contract	**oppandam** 8
control	**kaṭṭuppaaḍu** 8
convenience, facility	**vasadi** 5
cook	**same (-kkir-, -cc-)** 6
cooking	**samayal** 3
cool off	**aaru (-Ø-, -n-)** 15
core	**aḍippaḍe/ aḍippaḍai** 16
correct	**sari, sariyaana** 2
courage 15	**tayriyam, viiram**
cover (envelope)	**kavaru** 3
cow	**pasu** 5
cricket	**krikeṭ** 13
crore	**kooḍi** 16
cross street	**kurukku teru** 13
crow	**kaakkaa** 14
crowd	**kuuṭṭam** 5
cry	**aẓu (-r-, -n-)** 7
cultural programme	**kalainigaẓcci/ kale-** 16
culture	**paṇpaaḍu** 16
cure	**koṇapaḍuttu (-r-, -n-)** 12
custom	**paẓakkam** 7

D

daily	**denam** 6
dais	**meeḍe** 14
dampness	**iiram** 8
dark (become)	**iruṭṭu (-r-, -n-)** (with inanimate subj) 15
date	**teedi** 4
daughter	**maga(ḷ), poṇṇu** 5
day (24 hours)	**naaḷu** 2
day (of the month)	**teedi** 4
day after tomorrow	**naaḷekaẓicci** 6
day before yesterday	**mundaanaaḷu** 6
day of the week	**keẓame** 6
daytime	**pagalu** 6
decide	**muḍivu seyyi (seyr-, senj-)** 10
decision	**muḍivu** 10
deer	**maanu** 6
deficiency	**kore(vu)** 14
delay	**taamadam** 5
desire	**aase**

develop	**vaḷaru (-r-, -nd-)** 9
diarrhoea	**vayittupookku** 13
difference	**vittiyaasam** 12
different	**veere** 3
difficulty	**kaṣṭam** 7
diminish	**kore (-Ø-, -nj-)** 16
directly	**neere** 4
disappear	**mare (-r-, -nj-)** 7; **oẓi (-r-, -nj-)** 10
disease	**viyaadi** 2
distance	**duuram** 9
disturbance	**ragaḷe** 11
divorce	**vivaagarattu** 10
do	**seyyi (seyr-, senj-)** 5; **paṇṇu (-r-, -n-)** 7
doctor	**ḍaaktar** 8
dog	**naayi** 6
dollar	**ḍaalar** 7
donkey	**kaẓude** 14
door	**kadavu** 8
dosa (a kind of pancake)	**doose** 3
dot	**puḷḷi** 1
down	**kiiẓe** 8
dowry	**varadaccane** 10
draw (water from a well)	**ere (-kkir-, -cc-)** 5
dream	**kanavu** 7
dream (verb)	**kanavu kaaṇu (kaangr-, kaṇḍ-)** 7
dress	**ḍras** 8
drink	**kuḍi (-kkir-, -cc-)** 1
drive	**ooṭṭu (-r-, -n-)** 9
dry (become)	**kaa(y) (-r-, -nd-)** 14

E

each other	**oruttar** + **oruttar** (The first **oruttar** takes case marker) 10
easy	**leesu** 13
eat	**saapḍu (-r-, saapṭ-)** 1
education	**paḍippu** 7
effort	**muyarci** 12
egg-plant	**kattarikkaa(y)** 3
eight	**eṭṭu** 2
eight hundred	**eṇṇuuru** 2
eighteen	**padineṭṭu** 2
eighty	**embadu** 2
electric power	**karaṇṭ** 8
elephant	**yaane** 15
elephant calf	**yaanekuṭṭi** 14
eleven	**padinoṇṇu/-oru** 2
end	**kaḍesi** 14
end (intr)	**muḍi (-r-, -nj-)** 8
end (tr)	**muḍi (-kkir, -cc-)** 8
England	**Ingilaandu** 8
English	**Ingliṣ** 1
enough (be)	**poodum**; negative **poodaadu** 2
enter	**noẓe (-r-, -nj-)** 15
envelope	**kavaru** 3
environment	**suuẓnele/suuẓnilai** 10
equality	**samam** 10
eradicate	**oẓi (-kkir, -cc-)** 10
essay	**kaṭṭure** 9
essential	**avasiyam** 10
even	**kuuḍa** 5
evening	**saayangaalam** 1
event	**nigaẓcci** 15
everyone	**ovvoruttaru** 6
exactly	**sariyaa** 6
examination	**paricce** 6

excellent **piramaadam** 11
excuse **manni (-kkir, -cc-)** 5
expect **edirpaaru (-kkir-, -tt-)** 11
experience (verb) **paḍu (-r-, paṭṭ-)** 7
export **eettumadi** 8
extremely **mikka** 13
eye **kaṇṇu** 7

F

face **mugam** 7
fall **viẓu (-r-, -nd-)** 7
fall (of rain) **peyyi (peyyudu, penj-)** 7
familiarity **paẓakkam** 7
family **kuḍumbam** 10
famous **siranda** 16
fasten **kaṭṭu (-r-, -n-)** 8
father **appaa** 6
Father Christmas **kristumas taattaa** 16
faucet **koẓaa(y)** 5
fault **tappu** 5
fear **payam/bayam** 10
festival **tiruviẓaa** 7
festival (religious) **paṇḍige** 16
fete **viẓaa** 16
fever **juram** 6
few, a **sila**
fifteen **padinanju** 2
fifty **ambadu** 2
fight **saṇḍe** 7
file **fayil** 8
film **sinimaa** 7
finally **kaḍesile** 14
finish (intr) **muḍi (-r-, -nj-)** 8
finish (tr) **muḍi (-kkir, -cc-)** 8
fire **tii** 16
firecracker **veeṭṭu** 15
first **modal** 4
firstly **modalle** 15
five **anju** 2
five hundred **aynuuru** 2
flour **maavu** 3
flower **puu** 4
fly (insect) **ii** 4
food **saappaaḍu (saappaaṭṭ-)** 6
foreigner **veḷinaaṭṭukkaaran/-kaari** 15
forest **kaaḍu (kaaṭṭ-)** 7
forget **mara (-kkir-, -nd-)** 5
forgive **manni (-kkir-, -cc-)** 5
forgiveness **mannippu** 1
form **faaram, paaram** 4
forty **naappadu** 2
four **naalu** 2
four hundred **naanuuru** 2
fourteen **padinaalu** 2
fowl **kooẓi** 14
fox **nari** 14
France **Fraansu** 13
freedom **sudandiram** 10
freely **taaraaḷamaa** 6
Frenchman **Frencukkaaran** 13
Friday **veḷḷikkeẓame** 6
friend **naṇban** 16
fruit **paẓam** 6

G

game **aaṭṭam** 11
garment(s) **ḍras, tuṇi** 8
gasoline **peṭrool** 2
gather **kuuḍu (-r-, -n-)** 7

generally	**poduvaa** 10
gently	**meduvaa** 6
Germany	**Jermani** 13
get	**keḍe (-kk-, -cc-)** (with dative subj) 1
get off (a vehicle)	**erangu (-r-, -n-)** 6
get on (a vehicle)	**eeru (-r-, -n-)** 6
gift	**parisu** 16
ginger	**inji** 5
girl	**poṇṇu** 6
give	**kuḍu (-kkir-, -tt-)** 2
give up	**viṭṭukuḍu (-kkir-, -tt-)** 10
go	**poo (-r-, -n-)** 1
goat	**aaḍu (aaṭṭ-)** 7
good	**nalla** 3
goodness	**nanme** 9
goods	**sarakku** 8
government	**aaṭci** 9; **arasaangam** 8
gram	**graam** 3
granddaughter	**peetti** 6
grandfather	**taattaa** 6
grandmother	**paaṭṭi** 6
grandson	**peeran** 6
grasp	**piḍi (-kkir-, -cc-)** 4
grass	**pullu** 7
gratitude	**nanri** 5
green	**pacce** 5
greetings	**vaaẓttu** 16
ground	**tare** 8
grow, grow up	**vaḷaru (-r-, -nd-)** 9
gunshot	**veeṭṭu** 15

H

habituated (be)	**paẓagu (-r-, -n-)** 15
half	**are** 4
hand	**kayyi** 4
handle	**samaaḷi (-kkir-, -cc-)** 10
handwriting	**kayyeẓuttu** 13
happened	**aaccu** 5
happening	**nigaẓcci** 15
happiness	**magiẓcci** 1; **sandooṣam** 5
hardness	**valu** 6
have	**iru (-kk-, -nd-)** (with dative of subj) 2
he	**avan, ivan** 1
he (polite)	**avaru, ivaru** 1
head	**tale** 5
head office	**taleme aluvalagam** 11
headache	**talevali** 13
heal	**aaru (-r-, -n-)** 16
hear	**keeḷu (keekkir-, keeṭṭ-)** 7
hear about	**keeḷvipaḍu (-r-, -ṭṭ-)** 16
heaviness	**kanam** 5
height	**oyaraam** 16
hello (as a greeting)	**vaṇakkam** 13
hello (on telephone)	**haloo** 13
help	**odavi** 5
hen	**kooẓi** 14
here	**inge** 1
hesitate	**tayangu (-r-, -n-)** 7
hesitation	**tayakkam** 14
hide	**oḷi (-kkir-, -cc-)** 8
hide (oneself)	**oḷi (-r-, -nj-)** 8
Hindi	**Indi, Hindi**

hire	**vaaḍage** 5
hit	**aḍi (-kkir-, -cc-)** 2
home	**viiḍu (viiṭṭ-)** 2
homework	**viiṭṭuppaaḍam** 15
horn (of cow)	**kombu**
horse	**kudire** 6
hot	**suuḍu** 7
hotel	**ooṭṭal, hooṭṭal** 1
hotness (pungency)	**kaaram** 6
hour	**maṇi** 4
house	**viiḍu (viiṭṭ-)** 2
how	**epḍi** 3
how many	**ettane** 2
how much	**evḷavu** 3
humidity	**puẓukkam**
hundred	**nuuru** 2
hunger	**pasi** 9
hungry (be)	**pasi (-kk-, -cc-)** (dative subj; neuter ending on verb) 9
husband	**kaṇavan** 10; **viiṭṭukkaararu** 2

I

I	**naan (en-)** 1
ill-treat	**koḍumepaḍuttu (-r-,-n-)** 10
immediately	**oḍane** 1
import (noun)	**erakkumadi** 8
import (verb)	**erakkumadi seyyi (seyr-, senj-)** 8
important	**mukkiyam** 13
inauguration	**terappu/tiṟappu** 16
independence	**sudandiram** 10
India	**Indiyaa** 8
Indian (adj)	**Indiya** 10
individual	**tanippaṭṭa** 10
inject	**uusi pooḍu (-r-, ṭṭ-)** 13
injustice	**aniyaayam** 9
inland letter form	**inlaaṇḍ** 3
inside	**uḷḷe** 11
inspection	**taṇikke** 11
insufficient (be)	**poodaadu** 2
intestine	**koḍalu** 13
invite	**kuupḍu (-r-, -ṭ-)** 6
invoice	**billu** 3
irrigation tank or lake	**koḷam** 14
it	**adu, idu** 1
Italy	**Ittaali** 13

J

Jaffna	**Yaaẓppaaṇam** 3
Japan	**Japaan** 13
job	**toẓil** 12
join (intr)	**seeru (-r-, -nd-)** 8
jointly	**seendu** 10
journey	**pirayaaṇam**
juice	**caaru** 1; **juus** 3
July	**juulay** 6
jump	**kudi (-kkir-. -cc-)** 5
June	**juun** 6
jungle	**kaaḍu (kaaṭṭ-)** 7

K

Kanya Kumari	**Kanniyaakumari** 16
kill	**kollu (kolr-, koṇṇ-)** 7
kilogram	**kiloo** 3
kilometre	**kiloomiiṭṭar** 2
kind	**kanivaana**
kindness	**kanivu**
kite (bird)	**parundu** 16

kitten	**puunekkuṭṭi** 14
know	**teriyum** (past **-nj-**) (with dative subj); negative **teriyaadu** 5
knowledge	**arivu** 9

L

lady's finger (vegetable)	**veṇḍekkaa(y)** 3
lakh	**laṭcam** 16
language	**moẓi** 15
last (e.g. year)	**poona** 9
late	**taamadamaa** 5
laugh	**siri (-kkir-, -cc-)** 14
laugh, laughter	**sirippu** 14
leave	**viḍu (-r-, viṭṭ-)** 7
leave (on a journey)	**keḷambu (-r-, -n-)** 6
left (side)	**eḍadu** 4
leg	**kaalu** 5
leisurely	**nidaanamaa** 5
lentil (split)	**tovaram paruppu** 3
lesson	**paaḍam** 9
let go	**viḍu (-r-, viṭṭ-)** 7
letter (of the alphabet)	**eẓuttu** 12
letter (post)	**kaḍidam** 12
lie (untruth)	**poy/poyyi** 9
lie down	**paḍu (-kkir-, -tt-)** 7
life	**vaaẓkke** 10
light (in weight)	**leesu** 13
like	**piḍi (-kk-, -cc-)** (with dative subj) 5
like (manner)	**maadiri** 9
like that	**apḍi** 4
like this	**ipḍi** 2
likes and dislikes	**viruppu veruppu** 10
likewise	**adee maadiri** 7
line	**varise** 4
lion	**singam** 6
lip	**odaḍu** 2
listen	**keeḷu (keekkir-, keeṭṭ-)** 7
literature	**ilakkiyam** 5
litre	**liṭṭar** 2
little (a)	**konjam** 1
London	**Laṇḍan** 3
look after	**paattukka (-kiḍur-, -kiṭṭ-)** 8
look up	**paaru (paakkir-, paatt-)** 4
lorry	**laari** 13
lose	**tole (-kkir-, -cc-)** 9
loss	**naṣṭam** 15
lover (fem)	**kaadali** 13
lover (masc)	**kaadalan** 13
luggage	**saamaan** 3

M

Madras	**Meḍraas** 1
Madurai	**Madure** 3
mail	**tabaal** 3
mainly	**mukkiyamaa** 13
make	**paṇṇu (-r-, -n-)** 7
Malayalam	**Malayaaḷam** 12
Malaysia	**Maleeṣiyaa** 13
man	**aaṇ** 10; **aaḷu** 15
manage	**samaaḷi (-kkir-, -cc-)** 10
mango (ripe)	**maambaẓam** 3
mango (unripe)	**maangaa(y)** 3
manner	**maadiri** 9; **vedam** 10

manufacture	**tayaari (-kkir-, -cc-)** 8
many	**pala**
mark	**maark** 9
marriage	**kalyaaṇam** 10
marry	**kalyaaṇam paṇṇu (-r-, -n-)** 10
matter	**viṣayam** 6
may	**kuuḍum** 11
meal	**saappaaḍu** 6
meaning	**arttam** 13
measurement	**aḷavu** 9
meat	**kari** 7
medical treatment	**vayttiyam** 12
medicine	**marundu** 8
medicine (practice of)	**maruttuvam** 12
meet together	**kuuḍu (-r-, -n-)** 7
meet, encounter	**sandi (-kkir-, -cc-)** 6; **paaru (paakkir-, paatt-)** 2
meeting	**kuuṭṭam** 5
meter	**miiṭṭar** 2
metre	**miiṭṭar** 4
midday	**madyaanam** 6
middle class	**mattiyadara** 10
milk	**paalu** 1
millet	**keeppe** 14
mind	**manasu** 15
minister	**mandiri** 8
minute	**nimiṣam** 4
mist	**pani** 16
mistake (noun)	**tappu** 5
misunder-standing	**manastaabam** 10
model shirt (for measure-ment)	**aḷavu saṭṭe** 9
Monday	**tingakkeẓame** 6
money	**paṇam** 6
monkey	**korangu** 6
monsoon	**maẓe kaalam** 8
month	**maasam** 5
mosquito	**kosu** 7
mother	**ammaa** 5
mouse	**eli** 9
much	**adigam** 5
must	**-ṇum**; negative **veeṇḍaam** 5
must not	**kuuḍaadu** 11
mutton	**aaṭṭukkari** 10
my	**en** 1
Mysore	**Maysuur** 15

N

name	**peeru** 1
native (of place)	**sonda** 10
nauseous (feel)	**koḍale peraṭṭikiṭṭu vaa (varr-, vand-)** 13
nearby	**pakkam, pakkattule** 4
nearly	**kiṭṭataṭṭa** 10
necessity	**avasiyam** 10
need (noun)	**teeve** 7
need (verb)	**veeṇum**; negative **veeṇḍaam** 3
needle	**uusi** 13
neem tree	**veeppamaram** 9
neighbour	**pakkattu viiṭṭukkaararu** 6
new	**pudu** 3
new thing	**pudusu** 3
news	**viseeṣam, viṣayam** 6
newspaper	**patrikke** 9
next (e.g. year)	**aḍutta** 9
night	**raatri** 6
nine	**ombadu** 2

nine hundred	**toḷaayiram** 2
nineteen	**pattombadu** 2
ninety	**toṇṇuuru** 2
no	**ille** 2
noise	**sattam** 7
not	**ille** 2
novel	**naaval** 10
now	**ippa** 1
number	**nambar** 4

O

OK	**sari** 2
office	**aafiis/aapiis** 8; **aluvalagam** 11
officer	**aafiisar** 8
often	**aḍikkaḍi**
oil	**eṇṇe** 3
okra	**veṇḍekkaa(y)** 3
old	**paẓeya** 1
one	**oṇṇu**
one (adj)	**oru** 2
one and a half	**oṇṇare**
onion	**vengaayam** 3
only	**maṭṭum** 2
Ooty	**Uuṭṭi** 15
open	**tera (-kkir-, -nd-)** 8
opening	**terappu/tiṟappu** 16
opinion	**karuttu** 10
opposite side	**edirpakkam** 15
or	**alladu** 3
ordinary	**saadaaraṇam, saadaa** 2
organise	**naḍattu (-r-, -n-)** 8
other	**matta** 2
other (different)	**veere** 3
other than	**viṭṭaa(l)** 11
others	**mattavanga(ḷ)** 7
otherwise	**mattapaḍi** 16
ought	**-ṇum**; negative **veeṇḍaam** 5
out, outside	**veḷiye** 6
own (adj)	**sonda** 10
ox	**maaḍu (maaṭṭ-)** 6

P

paddy	**nellu** 3
pain	**vali (-kk-, -cc-)** (with dative subj) 9
palmyra fruit kernel	**nongu/nungu** 14
palmyra tree	**panemaram** 14
pardon (noun)	**mannippu** 1
pardon (verb)	**manni (-kkir-, -cc-)** 5
parents	**pettavanga(ḷ), appaa ammaa** 10
parrot	**kiḷi** 14
part	**pagudi** 15
particularly	**mukkiyamaa** 13
pass	**paas paṇṇu (-r-, -n-)** 8
passenger	**pirayaaṇi**
paste	**oṭṭu (-r-, -n-)** 3
path, pathway	**vaẓi** 4
patience	**porume** 8
pay (fee, debt)	**kaṭṭu (-r-, -n-)** 8
pen	**peenaa** 2
people	**jananga(ḷ)** 2 **makkaḷ** 12
permission	**anumadi** 8
petrol	**peṭrool** 2
pick up	**eḍu (-kkir-, -tt-)** 1
pickle	**uurugaa(y)** 6
picture	**paḍam** 7
pity	**erakkam** 7
place	**eḍam** 4

place, put	**vayyi (vakkir-, vacc-)** 8
plan (noun)	**tiṭṭam** 8
plan (verb)	**tiṭṭampooḍu (-r-, -ṭṭ-)** 8
plantain	**vaaẓappaẓam** 14
platform (railway)	**piḷaaṭfaaram**
play	**veḷeyaaḍu (-r-, -n-)** 6
playing cards (pack, deck)	**ciiṭṭukaṭṭu** 6
plentiful	**nereya** 7
police officers	**pooliskaaranga(ḷ)** 2
polio	**pooliyoo** 13
Pondichery	**Puducceeri 3**
possible (be)	**muḍiyum** 4; **kuuḍum** 11
pot	**koḍam** 7
potato	**uruḷekkeẓangu** 3
practice	**paẓakkam** 7
praise (verb)	**paaraaṭṭu (-r-, -n-)** 5
prepare	**tayaari (-kkir, -cc-)** 8
prescribe	**eẓudi kuḍu (-kkir, -tt-)** 13
prevent	**taḍu (-kkir, -tt-)** 8
prize	**parisu** 5
problem	**piraccane** 8
produce	**tayaari (-kkir, -cc-)** 8
profession	**toẓil** 12
professor	**peeraasiriyar** 1
protection	**paadukaappu** 15
provisions	**saamaan** 3
publicise	**veḷambarapaḍuttu (-r-, -n-)** 16
publicity	**veḷambaram** 16
pull	**iẓu (-kkir, -tt-)** 15
pungency	**kaaram** 6
puppy	**naaykuṭṭi** 14
purity	**suttam** 12
put	**pooḍu** (-r-, -ṭṭ-) 3; **vayyi (vakkir-, vacc-)** 8
put up with	**poru (-kkir, -tt-)** 10

Q

quarrel	**saṇḍe** 7
quarter (fraction)	**kaal** 4
question	**keeḷvi** 9
queue	**varise** 4
quickly	**siikram** 9, **veegamaa** 12

R

railway station	**rayilvee sṭeeṣan** 2
rain	**maẓe** 8
rainy season	**maẓe kaalam** 8
rat	**eli** 9
read	**paḍi (-kkir, -cc-)** 7
ready	**tayaar; reḍi** 11
reason	**kaaraṇam** 15
recital	**kacceeri** 16
redness	**sevappu** 8
relative (fem)	**sondakkaari** 16
relative (masc)	**sondakkaaran** 16
relaxation	**ooyvu** 1
rent	**vaaḍage** 5
research	**aaraaycci** 12
reservation	**risarveeṣan** 2
rest	**ooyvu** 1
restaurant	**(h)ooṭṭal** 1
return, give back	**tiruppu (-r-, -n-)** 9
return, go back	**tirumbu (-r-, -n-)** 8

rice	**sooru/cooru** 6
rice (as a crop)	**nellu** 3
rice (uncooked)	**arisi** 3
rice mixed in yoghurt	**tayirccooru** 6
right	**sari** 2
right (side)	**valadu** 13
roll	**uruḷu (-r-, uruṇḍ-)** 7
room	**ruum, are**
root vegetable	**keẓangu** 6
rope	**kayiru (kayitt-)** 15
ruined (be)	**keṭṭupoo (-r-, -n-)** 10
run	**ooḍu (-r-, -n-)** 6
run (noun)	**ooṭṭam** 6
run around/ after	**ale (-yr-, -nj-)** 8
running race	**ooṭṭappandayam** 15
rupee	**ruubaa(y)** 2

S

salt	**uppu** 9
Saturday	**sanikkeẓame** 6
say	**sollu (solr-, sonn-) collu** 2
scholar	**ariñar** 16
scold	**tiṭṭu (-r-, -n-)** 10
Scotland	**Skaaṭlaandu** 13
scream (noun)	**alaral** 7
scream (verb)	**alaru (-r-, -n-)** 7
sculpture	**sirpam/cirpam** 6
sea shore	**kaḍalkare** 6
seat	**eḍam** 4
see	**paaru (paakkir-, paatt-)** 2
see (e.g. a dream)	**kaaṇu (-r-, kaṇḍ-)** 7
seem	**paḍu (-r-, -ṭṭ-)** 10
self	**taan** (plural: **taanga(ḷ))** 2
sell	**villu (vikkir-, vitt-)** 2
send	**anuppu (-r-, -n-)** 7
service	**seeve** 12
set aside	**odukku (-r-, -n-)** 12
set off	**porappaḍu (-r-, -ṭṭ-)** 4
set out	**keḷambu (-r-, -n-)** 6
set up	**ame (-kkir-, -cc-)** 16
seven	**eeẓu** 2
seven hundred	**eẓanuuru** 2
seventeen	**padineeẓu** 2
seventy	**eẓuvadu** 2
sew, get sewn	**tayyi (takkir-, tacc-)** 9
she	**ava(ḷ), iva(ḷ)** 1
she (polite)	**avanga(ḷ), ivanga(ḷ)** 1
sheep	**aaḍu (aaṭṭ-)** 7
ship	**kappal** 16
shirt	**saṭṭe** 7
Shiva	**Sivan** 15
shop	**kaḍe** 4
shopkeeper	**kaḍekkaaran** 7
short(ness)	**kuṭṭe** 13
short cut	**kurukku vaẓi** 13
shortage	**kore, korevu** 14
siblings	**kuuḍa-perandavanga(ḷ)** 6
side	**pakkam** 4
sightsee	**suttipaaru (-paakkir-, -paatt)** 7
signature	**kayyeẓuttu** 13

silk	**paṭṭu** 9
sing	**paaḍu (-r-, -n-)** 7
Singapore	**Singapuur** 13
sir	**saar** 2
sister (elder)	**akkaa(ḷ)** 2
sister (younger)	**tangacci** 6
sit down	**ukkaaru (-r-, -nd-)** 2
six	**aaru** 2
six hundred	**aranuuru** 2
sixteen	**padinaaru** 2
sixty	**aruvadu** 2
sleep	**tuukkam** 7
sleep	**tuungu (-r-, -n-)** 5
slightly	**leesaa** 12
slip, be slippery	**vaẓukku (-r-, -n-)** 10
slowly	**meduvaa** 6
small	**sinna/cinna** 5
smoke	**poge** 13
smoke (tobacco)	**poge piḍi (-kkir-, -cc-)** 13
snake	**paambu** 5
snow	**pani** 16
so much	**avḷavu** 7
so, like that	**apḍi** 4
so, therefore	**adunaale** 5
social	**samuuga** 10
society	**samuugam** 10
soft	**medu, meduvaana** 6
softly	**meduvaa** 6
some	**konjam** 1
someone	**yaaroo** 5
somewhat	**konjam** 1
somewhere	**engeyoo** 5
son	**magan, payyan** 5
song	**paaṭṭu** 7
sorrow	**kavale** 7
sound	**oli** 4; **sattam** 7
sourness	**puḷippu** 6
speak	**peesu (-r-, -n-)** 5
special event	**viseeṣam** 6
speech	**peeccu** 7
speed	**veegam** 8
spend (money)	**selevaẓi (-kkir-, -cc-)** 10
spice	**masaalaa** 3
Sri Lanka	**Ilange** 11
stage	**meeḍe** 14
stamp	**sṭaampu** 3
stand	**nillu (nikkir-, niṇṇ-)** 4
start	**aarambi (-kkir, -cc-)** 8
start out	**keḷambu (-r-, -n-)** 6
station	**sṭeeṣan** 2
statue	**sele/silai** 16
stay	**tangu (-r-, -n-)** 5
stick (with glue)	**oṭṭu (-r-, -n-)** 3
still	**innum** 5
stitch, get stitched	**tayyi (takkir-, tacc-)** 9
stomach	**vayiru (vayitt-)** 9
stop	**nillu (nikkir-, niṇṇ-)** 4
stop (for bus)	**sṭaap** 4
storeyed house	**maaḍi viiḍu** 13
story	**kade** 7
straight	**neere** 4
street	**teru** 4
stripe	**kooḍu** 13
student (female)	**maaṇavi** 1
student (male)	**maaṇavan** 1
study	**paḍi (-kkir-, -cc-)** 7
style	**sṭayl** 9
subtract	**kaẓi (-kkir-, -cc-)** 8

suddenly **tiḍiirnu** 15
suffer **kaṣṭappaḍu (-r-, -ṭṭ-)** 7
suffering **kaṣṭam** 7
suffice **poodum** (negative **poodaadu**) 2
sugar **cakkare** 3
sugar cane **karumbu** 1
suggestion **yoosane** 9
suitability **poruttam** 9
sun **suuriyan** 11
Sunday **nyaayittukkeẓame** 6
sunshine **veyil** 2
support **aadaravu** 10
sweet (be (in taste)) **ini (-kk-, -cc-)** 1
sweetness **inippu** 6
sympathy **erakkam** 7
system **more** 12

T

table **meese** 4
tablet **maattire** 13
tailor **tayyakkaararu; ṭeylar** 9
take **eḍu (-kkir-, -tt-)** 1
take part **kalandukiḍu (-r-, -ṭṭ-)** 12
talk **peesu (-r-, -n-)** 5
tall **vaḷatti** 13
tamarind **puḷi** 3
Tamil **Tamiẓ** 8
Tamil Nadu **Tamiẓnaaḍu** 5
tap **koẓaa(y)** 5
taste **rusi** 15
tasty **rusiyaa(na)** 15
taxi **ṭaaksi/ṭæksi** 2
taxi driver **ṭaaksikkaaran** 2
tea **ṭii** 3
teach **paḍippi (-kkir-, -cc-)** 12
teacher **aasiriyar** 9
tear **kiẓi (-r-, -nj-)** 9
television **ṭi vi** 8
temple **kooyil** 11
ten **pattu** 2
terrible **bayangaramaana** 7
than **viḍa** 12
thanks **nanri** 5
that **adu** 1
that (adj) **anda** 1
that day **aṇṇekki** 1
that many **attane** 1
that much **avḷavu** 7
then **appa** 1
then (next) **peragu** 4
then (on that day) **aṇṇekki** 1
there **ange** 1
therefore **adunaale** 5
these (adj) **inda** 1
these (things) **iduga(ḷ)** 1
they (human) **avanga(ḷ)**, **ivanga(ḷ)** 1
they (neuter) **aduga(ḷ)**, **iduga(ḷ)** 1
thing **saamaan** 3
think **yoosi (-kkir-, -cc-)** 10
thirteen **padimuuṇu** 2
thirty **muppadu** 2
this (adj) **inda** 1
this (thing) **idu** 1
this much **ivḷavu** 1
those (adj) **anda** 1
thought **yoosane** 9
thousand **aayiram** 2
thread **nuulu** 7
three **muuṇu** 2

three hundred	**munnuuru** 2
Thursday	**viyaazẓakkezẓame** 6
ticket	**ṭikkeṭ** 8
tie	**kaṭṭu (-r-, -n-)** 8
tiger	**puli** 6
tiger cub	**pulikuṭṭi** 14
time	**neeram** 2
time (marked for doing something)	**samayam** 15
time (o'clock)	**maṇi** 4
time (occasion)	**taḍave** 8; **veeḷe** 10
tired	**kaḷeppaa** 5
tiredness	**kaḷeppu** 5
Tiruvannamalai	**Tiruvaṇṇaamale** 16
titbit (in a newspaper)	**tuṇukku** 14
title	**talappu** 12
today	**iṇṇekki** 1
toddy	**kaḷḷu** 14
together	**seendu** 10
toil	**ozẓeppu** 5
tolerate	**poru (-kkir-, -tt-)** 10
tomato	**takkaaḷi** 3
tomorrow	**naaḷekki** 5
tongue	**naakku, naa** 16
tooth	**pallu** 8
town	**uuru** 3
train	**ṭreyn** 4; **rayilu** 13
traveller	**pirayaaṇi**
treat	**koṇazpaḍuttu (-r-, -n-)** 12
treatment (medical)	**maruttuvam** 12
tree	**maram** 2
truck	**laari** 13
try	**paaru (paakkir-, paatt-)** 2; **muyarci paṇṇu (-r-, -n-)** 11
Tuesday	**sevvakkezẓame** 6
turn (e.g. at a corner)	**tirumbu (-r-, -n-)** 13
TV	**ṭi vi** 8
twelve	**panireṇḍu** 2
twenty	**iruvadu** 2
two hundred	**eranuuru** 2

U

uncle (father's elder brother)	**periyappaa** 6
uncle (father's younger brother)	**cittappaa** 6
uncle (mother's brother)	**maamaa** 6
undergo	**paḍu (-r-, paṭṭ-)** 7
understand	**puriyum (-nj-)** (with dative subj); negative **puriyaadu** 5
unfairness	**aniyaayam** 9
unhurriedly	**nidaanamaa** 5
until	**varekkum** 15
untruth	**poy/poyyi** 9
up to	**varekkum** 15
urgency, urgent	**aaccariyam** 15
USA	**Amerikkaa** 7
use	**payanpaḍuttu (-r-, -n-)** 12
usefulness	**payan** 12
usual	**vazẓakkamaana** 7
usually	**vazẓakkamaa** 7

V

vada (a savoury) **vaɖe** 6

van **væn** 6

vegetarian(ism) **saivam** 7

very, very much **mikka** 13

very, very much **romba** 1

village **kiraamam** 7

vocation **toʐil** 12

vomiting **vaandi** 13

W

wait **kaattiru (-kk-, -nd-)**, **kaa (-kkir-, -tt-)**, **iru (-kk-, -nd-)** 2

wait for **edirpaaru (-kkir-, -tt-)**

walk **naɖa (-kkir-, -nd-)** 1

walk, gait **naɖe** 12

wall **sovaru** 4

wander **ale (-r-, -nj-)** 8

want **veeɳum**; negative **veeɳɖaam** 3

warm up (intr) **kaa(y) (-r-, -nd-)** 14

wash **kaʐuvu (-r-, -n-)** 4

water **taɳɳi** 5

way (manner) **vedam** 10

way (path) **vaʐi** 4

we (exclusive) **naanga(ɭ) (enga(ɭ)-)** 1

we (inclusive) **naama(ɭ) (nam-)** 1

wedding **kalyaaɳam** 10

Wednesday **budankeʐame** 6

week **vaaram** 2

weep **aʐu (-r-, -d-)** 7

well (adverb) **nallaa** 4

well (for water) **keɳaru (keɳatt-)** 5

wetness **iiram** 8

what **enna** 2

what day **eɳɳekki** 4

wheat **koodume** 3

wheel **cakkaram** 11

when **eppa** 3

when (on what day) **eɳɳekki** 4

where **enge** 3

which (adj) **enda, edu** 3

which one **edu** 3

who **yaaru** 1

who (which female person) **eva(ɭ)** 2

who (which male person) **evan** 2

who (which male person (polite)) **evaru** 2

who (which persons) **evanga(ɭ)** 2

whole **muʐusum** 9

why **een** 4

wife **manevi** 10, **viiʈʈukkaari** (informal) 2

wildlife sanctuary **saraɳaalayam** 15

will not **maaʈʈ-** 5

wine **oyin** 10

wind **kaattu**

withdraw **velagu (-r-, -n-)** 12

within **uɭɭe** 11

without **illaama(l)** 7

woman **peɳ** 10

wood **maram** 2

word **vaartte** 16

work **veele** 5

world	**olagam** 9
wound	**puṇṇu** 16
write	**ezudu (-r-, -n-)** 5
writing	**ezuttu** 12

Y

year	**varuṣam** 6 **aaṇḍu** 16
yes	**aamaa** 1
yesterday	**neettu** 6
yet	**innum** 5
yoghurt	**tayiru** 6
you (plural and polite)	**niinga(ḷ) (onga(ḷ)-)** 1
you (singular)	**nii (on-)** 1
young (of birds, and one or two other animals)	**kunju** 14
young of an animal	**kuṭṭi** 15

Z

zoo	**mirugakkaacci saale** 6

Index of grammatical terms